The Reconstruction Ku Klux Klan in
York County, South Carolina, 1865–1877

ALSO BY JERRY L. WEST

*The Bloody South Carolina Election of 1876:
Wade Hampton III, the Red Shirt Campaign for Governor
and the End of Reconstruction* (McFarland, 2010)

The Reconstruction Ku Klux Klan in York County, South Carolina, 1865–1877

JERRY L. WEST

McFarland & Company, Inc., Publishers
Jefferson, North Carolina, and London

> The present work is a reprint of the library bound edition of The Reconstruction Ku Klux Klan in York County, South Carolina, 1865–1877, first published in 2002 by McFarland.

LIBRARY OF CONGRESS CATALOGUING-IN-PUBLICATION DATA

West, Jerry L.
　The Reconstruction Ku Klux Klan in York County, South Carolina, 1865–1877 / Jerry L. West.
　　p.　cm.
　Includes bibliographical references and index.

　ISBN 978-0-7864-4343-7
　softcover : 50# alkaline paper ∞

　1. Reconstruction — South Carolina — York County.　2. Ku-Klux Klan (1866–1869).　3. York County (S.C.) — Race relations. 4. York County (S.C.) — History — 19th century.　I. Title.
　F277.Y6W48　2010
　975.7'43041 — dc21　　　　　　　　　　　　　　　　　2002003340

British Library cataloguing data are available

©2002 Jerry L. West. All rights reserved

No part of this book may be reproduced or transmitted in any form or by any means, electronic or mechanical, including photocopying or recording, or by any information storage and retrieval system, without permission in writing from the publisher.

On the cover: Illustration of two members of the Ku Klux Klan in their disguises in: *Harper's Weekly*, v. 12, 1868 Dec. 19, p. 813, Library of Congress; background ©2010 Shutterstock

Manufactured in the United States of America

McFarland & Company, Inc., Publishers
　Box 611, Jefferson, North Carolina 28640
　www.mcfarlandpub.com

To Dianne, a faithful
wife and loving mother

Acknowledgments

I owe a great debt to Dr. Allen H. Stokes, director of the South Caroliniana Library, for allowing me to work with the Mary Davis Brown Diaries. Extracts from her writings lace this publication and offer unique information and insights into the years and subjects being examined. With increased transcription and usage of the Brown Diaries, it has become evident that they are of considerable importance and ought to command the attention of a university press. The involvement of a professional historian in what once was going to be a local history effort would be crucial to maximize the use of this material among a wide variety of users.

A very special appreciation is extended to "the man with a big, red pencil"— Frederick C. Holder of Oconee County. As this manuscript began to develop, Fred freely gave of his time and expertise, reading draft after draft of the text and hundreds of footnotes, offering detailed criticism, and resolving inconsistencies— most of which he did with reasonably good humor.

Further gratitude is given to the late Elmer O. Parker, Jr., of Columbia, for allowing me to use his unpublished paper on his ancestor, Samuel Gordon Brown. More locally, I wish to thank Heather South of the Historical Center of York County for taking time to read the manuscript, and for her encouragement when it was needed the most.

To Mary Malleny and her associates at the York County Public Library in Rock Hill, my gratitude for important directions to tidbits of Klan information scattered throughout the collections in the Nan Weller Carson History Room; for their patience in answering my many questions;

for sharing with me their valuable time; and for allowing me to monopolize the film reader and copy machine.

I am deeply indebted to Wade Fairey, who, when he was Director of Historic Brattonsville, started me on my quest for local history. Had Wade not awakened an excitement for history within me, this book would never have become a reality.

Contents

Acknowledgments vii
Preface xi
Introduction 1

1 — Opening Scenes to Fury 15
2 — Advent of the Ku Klux Klan 34
3 — A Threat of Violence 45
4 — The Klan Wars 64
5 — Federal Intervention 77
6 — Colonel Merrill Begins Arrests 89
7 — The Klan Trials 97
8 — Peace Returns to York County 109

Appendices

1 — Oath, Constitution and Bylaws of the Ku Klux Klan 119
2 — Captain James Williams 123
3 — James Rufus Bratton, M.D. 126
4 — John Hannibal White 131
5 — Elijah Ross Sepaugh 134
6 — York County Men Imprisoned at the Albany Penitentiary 137

Contents

7 — Prison Life at the Albany Penitentiary	139
8 — Presidential Pardons	143
9 — Samuel Gordon Brown	145
10 — An Act to Provide for the Protection of Persons, Property and the Public Peace. No. 337	155
11 — Union League Oath	159
Notes	161
Bibliography	197
Index	201

Preface

I wish I could say that this book is the product of a planned effort, but the truth is, its beginnings were purely accidental, developing out of an attempt to write a preface for a paper on Reconstruction. At the time I was writing that preface, I had in mind to include only a paragraph or two on the Ku Klux Klan of York County and its effects on elections during that period — but curiosity got the best of me. One bit of information led to another until the research became obsessive, consuming more than two years of study. Having no plan and armed with only curiosity, I believe I have written this book objectively and without an agenda.

As my research continued and a sizable amount of material came together, I set a goal to make this book a definitive work on the Ku Klux Klan of York County. I had hoped to ease the work of later researchers who chose to study or write on this subject. With this goal in mind, I made strenuous efforts to locate and review every available resource on the subject.

In the beginning, I had little comprehension of the complexity of the Ku Klux Klan and its interaction with Radical Republicans, white Democrats and black freedmen. While I attempted to explain the organization's motivation, I seriously doubt I have been able to fully define the mental complexity that led to the violence it unleashed.

The importance of this book is found in its scope. In the past several years a number of scholarly books and papers have been published about the Reconstruction Klan, but these have dealt with the subject on a statewide or Southwide scale. This work, however, limits its scope to York

County. While some small papers have been done on Klan activities on the county level, I have not yet seen any in-depth study that limits itself to one county. Perhaps this book's publication will inspire others in other counties to produce similar works.

Hopefully this book will clarify some misconceptions about the Reconstruction Klan and disentangle it from later organizations that used the same name. The Reconstruction Klan stands alone in its origin and has no connection with the Klan that appeared in the early part of the 20th century, or today's counterpart which marches under the battle flag of the Confederacy. There are no reports of the Reconstruction Klan posting fiery crosses, nor did they have an ax to grind with Jews or Catholics. Yet, the Reconstruction Klan was a paramilitary group with political aims and which used violence and intimidation to achieve its goals.

Doing most of my research from my home or nearby libraries, I found the *Yorkville Enquirer* was the handiest and the richest source. Much of my research centered on the 1865 to 1876 editions of this local newspaper which are housed on microfilm at the York County Library at Rock Hill and the York County Historical Center in York. Although eyewitness accounts and histories written in the early part of the 20th century were much used, great care had to be exercised in separating prejudicial statements from facts. Another substantial and valuable resource was the papers of Governor Robert K. Scott, archived at the South Carolina Department of Archives and History in Columbia. Two government publications, *Report of the Joint Select Committee to Inquire Into the Condition of Affairs in the Late Insurrectionary States* and *Testimony Taken by the Joint Select Committee to Inquire Into the Condition of Affairs* in *the Late Insurrectionary States* (Vol. I, II and III), are a must in researching the Klan.

Numerous books, master's theses, published and private papers were used in this research. Many of these have longstanding acceptance as being excellent on the subject; therefore it is difficult to choose one or two as recommended reading. However, of the more recent publications, I would recommend: *The Great South Carolina Ku Klux Klan Trials 1871–1872* by Lou Faulkner Williams (Athens: University of Georgia Press, 1996) and *The Federal Government's Attack on the Ku Klux Klan: A Reassessment* (South Carolina Historical Magazine, January 1997).

Dr. George C. Rogers, Jr., the dean of South Carolina historians, used to stress to his students that our state's history has been, in essence, a lengthy conversation about race. From 1670, when Charles Town was established on the banks of the Ashley and Cooper rivers, Africans and whites have been involved in a conversation, often a heated one, concerning the relationship between two South Carolinians: one black and one white. Their dialogue has gone on since slavery came to South Carolina, fully formed, arriving with the first Barbadian colonists.

Race was at the center of the debate at the secession convention in 1860. Like a sleeping serpent, South Carolina's destiny was shaped — or distorted — by its addiction to human bondage. As we know from four traumatic years of Civil War, South Carolina paid a terrible price for its one-sided conversation about race.

This book looks at the aftermath of that war — the Reconstruction Era, with its battles between liberated African-Americans and angry Ku Klux Klan members, focused again on the conversation about race. The state's citizens, black and white, tried from 1865 to 1877 to outshout each other in a new era of conversation. As this study demonstrates, by Reconstruction's end, the state's people still had a tremendous distance to go before they heard — and understood — one another.

Introduction

> Every man hates to have a superior, but no man is willing to have an equal, every man desires to be superior to all others.... We may look as wise and moralize as gravely as we will; we may call this desire of distinction childish and silly; but we cannot alter the nature of men.
> — *John Adams*

"The moon was now shining brightly, and its light shimmering on the silent horses and men with their tall spiked caps made a picture such as the world had not seen since the Knights of the Middle Ages rode on their Holy Crusades." Such was the description of Thomas Dixon, writing in 1904 about a night ride of the Reconstruction Ku Klux Klan.

One should try to imagine in the year 2002, men riding through a yard on a dark night, shouting obscenities, firing weapons, or perhaps leaving an ominous coffin at a doorstep, or throwing paint on a house because its residents are black or members of a minority political party. One should try to imagine having the fear that bands of masked marauders may break into your house and physically assault you or your family at any time. One should try to imagine the animosity people feel for a government that is opposed to their views, opinions, and way of life. One should try to imagine having all of one's constitutional rights withheld, being arrested and held indefinitely in jail without a hearing, and the climate of fear arising from rumors of pending arrests of many others. One should try to imagine having to flee from his own home, leaving his family for an indefinite period of time when he knows those family members are going to suffer because of his absence. Then one can perhaps imagine some of the concerns and feelings that existed in York County during the Reconstruction years from 1868 to 1876.

The 1870 census, although suspect in its accuracy, gives York County a total population of 24,286 which was nearly equally divided, the blacks having a slight majority. Approximately 1,500 people, also equally divided between black and white inhabited the courthouse town of Yorkville, the largest cluster of people in the county in 1870. Yorkville was the county's commercial center — a pretty little town with its main street lined with "Trees of India." There were several large dry-goods businesses as well as smaller specialty stores, including a bakery, green groceries, and millinery and shoe shops. One of several hotels was Rose's, which was built in 1852 by doctors J. Rufus Bratton and E. A. Crenshaw and purchased later that year by William Edward Rose. Rose, it was reported, developed the establishment into one of the most "modern" hotels in the upcountry, and was mentioned in Columbia and Charleston newspapers. In April 1865, the fleeing Confederate Cabinet members visited the hotel while President Jefferson Davis stayed next door at the home of Doctor Bratton. During their overnight stay, Confederate Secretary of War, General Breckinridge, made a speech from the second-floor balcony charging the people of Yorkville to "keep the faith." The hotel boasted a bar, restaurant and shuttleservice to the depot some blocks away. During military occupation, Colonel Merrill's investigative office was in the hotel, and it became a center of military activity, as well as a favorite haunt of Republican leaders.

York County was moderately prosperous and made up of a few large plantations and many smaller farms raising corn and cotton. While a large percentage of the people still lived in log houses with frame additions of a more recent construction, many two-storied "I" houses of stylish design had been built by middle- and upper-class farmers.

Yorkville served as an end-of-the-line or terminus station for the King's Mountain Railroad between Yorkville and Chester, but the small town of Rock Hill, incorporated in March 1869, that served as the junction between Charlotte and Columbia, was moving toward superseding Yorkville in commercial importance. The telegraph did not arrive in the county until April 1870. At that time an office was opened in Rock Hill and Yorkville. Another line, between Chester and Yorkville, was completed in September 1871. Yorkville and the county, as well as some surrounding areas, were served by one newspaper, the *Yorkville Enquirer*, owned and published by Lewis M. Grist. Described as a "Democrat paper," Grist reported in December 1866 that the *Enquirer* was the largest newspaper in South Carolina outside the Charleston area.

Introduction 3

For several years after the Civil War and during the first year or so of Reconstruction, the South seemingly sat in sackcloth and ashes, patiently waiting for some sign of hope and direction to rise from among the ruins. Conservatives, soon faced with the reordering of their homeland, suffered great frustration by floundering in a society in the midst of major social and economic adjustment. Though the whites had long held tight rein over politics, finances, justice and religion, they suddenly had to consider the notion that they were no longer privileged and must share control. This loss of power and political expression, coupled with their dissociation from the emerging society, contributed to their anger.

Immediately following the close of the Civil War, the South was in an agitated social revolution. Raging within its borders was a war of ideas and ideals that unsettled and unhinged the peace of the people. The fixtures of stagnancy and status quo that had been a feature of the agricultural South prior to the war swirled about in a whirlpool of flux. Demographics had acutely changed; the right to vote had been given to the black race; not only had the white majority ended, but also in some areas whites became the minority. Living under Republican rule, many whites found that the grievances of freedmen took precedence over white concerns and problems.

To compound the situation of whites, emancipated black men found a platform. Their voices were being heard in the South from every hall, every ballot box and in every state government. This newfound voice was difficult for whites to accept and any departure from the white Democratic Party was seen as an act of disloyalty. Since slaveholders had considered their slaves as "our family" or "our people" this justified their claims of absolute obedience.[1] The blacks were forming their own religious and political societies apart from white leadership. This angered and chilled the hearts of former masters like Doctor J. Rufus Bratton who recorded, "The man Bob and his family I sent away from the farm early in 1868 on account of his radical politics."[2] Perhaps a less obvious reason for Bob's dismissal might have been the inability of Bratton, as well as others, to cope with the new system of labor. Many white farmers and planters, used to being masters over a bound labor force, and controlling every aspect of their lives, found it frustrating to deal with freedmen who could come and go at will. No doubt, this frustration led to irrational actions by former slaveholders.

Months before the Ku Klux Klan lifted its hooded head, certain leaders in the state, evidently seeing the strong possibility of conflict, offered a warning to the freedmen thereby setting the tone for the next decade. On 29 August 1867, in Belton, South Carolina, a large number of citizens from Anderson and surrounding counties gathered to hear various state officials discuss the developing political situations.³ Governor Orr, whose home was in Belton, spoke more directly to the whites urging them to register, and vote for a contention. Turning to the assembled blacks he "minded them that if they attempted oppression of the whites now, while in the majority, it might be visited upon them in the future, when the balance of power would be different.... He disabused their minds of the idea that they would obtain lands from the Government."⁴

Another speaker, J. P. M. Epping of Charleston and a United States marshal, gave his full attention to the freedmen and echoed Governor Orr's tone and warning, "but advised the blacks to adhere to the Republican party, and recommended to them the Union Leagues."⁵ He agreed with the Governor that the freedmen should not expect any lands to be given to them. Epping admonished them against any conflict with the white population, "declaring they would find 32,000,000 whites against 4,000,000 blacks, and that the conflict would be short, and result in their extermination."⁶

As a result of the South's constant agitation of the slavery question before the war, the North became aroused against what it called the aggressions of the slave power and succeeded in forming a new political party in 1856. This party, the Republicans, embraced a majority of the former Whigs of the North, the Free Soilers and the Abolitionists. The new party was purely sectional, having no following outside the Northern states. In the presidential election of 1856, the National Republicans carried 11 Northern states and polled 1,341,264 votes; but in 1860 it was strong enough to elect a president through northern votes alone. From the outset, the South feared there was no safety in the Union unless the Republican-controlled Congress gave them some new guarantees. This fear continued during Reconstruction.

When governments of the Southern states were newly reformed, they were generally controlled by the Republican Party⁷ as the Radicals of Congress intended. South Carolina was suffering under many dishonest, extravagant and incompetent officials; many were carpetbaggers. As Yankee opportunists poured into the South they may have thought their work would be easy, but they had not anticipated the strong determination that lay just out of sight. Southerners may have had to admit to defeat in war, but it was quite another for them to accept domination. By the time of Reconstruction, most Southerners had firmly developed a defensive attitude believing anything and everything conceived in the North, or by a Yankee, was at best humbuggery and at worst evil. As the pressures of disenfranchisement and Reconstruction developed, white Democrats withdrew into a mental bunker and proposed to stand at all costs against more changes to the life they earlier had known. When this stand was taken, a bloody conflict was prophesied. With relish Radical Republicans using the black vote worked to overhaul the South's society and change it from its old ways; but the appearance and vigor of the Ku Klux Klan wrecked their plans.

In the spring of 1868, the emergence of the Ku Klux Klan burst upon the Radicals without warning. The violence not only disrupted the complacency of the Radicals, but eventually brought Reconstruction to a halt. Regardless of the Klan's bleak prospects, the robed knights of York County never considered a truce. Their cause represented a deep commitment; they believed in themselves; they believed they were right; and they believed right would ultimately win. With this temperament, Klansmen fashioned one of the hottest political and social battles the state has ever known.

The height and depth of the Klan's power must not be underestimated, especially in York County. As this struggle continued throughout the South—sometimes overtly, sometimes covertly—the Klan reigned more completely and supremely in York than it did in any other southern county and nowhere could the term "reign of terror"[8] be more aptly applied. During the Klan's tenure, the county received more national publicity and governmental attention than any other in the South.

In short, the Ku Klux Klan was spawned out of frustration and anger created from a feeling of a loss of control, isolation from government, loss of faith in government, and the inability to find a place in a society in flux. In the summer of 1869 Governor Scott increased the value of land and further elevated property taxes, and at the same time, denied any repeal to be made to the courts. Furious over the denial of constitutional rights to appeal, property owners publicly declared that the governor was courting open rebellion.[9] Self-appointed warriors emerged from the ash heaps of a decimated society vowing to protect the white race from political bondage and obliteration by miscegenation. Rife with symbols, religious overtones and rhetoric, the Klan offered promise of a renewed commitment to white supremacy—a commitment that would prevail over perceived evils and guarantee mastery. Although dominion was lost via the Civil War, perhaps because of the sin of pride, the Klan gave belief that it could be regained.

The Klan of York County, as well as the entire South, was a product of white opinions and acceptable behavioral patterns of the times; it was a natural product of the South's violent history. Though the Klan supposedly was an all-male organization, in 1933, Lucy Zipporah Smith Howell related that she and Miss Willie Williams were "initiated into the fraternity, oath and all," and that their part was to make the robes and masks for the members and take care of them.[10] While only a few women actually took the oath, the klan was supported and approved as "necessary" by most women, and one of the touted reasons for it existence was that "it was for the protection of white womanhood." It is not beyond reason to believe that the white opinion would have trickled down even to children, and that they would have reflected it in their play and childish prattle. The old southern attitudes of rights, honor and womanhood were intricately woven into the robes of the Klansman. The South was a somewhat closed society that had changed its mental attitudes very little from its formative period; the Klan was not foreign but a natural progression of that society. Regarding the white participants of York County, it might be said on the one hand that they were a product of their times; on the other, in an atmosphere of intolerance, the majority of them simply were in the wrong place at the wrong time and some were apprehended.

The events in York County surrounding the Ku Klux Klan were not completely unique among South Carolina Piedmont counties, but seemingly they were more numerous there and more severe. This being the case, York County is a good study subject, and the variety of data now available provides the opportunity to examine this single county in considerable detail, and to offer some minor corrections to widely recognized scholarly studies.

Initially, the Federal Government's approach to the violence in the late 1860s and early 1870s was weak. Later attempts to control it generally proved ineffectual. One scholar in reevaluating the Klan in South Carolina succinctly sums up the federal effort: "In the end, it was the Klan that scored the strategic victory, for by forcing federal action, it revealed the inadequacies of the enforcement program for all to see — and for some in the South to use."[11]

When one views the violence evoked by the Ku Klux Klan one must stand amazed and subsequently wonder about the psychological origin of such brutality. Over the course of time, a number of sociological suggestions have been made, many of which are adequate. There is, however, one aspect that has been somewhat ignored that evidently had a direct bearing on the rise of the Klan. The presence of religion and mythology and its influence upon the South must be considered.

Religion rested at the heart of the Southerner — rich or poor, black or white, saint or sinner — all were (and are) haunted by God and the devil. Beginning soon after the American Revolution with the rise of evangelicalism in the South and continuing through the Federal period, religion and Old Testament mythology were delivered by preachers to a receptive population.[12] The Biblical stories of patriarchs founding a nation ordained by God were applied to the South, and Southerners identified themselves as new Israel carving out a paradise from the wilderness. To them, God was the planner of the South and its agricultural life; it was easy to believe that "he who lives close to the sod, is close to God." Believing themselves to be chosen and blessed, their theology penetrated all segments of their society. The religious stereotypes of the 18th and 19th centuries were so strongly imbedded in the southern antebellum Protestant that they wrote and spoke in intense religious terms—terms often dismissed as simple rhetoric by contemporary readers.[13] In 1860, when South Carolina seceded from the Union, men in Charleston employed such terms when they shouted, "We have pulled a temple down." Continuing with this particular brand of thought, they considered five years later that they had been overrun by the power of a foreign god. If they were worthy of their God, they had to fight.

Through the early and various waves of revivalism that swept the southland, a language of Zion was quickly incorporated into southern culture and the symbols of revivalism could easily be used to support order, freedom and justice. The call for repentance was developed into a call for men and women to unite in the struggle for justice, and the call to separate from sin allowed the Southerner to distinguish between friend and foe.[14]

While God haunted the heart of the Southerner, the preferred spirit was Satan. The wholesale acceptance of this entity provided the Southerner with an easy explanation for evil, and at the same time allowed them to be excluded from certain responsibilities. A 20th century comedian aptly epitomized this mentality when he declared, "the devil made me do it." Nineteenth-century evangelical preachers used the devil to awaken the layman and keep them and their family within acceptable religious boundaries.[15] The devil and devil imagery were among the strongest of southern dogmas.

The Southerner's ability to identify the devil and project that imagery onto others was often noted. In the Fairfield *Herald*, one such example appears in which Republican Party members are described as "gibbering, louse-eaten, devil worshipping barbarians, from the jungles of Dahomey, and peripatetic buccaneers from Cape Cod, Memphremagog, Hell, and Boston."[16] Carpetbaggers were described in the same imagery:

> The devil invented snakes, fleas, scorpions, tarantulas, centipedes, mosquitoes, gnats, hyenas, owls, buzzards, hawks, vultures, alligators, Stingarees [sic], gars, sharks, chigres [sic], and vampyres [sic], and to concentrate all the meanness and deviltry in creation, he put them in a cauldron and boiled them down and produced a carpet bagger, as the grand masterpiece of Satanic hate.[17]

Yet another, extolling the secret labors of the Ku Klux Klan against "the wicked, the ungodly and the perjured" stated they would "soon feel the keen edge of the sickle and the invisible boring of the white ant."[18] Such imagery assisted the Southerner in reenforcing his belief in man's evil nature and justifying corporal punishment in the home, school and prison. Since the devil was making them do it, they chose to literally "beat the Devil out of them." Being constantly admonished to be ever mindful of the infernal nature in all men, it was natural for the evangelical Southerner to conclude that the Negro race shared in this hellish nature. Although they may have recognized the devil in themselves, they undoubtedly could see it all the more clearly in the black man. When Klansmen whipped or beat a black man, they could with minimal effort convince themselves that they were doing a service for both the man and society.

Religious mythology was also a large part of the southern system of slavery. The system was seen by most as an institution that afforded a better life and possibly a way of salvation for the black man who fortuitously had been rescued from the dark jungles of Africa and introduced to the white man's civilization. The slave master argued slavery was supported by the Bible and an extension of God's law, and saw himself as a steward over a lesser people. Often ministers and laymen pointed to the account of Paul and Onesimus as sufficient justification for slavery. Yet, justification for this system was glaring when nearly all white nations had forsaken the institution.[19]

Seeming to agree, though indirectly, with the influence religion had on the Southerner, W. J. Cash offers an explanation as to why Klansmen perpetrated acts of such violence and brutality considered reprehensible by Federal authorities at the time and now by both Northerners and Southerners in the 20th century. Cash suggests that Klansmen may have found it necessary "to hold fast to their own, to maintain their divergence, to remain what they had been and were." Cash also agues that an "all too great attachment to racial values and tendency to justify cruelty and injustice in the name of those values" characterized the southerner of the past and remained to the 1930s when Cash was writing. Though Cash's *The Mind of the South* has been criticized by many prominent Southern historians since 1941, he remains a powerful voice.

There may be other less easy ways to explain rationales that allowed Klansmen to justify their actions. Blacks were seen as a superstitious lot who, at worst, were evil brutes and at best, docile animals.[20] It was commonly believed that the black man's nature exhibited a proclivity toward lawlessness and savagery that constantly involved him in crime. "Everybody knows," wrote Reverend W. H. Campbell, "that when freed from the compelling influence of the white man[,] he reverts by a law of nature to the natural barbarism in which he was created in the hot jungles of

Africa."[21] As long as this image that the black man was somehow inferior or subhuman could be maintained, it served to justify many cruel acts.

Writing from Bluffton, South Carolina, in 1876, planter Mellichamp speaks of his racial and evangelical attitudes common to the South while telling about his house catching afire. "It would have burned down in a short time had it not been for the presence of mind of an old servant of mine, & the crowds of my negro patients [?] who came in howling, — yelling, screaming — and leaping like demons (or will you say monkeys?) — upon the shed, — some climbing the pillars— and all working as if mad!"[22] Almost certainly, his use of the word "demons," and "monkeys," would not have appeared a few decades later in describing a similar incident. Referring to their appearance as demons is clearly taken from religious language so casually used by Southerners, while the word monkey hints at his belief of their subhuman existence.

The close of the Civil War produced wholesale romanticism of the Old South as a spurious harvest was reaped regarding honor-bound admiration and protection of southern womanhood. This admiration and protection, however, ignored a large population of women. The Klan's Constitution, which states, "Females ... shall ever be special objects of our regard and protection," obviously was selective among womanhood. This is evidenced through the account of Richard M. Jolly of Gaffney in Spartanburg County (now Cherokee County), a self-professed Klansman.

> In that year [1868] I had an excapede [sic] with a negro who had risen above her state at a sale of my mother-in-law's. She told some one in her smart set that my mother had told a lie. When I heard it I could not contain my wrath. I asked if she had said it. The woman replied that she had whereupon I knocked her down and was on the point of using a chair to finish the job when she scrambled up and ran for her life. I attempted to get a gun, but was stopped ... [and] reminded ... that night would come.[23]

Over the last several years, a number of books and articles have been published concerning the Ku Klux Klan in South Carolina; all giving at least some attention to its activities in York County. Up to this time there has not been a publication, however, that has dealt specifically or in depth with this segment of York County's history. It is hoped that this work will fill that gap. As the title of this work implies, it is limited to the Klan within York County, venturing out of this boundary only when some incident reflects heavily on the county's people or events. The focus of this publication is to highlight the central figures of the Klan and reveal the depths to which the organization penetrated the social and political fabric of the area during the Reconstruction years.

Warning needs to be given concerning the casual reading of any discussion on behavior during the Reconstruction Period; this work is no exception to that rule. Judging the role of 19th century participants from our perspective is not only difficult, but that judgment will invariably be tainted by 21st century biases. In reading any history, one must lay aside preconceived political and social notions. Elizabeth Fox-Genovese aptly said, "We have traveled so far down the road of identity politics that it has become all but impossible to understand that good people, and even great people may honestly defend positions and causes that we ourselves find repugnant."[24]

A superficial look at the activities of the Ku Klux Klan will place white Democrats in a most unfavorable, though perhaps deserved, light. On the other hand, a casual reading may cause one to envisage white Republicans as a compassionate vanguard of civil rights. With Klan violence so glaring, it would be easy to overlook the corruption and manipulation of the Reconstruction government promoted by the Radical elements of the Republican Party. In fact, both Democrats and Republicans were using the black man as a tool for supremacy. The Democrats were hoping for "business as usual" in the South, and Republicans were struggling to keep control of national politics; caught in the crossfire of this political war were the freedmen. It is fair to say that both parties would have been content had African-Americans not been present. Since they were, though, and since they represented a large block of votes, black men important to both.

Preconceived notions have led many whites today to entertain the idea that the Ku Klux Klan acted as moral guardians of the postwar years. This belief is clearly not grounded in truth. It may be that the Ku Klux Klan of the early 20th century has been confused with the earlier Klan of the Reconstruction era. Although the Klan movement of the second decade of the 20th century did, indeed, exert some judgment on immoral behavior, the Reconstruction Klan had little motivation to improve morality It cannot be over stressed that the Klan of the 19th century should never be interpreted as a watchdog of morality since it was motivated by politics only.

It is agreed that the Reconstruction Klan in York County levied occasional punishment for unacceptable behavior (as took place on the Hullender farm in Cherokee County, in the case of the whipping of a man who frequented a house of ill repute), but these occurrences were few. The few cases dealing with morality play a minor role in the Klan's history when compared with the overwhelming acts that were solely of a political nature.

An excellent example of how one-sided the Klan was in its moral judgment is found in the transcript of the Klan trials. When a Chester

County black woman gave birth to a child fathered by a white man, the Klan not only punished the woman but her stepfather as well, and did nothing to the man who had committed adultery with her. Furthermore, testimony proved that the state of South Carolina had never seen fit to create a law against bastardy between a white man and a black woman.[25] Another example of this biased moral code is found in how a York County black woman was punished for bearing seven children for her ex-master. The reason the Klan gave for whipping the woman was that she had made herself a "nuisance" to the man's wife; there was no consideration of his contribution. These examples serve to prevent us deceiving ourselves about the true aims of the Klan. From its inception the Reconstruction Klan was a political force — not moral guardians — and remained so during its existence.

Another misconception regarding this paramilitary organization involves the reason the Ku Klux Klan was organized in the first place. Typical histories of the Klan written just after the turn of the 20th century — some forty years after Reconstruction — often state that the Klan had been organized to end the burning of private property and disarm the black militia. In their obvious attempts to justify its formation, these historians ignored the fact that the Klan existed before the formation of the militia units and before there was any reported arson of private property in the county. An 1868 article in the *Yorkville Enquirer* clearly defines the work of the Klan as being political in nature and designed "to thwart Radicalism, [and] arrest negro domination in the South."[26]

A third misconception involves the thinking that the developing situation in the immediate postwar years warranted violence or made it necessary. Surely we have come to a place in our history that we can see that violence provokes violence and that violence executed by vigilantes is never warranted. When the present study was in the early stages, the Oklahoma City bombing took place and sharply affected the writer's thinking and, consequently, the writing of this history. A few days after the tragedy I went back to the draft and made a definite change in its mood by exchanging words that strengthened the horror of vigilante rule. It is certainly agreed that the advent of the Ku Klux Klan in York County totally stymied the Federal government and hastened its retreat from the South. History, however, proves that had the white Democrats patiently endured the inequities of Reconstruction the Northerners would have tired of their labors and abandoned them on their own.

Though not necessarily a misconception, but perhaps more a lack of understanding, is the difference with which Southerners and Northerners dealt with the presence of African-Americans in the 19th century South. Although some might contend that the South was a pluralistic society because the black race was mightily present, pluralism was only superficial. Truly many whites brought their slaves into close association and treated them "like family," but the race as a whole was ignored. Somewhere it has been said that Southerners had great appreciation for blacks as individuals, but had little regard for them as a race. On the other hand, Northerners supposedly extolled the race in general, but had little regard for them as individuals. If this is true, it would explain the two subcultures' approaches to race issues. Either way, blacks were so mentally detached and segregated by whites from the local society that they existed as a mere dark shadow on a white society.

Emancipation and the granting of full civil rights to the once enslaved race nearly guaranteed social turmoil. Southern white adults born prior to the Civil War were a privileged lot. They had grown up in a society that remained nearly constant and offered little opportunity for demonstrations of tolerance. Only sporadically did they have to acknowledge a few who were unlike themselves. Roman Catholics and Jews scattered throughout the Piedmont offered little challenge to the largely white Protestant population. The Old South had its own brand of religion, music, food, social patterns and dialect; variances were marginal and tolerated with minimal effort.

As one reads this account of the Ku Klux Klan in York County, it will be obvious that South Carolina's governor, Robert K. Scott, was one of the major players. Scott's adamant approach to unpopular policies persistently caused white Democrats to square off with him. While in office Scott was relentless in promoting the Republican Party over good leadership; yet, some years after leaving office he reflected on the era with some regret regarding the polices of the Federal government which he enforced with fervency. The ex-governor said that he regarded the Reconstruction Acts a mistake. He then believed that the Federal government would have done better if practical provisions had been made to benefit the South, and if Congress had organized a provisional government that would have established schools to educate the ignorant.

Evidently seeing clearly the ill influence of the Radical Republicans among the freedmen and their lack of education, he was assured that had they promoted education and not politics, blacks then would have been better qualified to govern themselves. In retrospect he counted the "onerous tax on cotton" to have ruined South Carolina's financial recovery because it drained vast sums of money from the state. Regarding the enfranchisement of blacks, he was less than complimentary to his own political party; he said, "Many Republicans are opposed to colored citizenship, and have refused to make all men equal before the law. They believe this is a 'white man's government,' and 'if the class combines with other hostile elements, you will find a party in the United States sufficiently strong to eliminate the colored man entirely from any part or influence in politics.'" Well after the Reconstruction era, he admonished blacks to "stand aloof from all political parties," and recommended they form their own party since they had little hope of constructive actions from either the Republicans or the Democrats. Scott wisely concluded that each party would affiliate with the black man only so long as it promoted that party's supremacy.

1

Opening Scenes to Fury

"...Disappointed Hopes and Aspirations."

Voter registration began in York County on Thursday, 17 August 1867, and continued until 5 o'clock P.M. the following Saturday. It proceeded quietly with 706 individuals registering—369 whites and 337 blacks—with whites obtaining a majority of 32. Each person hoping to register had to "solemnly swear in the presence of Almighty God" an oath of loyalty to the United States, particularly in the following words:

> That I have never been a member of any State Legislature, nor held any executive or judicial office in any State, and afterwards engaged in insurrection or rebellion against the United States, or given aid or comfort to the enemies thereof, that I have never taken oath as a member of the Congress of the United States or as an officer of the United States, as a member of any State Legislature, or as an executive or judicial officer of any State, to support the Constitution of the United States, and afterwards engaged in insurrection or rebellion, or given aid or comfort to the enemies thereof; that I will faithfully support the Constitution and obey the laws of the United States and will to best of my ability encourage others to do so.[1]

A second round of registration took place early in the following September,[2] and by September 24, all registration returns were reported except those of the Bethel Precinct. Tallies revealed 1,870 whites enrolled with blacks totaling 1,908 and having a majority of 38. McConnellsville and

Rock Hill showed a heavy percentage of blacks,[3] and it was expected that Bethel returns when made available also would report a black majority. The only areas exhibiting an overpowering number of prospective white voters were Bethany and Boydton in extreme western York County. Revised county returns later made to the Military Headquarters in Charleston showed that 1,990 whites and 2,029 blacks had registered.

Military Order No. 98 which was issued 16 October 1867 by General E. R. S. Canby, Commander of Federal forces in the Carolinas, required an election to be held on Tuesday and Wednesday, 19 and 20 November. Those casting ballots could mark "Yes" or "No" for calling a convention to draft a new constitution for South Carolina; those voting "yes" could then write in their choice for a delegate.[4] Though the figures for statewide registered voters stood at over 125,000 (46,346 whites and 78,982 blacks), only 71,807 cast their vote. In favor of the convention were 130 whites and 68,876 blacks; voting against it were 2,808 whites. This lack of white voter participation was reflected in York County. Out of a total of 4,084 registered voters only 1,773 cast their ballots. Of the 2,311 who did not vote, only about 350 were black. The newspaper reported that "...very few of the whites voted, not exceeding sixty!"[5]

The Convention to frame a constitution and civil government according to the Reconstruction Acts of Congress opened in Charleston on 14 January 1868, in obedience to General Canby's General Order No. 160 issued 28 December 1867. Delegates from York County were J. L. Neagle[6] (R/white), William E. Rose (R/white), J. W. Mead (R/black) and J. Hannibal White (R/black). This convention labored over 50 days before the new state constitution was ready for submission to the voters.[7]

In Alabama white voters successfully prevented the ratification of a new state constitution by refusing to vote, causing it to be defeated for the lack of a majority. To prevent white voters in other states from attempting the same thing, Congress passed a Fourth Reconstruction Act in the first quarter of 1868 "providing that a majority of the votes cast was sufficient to ratify a [state] constitution."[8] In other words, a small number voting would not prevent an election from being declared valid.[9]

In preparation for the April 14, 15 and 16 vote on the Constitution and the simultaneous election of those who would hold various legislative and state offices, the boards of registration were ordered to open their books for final revision. The count of eligible voters appearing in the area newspaper, though lacking the county's third military precinct,[10] was given as 2,065 whites and 2,072 blacks, showing that an additional 75 whites and 43 blacks had registered. Whites had narrowed the black majority to only seven in the reported areas,[11] suggesting that a concerted effort had been made to register as many whites as possible.

1. Opening Scenes to Fury

Looking south on Congress Street, Yorkville, SC.

The mid–April election would offer voters the opportunity to elect members of Congress, a Senator and four Representatives to the Legislature, the Governor, Lieutenant Governor, Secretary of State, and Comptroller General. Since it would be this newly elected government that would determine the future rights for everyone in South Carolina, their decisions would be crucial to members of both races. On 6 April 1868, a mass meeting of conservatives from across York County gathered at the courthouse square to amend the Democratic ticket for the Legislature. By 11 A.M. the crowd was as large "as any political exigency ever brought here before."[12] This seemingly benign scene was the beginning of some of the most tumultuous events to take place in York County since the Revolutionary War. During the beginning of the Reconstruction, from late 1867 and into early 1868, attention mainly focused on the Union League and the Democratic Conservative Clubs; but after the spring of 1868 the key players were the Federal government and the Ku Klux Klan.

A number of studies previously done on the Ku Klux Klan have frequently repeated a near traditional view that the name was taken from the Greek meaning, "a circle of friends." However, in 1934, W. B. Romine offered an interesting suggestion as to the origin of the name. Admitting she was without documentation, she believed it was derived from Mexican mythology concerning Cukulcan, the god of light. To support her theory, she relates that 30,000 men from Tennessee volunteered for service during the Mexican War and would have become familiar with the Mexican myth.[13] The myth certainly may have had some poetic appeal to their sons and nephews who heard the story of Cukulcan, who was always seen in conflict with the vampire god of darkness and bringing forth the dawning of a new day by his victory over lightlessness. This theory certainly fits the Southern imagery of good against evil, light against darkness.

Apparently there is an endless string of theories. The *New York Tribune* suggested the organization's name was derived from the sound of a rifle being cocked. This is apparently what is being referred to by the *Augusta Chronicle* in its reporting of a civil disturbance at Hamburg, South Carolina, "a game of chuck-a-luck," in the fall of 1869.[14] Still yet, the *Charleston Republican* claimed it was named for a Texas desperado, Nal. K. Xulkuk, who supposedly avenged any wrong done to him, his partners or country. Spelled backwards, his name becomes Kuklux Klan. Another newspaper, The *Memphis Appeal*, believed the name was taken from an ancient Jewish manuscript entitled, "A True and Authenticated History of the Great Rebellion of the Hebrews against King Pharaoh, B.C." In the text the name was spelled Cu Clux Clan, which in English means the Straw Club. The account dealt with a rebellion by Hebrew brick makers who had to carry their own straw, and with the proverb, "Straws show which way the wind blows."[15]

The Union League was the first new, political group to form in York County following the Civil War. The nearly all-black organization first emerged in the North as a patriotic body supporting the Lincoln Administration and the war that was being waged.[16] In the spring of 1867, the league's national leaders decided to assist in the establishment of Republican Clubs throughout the South. Realizing that speakers would be more effective than printed materials when dealing with illiterate freedmen, funds from the Republican Party were funneled to South Carolina organizers who canvassed the state.[17] Throughout the summer and fall of that year these organizers traveled the back roads to churches, schools, plantation quarters, and small shacks and cabins used by black laborers. Whenever the speakers made their appearance they had no trouble drawing crowds; black men, women and children rallied to meeting places eager to hear of forestalled rights as well as social changes that soon would transform their lives.[18]

As chapters of the Union League were organized, blacks commenced the process of developing a much-needed cohesiveness and they began to emerge as a major factor in southern politics. The world of ex-slaves started to burst with excitement. During the summer of 1867 freedmen laid hold to their new rights with camp-meeting enthusiasm. A local chapter of the league often served as a center to learn about political rights, upcoming elections, various Reconstruction acts, and political platforms. Members might come to a meeting and spend hours listening to someone read aloud from newspapers and pamphlets.[19] Freedmen in York County, as well as those in other parts of the Second Military District[20] that comprised all of South Carolina and North Carolina, joyously united with the developing political movement. Prior to the 19–20 November 1867 referendum on holding a state constitutional convention, nearly 90 percent of the state's eligible black voters, and more than eight out of every ten blacks in York County, had registered.[21]

Although little subject matter connected with Union League in York County is available, segments of its operations can be gathered from information about other chapters of the league in South Carolina. Union League chapters were more than information centers. They were a combination of a political machine, labor union, tribunal, educational system, moral council, and rental protection agency. They addressed social welfare, assisted in marketing agricultural products, secured health care from physicians who would wait for end of year payment, and reviewed legal judgments against members and labor problems.[22] In legal matters, leaders acted as mediators on behalf of members who had been excluded from civil procedures by local law enforcement officers. On some occasions, league members claimed the authority to perform citizen's arrests or secure a suspect until a warrant could be obtained. When law officials were slow to act, members sometimes would serve warrants; when authorities claimed ignorance, a league might conduct its own investigation regarding a Klan raid or other happening. In some instances, league members formed into a community watch force and defended Republican office holders who otherwise might have met with violence or expulsion from office.[23]

One of the first activities of the Union League in York County was an organizational "Grand Mass Meeting" scheduled at the Yorkville courthouse in July 1867. Disgruntled white farmers saw little need for the gathering, concluding that it only provided an opportunity for those attending to "mood over their disappointed hopes and aspirations." Their real opinion was that a faceless, subhuman labor force would "become distracted [and] the crops suffer serious injury."[24] Though the *Yorkville Enquirer* saw little need to report much about the meeting, it did publish portions of what purportedly was a league order book's instruction for passing oneself as a "Leaguer." When questioned: "Give the 'Four L's' as follows: right hand raised to Heaven, thumb and third finger touching their ends over the palm and pronounce 'Liberty.' Bringing the right hand down on a line with the shoulder, pronounce 'Lincoln.' Dropping the hand open at your side, pronounce 'Loyal.' With your hand and fingers downward in the chest, the thumb thrust into the vest or waistband, across the body, pronounce 'League.'"[25]

In an October 1867 issue of the *Yorkville Enquirer*, a white Democrat offered his opinion of the league and warned against membership:

> ...to this so-called patriotic organization, I deem it my duty to caution the public against it. It is gotten up chiefly by aspirants for political advancement, who see no other chance to get office. These men seek to create the impression that to be truly patriotic, everybody ought to join the Union Leagues. Those who are so confiding as to take this advice, are immediately bound by solemn oaths to vote for none but loyal; but they are not left at liberty to judge for themselves, as to who are loyal. The heads of the League assume this duty....
>
> Strange as it may seem, this trap for votes is meeting with considerable success through the country, and is catching not a few victims in our District. Quite a number of voters have bit at the bait of extra patriotism which the Leagues offer as an inducement to its dupes, and have pledged themselves, blindfold, to its requirements.[26]

In York County, as well as in other parts of the Piedmont, the Union League was more prevalent than in the low country. The former slave population had a direct influence on the formation of the league. The rolling Piedmont was composed of farms that required smaller patchwork fields, and it was here that less affluent farmers of the upcountry often worked closely with their slaves. This association afforded blacks an opportunity to become more knowledgeable about politics than their low country counterparts.[27] After emancipation, upcountry freedmen quickly grasped the meaning of their franchise and were eager to learn more about their rights. Seeking information about their constitutional liberties and how they might practice them, yet being suspicious of their former masters, they turned to the waiting arms of the Republican Party. Befriended by white Republicans who formed the league, blacks filled meeting halls to obtain advice about methods to elect a friendly government. The political education they received made them vocal and zealous members in the Republican Party, and simultaneously made them distrustful of the Democratic Party.[28]

Although a few white men of some standing provided direction and expounded ideology within the ranks of the Union League, membership in the league was composed primarily of black Republicans. It must be stated that even though the national, state and county Republican Party embraced the blacks, racial barriers and social mores of the times remained unabridged. This is illustrated by an incident involving a small group of men traveling from Yorkville to conduct a league rally in western York County. Among this party was a black legislator, the Honorable John

Mead. All agreed he was educated and respectable; yet when they arrived at the home of Captain Faris (white) for a meal, they experienced a problem with seating. Captain Faris was not willing to have his family sit with Representative Mead; the other men, all whites, sympathized with the Captain. Faris agreed to set a long table and seat Mead at the furthermost end while the whites were clustered at the opposite end. Later, when sleeping accommodations were being arranged, none of the white men wanted to share a bed with the black man, though as one Republican later claimed, "it was a customary habit with the old scalawags and carpetbaggers." A compromise arrangement was reached when Faris agreed to place a pallet on the floor for the representative.[29] Old social habits and prejudices were slow to die, even in the political arena that called all men equal.

Some white Republicans who claimed freedmen could not trust their former Democratic masters felt comfortable in lying to their black counterparts. Much to the consternation of Democrats, some of the league's white leaders deceived black members by telling them that the admittance oath required inductees to vote only the Republican ticket. As one of these leaders explained years later, "Leagues were extended for no other purpose than to carry the election, and impose upon the ignorant that they were compelled by oath to support the nomination or else be exposed."[30] The Union League was soon seen as a political thorn in the side of the Democrats, and thus became a primary target of the Klan.

From the outset of their emancipation in 1865, freedmen were forced to exercise political practices in relation to the land and labor structure. The control of manual labor was the immediate concern of white Democrats who, more often than not, viewed black Republicans as unsuitable employees. A laborer might easily be denied rental privileges on the simple ground that he failed to vote the Democratic ticket, or he might be driven off a farm or be denied pay for attending Union League meetings. Social and political power, it was seen, could only be secured through land reform.[31]

For this reason, soon after its organization the Union League undertook the issues of labor as part of its political work. The rural chapters of York County were included with others in the state league that advanced the movement to standardize yearly tenure agreements. Regardless of these efforts such arrangements were not easily negotiated, and some blacks were forced to act in ways they saw as being in their family's best interest. As an example: in some parts of the state, blacks who voted with whites were awarded "certificates of democracy" which almost assured them employment, a house and the white landowner allowing them the use of a small amount of land. As white tactics became more violent, increased night raids by Ku Klux Klansmen assisted planters in achieving

Perhaps an African American rally of the Union League in Yorkville during Reconstruction.

a degree of political domination of laboring blacks and in controlling their political behavior.[32]

The Conservative Clubs of the Democratic Party[33] began forming immediately after the April 1868 election, which had been a rude awakening for the white Democrats. Most white Democrats, who commonly called themselves Conservatives to appeal to members of the old Whig Party, had wrongly speculated that the Union League was of little consequence. They further persisted in believing that the influence of the Radicals of the Republican Party, as well as support for them, was declining. Prior to the spring 1868 election, they had little concern about the Radicals ever gaining control of county politics; but the outcome proved to white Democrats that blacks were going to vote solidly Republican unless convinced to do otherwise. Conservative tactics through late 1868 would remain simple: they would take a peaceful approach in dealing with the blacks, who, they believed, would eventually come to the Democratic Party and help trounce the self-righteous Republicans through a united vote.

Throughout the state and the entire South, a move was promoted to form Conservative Clubs to register white voters and plant strategy for winning local and national elections. On the same page as the results of the April election, the editor of the Yorkville paper urged Democrats to form Democratic Clubs; one such article demanded, "Organize! Organize!" and in another he charged white Democrats:

> The contest for district officers is soon to come off and we will have then an opportunity to wipe out the disgrace of our late defeat. Therefore let every man [begin] to work at once. Organize Conservative Union Clubs throughout the District, put these organizations in communication with a central organization at this place, and then strive to perfect and enlarge in every possible way these organizations. By these we can succeed. If we neglect them, we may fail again. We all acknowledge that success in the coming election is a matter much more important than that which engaged our attention last week. It will be criminal in us to sleep over our fortunes now.

Faced with the potential of suffering future losses at the polls and chided into action by the editor of the *Yorkville Enquirer*, the Democrats soon after the April elections formed themselves into community Conservative Clubs. On April 20, the Yorkville Conservative Club, acting as unofficial headquarters for all such groups in the county, offered a resolution allowing black conservative membership, thus suggesting the Democratic Party's awakening awareness of the black voter. Obviously, white land-holding farmers were hoping to siphon power from the Radicals rather than to secure a majority voting strength through cooperation with the county's blacks. Many Democrats remained unconvinced that the fall of Radicalism could be accomplished by seeking the black vote. Nonetheless, a resolution allowing black membership in the clubs was adopted in 1868:

> *Whereas*, we desire for the future as in the past, that kindly relations should be cherished towards the colored people; and that we will afford them every opportunity and privilege in our power whereby they may become instructed in the duties of citizenship, and in furtherance of these views, be it
> *Resolved*, That the colored people be invited to attend the meetings of this club, and that such as choose to do so, be invited to enroll their names as members of the same.
> *Resolved*, That we, the members of this Club, do cherish, patronize, and otherwise uphold and sustain those colored persons who have patriotically and intelligently decided that the interests of all classes in this State are identified with each other, and who have voted to sustain this principle; and we do further pledge ourselves to prefer those persons who are members of this Club, in the matter of employment and wages, over and above all other persons whosoever.[34]

Across the state, and certainly in western York County, numbers of Conservative Clubs were organized. Not since a few weeks before

Secession had the area known such political activity. Although the first club mentioned in the *Yorkville Enquirer* is the "Conservative Union Club of Clark's Fork,"[35] other clubs already had been formed in Yorkville and the surrounding areas.[36] The Clark's Fork group, meeting a few miles west of the county seat, convened at Allison's store on Saturday, April 25. Following the example set by the Yorkville Club, they adopted a resolution to receive black men into the organization.[37] The following Saturday, May 2, two new Conservative Clubs were organized: the Blairsville Club[38] and the Rock Hill Club.[39] On Saturday, May 16, an all-black club was formed in Rock Hill. The editor of the county newspaper boasted that these "colored people" were "awaking to their true interests and cutting themselves loose from oath bound societies, and the influence of persons who are luring them on to destruction."[40] At the Bullock's Creek Presbyterian Church in the extreme southwestern corner of the county, area white men met on May 9 and organized the Bullock's Creek Club.[41]

Sometime prior to the meeting at Bullock's Creek, two clubs in western York County had organized: "Pine Grove" near Antioch Baptist Church in the northwestern corner of the county, and "Whitaker" near present day Blacksburg (now Cherokee County). Both boasted that part of their membership was "colored." Two additional clubs were formed in western York County during the last week of May: the "Buffalo Club," and another that met at Wylie's Store and designated itself the "Hickory Grove Club." The latter group consisted of sixty-eight members of which 17 were black.[42]

The efforts of the clubs are not immediately obvious. When the boards of registration completed a revision of the voter list on May 23 in preparation of the upcoming election,[43] whites held a majority of 32 — only 39 more whites than were registered at the time of the April election. Although one observer claimed the white majority resulted from some blacks migrating from the county, the completed and revised list of eligible voters gave as totals: whites, 2119, and blacks, 2087,[44] or 15 more blacks than were registered in mid–April.

Evidently something less obvious than changes in voter registration had occurred before the June election, since the Democrats took every position on the ballot. Considering that the local newspaper reported that the election had progressed without any incident, we are left to assume that black suppression had advanced to overwhelming proportions by that time. It is of some interest to note that the *Yorkville Enquirer* reported 1,629 whites cast their ballots and only 452 blacks.[45] Obviously something had prevented black voters from casting their ballots. No doubt rough tactics used by Democrats or perhaps Klan members had secured the polls as they would do in the following November elections. The result of the June election follows with the Radicals or Republicans in italics.[46]

Sheriff		Probate Judge	
R. H. Glenn	1874	F. C. Harris	1853
D. T. Barrett	198	*J. C. Simpson*	197
County Commissioner		**School Commissioner**	
M. O'Connell	198	*James Bynum*	209
J. R. Faris	202	Robert Lathan	1843
W. E. Kell	142	**Coroner**	
P. Garrison	1840		
B. F. Briggs	1830	*Amos Biggers*	197
C. Whisonant	1832	J. E. Jefferys	1847
		Clerk of Court	
		J. F. Wallace	1867

Encouraged by the election, whites then pressed to extend and strengthen the Democratic Party in preparation for a good fight in the November election. On August 18, the Yorkville Club elected new officers. At the same time the members decided to hold a countywide meeting on the 29th after they received a letter from Colonel John P. Thomas of Columbia, offering to address the membership. Thomas had only recently been nominated as a Democratic Party Presidential Elector for the state.

At their national convention in New York on July 4, the Democrats nominated Horatio Seymour of New York for president and Frank P. Blair, Jr., of Missouri for vice president. In line with the thinking of the York County Conservative Clubs, the Democratic platform denounced Reconstruction and the policies of the Republican Party. The Yorkville Club's corresponding secretary was instructed to invite Major E. C. McClure of Chester, Democratic Party Presidential Elector for the state's 4th Congressional District,[47] as well as General E. M. Law and Colonel A. Coward, both of whom were to address the meeting following Colonel Thomas. In a carefully designed ploy, a special invitation was to be extended to the black membership. On August 22, a few days following the Yorkville Club meeting, the McConnells Club formed.[48] On the Monday thereafter, August 24, the Bethesda Club organized. This club adopted a typical constitution, but lowered the age limit from 18 to 16.[49]

The meeting of 29 August initiated and hosted by the Yorkville Club was a political success and long remembered by the citizens of York County and the surrounding area. Several columns in the *Yorkville Enquirer* described the events of the day and gave full accounts of prayers and speeches. The town was filled with an assemblage of 2000 white men and women as well as 200 blacks who ignored "the slavish orders of the Leagues [and] had come out to hear the other side of the question...." About 10 o'clock that morning, Colonel Thomas, called the "Ajax Telemon of the South Carolina Democracy," and a number of passengers coming from Chester and points south, disembarked from the train and were greeted by a salute from an artillery piece.

As soon as the crowd could be ordered, Colonel W. H. McCorkle, marshal of the day, assembled the people at the public square for the raising of the Seymour and Blair Flag. "The band struck up a lively air — the cannon thundered a salute, and the flag gracefully threw folds to the breeze amid the shouts and huzzas of the multitude...." Colonel W. B. Wilson dedicated the flag to the cause of constitutional liberty and right as found in the Democratic Party, after which a procession led by the Chester Brass Band proceeded down Congress Street to a large platform constructed specifically for the meeting. The 20-by-24, foot stage was decorated with green foliage and boasted the flag of the Constitution. Among others seated with Colonel Thomas were Captain I. D. Witherspoon, president of the Yorkville Club, Reverend Robert Lathan, pastor of the local Associate Reformed Presbyterian Church, Colonel T. Stobo Farrow of Spartanburg, General E. M. Law, Colonel A. Coward, William C. Beatty, Esq., and Colonel W. H. McCorkle.

Reverend Lathan opened with a brief prayer, after which Colonel Thomas was introduced. He proceeded to trace the origins of the Democratic Party back to 1787 and then offered the Jeffersonian theory of states' rights and limited federal powers. Pointing out that the two dividing issues of slavery and secession had been settled, he cited the new issues of constitutional invasion and despotism. "The Howard Amendment was first submitted. What was the substance of that Amendment? It was that all that had taken an oath of office prior to the war, and afterwards engaged in it, should be deprived of holding office. That is, you were called upon to put the brand of infamy upon those who led us in the war and in the councils of the State. It was to make us lose our self-respect.... History records the atrocities of Ghengis Khan, the Great Conqueror, and of Attila, the Scourge of the World, but it has been reserved for modern radicalism to improve upon these barbarities, and subject a conquered people to the dominion of their former slaves. Nowhere will you find perpetrated, such acts of despotism as have been accomplished in this land."[50]

Following limited remarks by Colonel Farrow, General Law took the podium. He, like Thomas, denounced the Radical Republicans and argued the Reconstruction Acts to be unconstitutional. Ending the speech, Law spoke directly to the blacks gathered for the occasion, charging them to realize they were but mere tools to the Radicals who were using them for their own selfish ends. At the conclusion, the throng moved down the street to the Kings Mountain Hotel[51] where owner Thomas Davis greeted them under the Blair and Seymour Flag. Throughout the day, cheers went up and Theodore Parrish fired a piece of artillery whenever the speech-makers pleased the crowd.[52]

Sometime during the festivities, the Yorkville Club met with 14 delegates from various county clubs to form a Central Democratic Club. Doctor A. P. Campbell, who was temporarily serving as chairman, appointed R. E Guthrie secretary. On a motion by Samuel G. Brown of Sharon, a committee was appointed to nominate permanent officers; those installed were Doctor J. Rufus Bratton, president; Colonel Robert M. Kerr and Colonel W. H. McCorkle, vice presidents; D. D. Moore, secretary; R. E. Gunthrie, corresponding secretary; Major A. A. McKenzie, treasurer. A mass meeting was proposed for Thursday, September 18, and another the following day at Rock Hill. In preparation, Doctor Rufus Bratton called a gathering of delegates from each of the clubs.[53] Those attending were:

Yorkville	J. G. Enloe
Bethel	J. Leander
Clay Hill	Captain J. C. Phillips
Wylie's Store	Thomas McGill, Esq.
Allison's Store	Doctor J. W. Allison
Bethany	Doctor A. P. Campbell
Blairsville	R. A. Black
Bullock's Creek	James Blair
Fort Mill	J. H. Faulkner
Rock Hill	W. L. Roddy
Buffalo	Henderson Martin
Antioch	Ira Hardin

Within a few days of the delegates meeting, the Turkey Creek Club was formed on September 3. The organization of that club, along with the McConnellsville and Bethesda clubs that had formed less than a month earlier,[54] completed the influence of the Conservative Clubs and blanketed the entire western portion of York County.

It was already apparent to the Democrats that various enticements, meetings, peaceful parades, and picnics would not attract black voters away from the Republican Party; thus an approach both rough and violent was considered. The alteration in tactics was openly proclaimed: "The bonds of the league have become more close.... We will have to change our tactics to meet this new state of things. The difficulties in the way of bringing over the negroes to our side, are becoming greater...."[55] Not until the violent activities employed by the Ku Klux Klan did the area again witness such concerted opposition to the Radicals.

Building on the political excitement generated by the late–August gathering when Thomas spoke, a public meeting was held at the York courthouse on Monday, September 7, to consider the question of a compromise on debt.[56] Like all the southern states, South Carolina and its citizens were reeling under the weight of debts incurred during the Civil War. Businessman J. Newman McElwee was seated as chairman, and R. Springs Moore served as secretary. McElwee was a creditor of over $30,000, but he was ready to commit the debts to flames if all would do likewise for the betterment of the country. Charging that the white people of York County had no representatives in Washington or Columbia, and that the property of the entire county would not pay 50 cents on each dollar owned as debt, he declared the only option left was a compromise between debtor and creditor. "Yes, fellow citizens, a liberal, just and equitable compromise will restore harmony; unite the white people; exhume morality and social feeling; pay more debts and bury Radicalism in York District in an infamy so deep and so profound, that nothing short of resurrection will ever reach it."[57] Those attending resolved that the chairman establish a committee consisting of 11 men from both regimental areas of the old district to prepare a report and resolution on a compromise on debt, and that the committee make a presentation at a meeting in October. Those appointed by the chairman were:

Western Regiment	Eastern Regiment
Doctor J. R. Bratton	Colonel Cadwalder Jones
John O. Crawford	Colonel A. B. Springs
W. A. Moore, Esq.	W. L. Roddy
Colonel W. H. McCorkle	Colonel John M. White
Reverend R. A. Ross	A. F. Hutchinson
J. N. McElwee, Sr.	L. H. Massey
Doctor R. T. Allison	John S. Bratton
William Oates	John R. Patton
J. C. Chambers	J. H. Adams
William McGill	Peter McCallum
James Brian	Samuel Anderson

The mass meeting of the county Conservative Clubs on September 18 gave evidence that the people of York County were "keenly alive to the issues to be determined in the coming election." The *Yorkville Enquirer* reported that proof of the people's concern was "afforded in the frequency of political gatherings and the attentive interest and large outpourings of the people that characterize them."[58] Much like the late–August meeting, a large garlanded platform held the speakers. Z. B. Vance, an ex-governor of North Carolina, arrived by train at 10 A.M. from Chester, where he had spoken at a barbecue hosted by that county's Democratic Club. The crowd of about 2000 people at York were led in prayer by Reverend T. R. Gaines, after which Captain I. D. Witherspoon, acting as chairman of the event, introduced the governor. Vance gave the principal address and reportedly kept the crowd "spell-bound" for three hours!

Two black Democrats, James Minor and William Stowers, took the stand following Vance. Minor spoke to the men of his race in a "...plain, sensible, and to the point" manner, and Stowers closed the event with a short speech. Amid a large number of men carrying torches the group moved down the street to the Masonic Hall, where the ladies of the Episcopal Church hosted Vance as their guest of honor at a type of fair. Craving more oratory, the crowd issued vigorous calls to the governor. He declined, saying that if the people of South Carolina wore him out with speechmaking, then "scallawagerie would have a fine time in North Carolina." The crowd, determined not to be so easily quelled, managed to elicit short speeches from Colonel W. B. Wilson, Colonel J. D. Wylie of Lancaster County, and Colonel L. M. McAfee of Shelby, North Carolina. The din of drums and horns continued on into the morning hours.

With the November elections approaching, the month of October was spiked with large gatherings where political drums were beaten and the participants thrilled over possible victory at the polls. The Allison Store and Wylie Store Conservative Clubs met at the "Berry Place" in western York County, on Saturday, September 26. At that time chairman Doctor R. T. Allison with the assistance of Theodore A. Moore, secretary, announced plans for a mass meeting of the "Democracy of Western York County" at Whiteside's Mill on Wednesday, October 7.[59]

Attending the festivities at the mill were Democrats from all over the county. The local black Democrats and some of the committee of arrangements were seated under the Seymour and Blair flag, while the all-black Yorkville Colored Club rested under their symbol — "a mighty mule on canvas."[60] After dinner the audience reassembled at the stand, and Major E. C. McClure, Democratic Party Presidential Elector for the fourth Congressional District, made a short speech. Next, Reverend R. A. Ross[61] came to the stand and defined his position from 1832 to the present time within the Democratic Party. He finished his talk by exposing the rottenness of the Radical platform and declared his intention to vote for Seymour and Blair. Primus Ellis rose and made a few remarks in total agreement with Reverend Ross. He urged the blacks to quit the Union League and unite with their "old masters who were their best friends."[62]

Amid all the Democratic rallies, picnics and meetings, the Republicans attempted their own mass political gathering in Yorkville on October 9. The turnout was puny compared to the Democratic meeting of mid–September. A biased observer reported that early in the morning "a number of local Mongols of the party could be seen on the wing, hurrying to and fro, trying to produce a moderate degree of enthusiasm among their deluded followers, but with little success, as was afterwards demonstrated." A claimed head count of the Republicans, purportedly taken as they marched down Congress Street, revealed only 108 freedmen present. The march of the Radicals terminated at "Hannibal White's Grove," not far out of town, for political speeches. Alexander S. Wallace, candidate for Congress, P. J. O'Connell, and Hannibal White, members of the Legislature from York, and Lucius Windbush from Chester, addressed the group.

Wallace, being a local turned Republican, was particularly hated by white Democrats. He was prone to call the Democratic Party a "slaveholding party," which the Democrats found to be disgusting since he had remained a slaveholder to the end of the war. But at least one man, S. B. Lathan, recalled that Wallace had initially made an honest effort toward bipartianship. In 1933 Lathan claimed that just after the war Wallace had tried his best to get at least ten good white men to organize an effort to lead the freedmen along Democratic Party lines, but the whites refused and the freedmen followed after the Radicals and carpetbaggers.[63]

Seemingly the Democrats took every opportunity to slander Congressman Wallace. On one occasion, after Wallace had attended the 1869 Republican Convention, they reported he acted the part of a "ladies man, basking in the smiles and sweet words of all the ladies attending — but, all the ladies were colored." About the same time, with hopes to turn the black Republicans against Wallace, the Democrats dredged up a bill Wallace had introduced to the House on 26 November 1858 to authorize the sale of free blacks back into slavery if they committed crimes. Although Wallace was hated by white Democrats, he succeeded in regaining their confidence a few years after Reconstruction; one man recalled, "Mr. Wallace was a much hated man in those days but time has softened some of that and really Mr. Wallace was never as he was painted. And as a matter of fact, he was not so different from many folks of this day. His politics helped him to get into office and hold it, and there's a many loud-mouthed Democrats for office getting only. If being a Republican would land him in Congress or in a good paying soft job there are not so many of them who would turn the jobs down."[64] Wallace was born 30 December 1810 and died 27 June 1893 and is buried in Rose Hill Cemetery in York. His tombstone reads, "A self made man. He became a member of the S.C. Legislation, Collector of Internal Revenue and member of U.S. House of

1. Opening Scenes to Fury

Home of U.S. Senator Alexander S. "Buttermilk" Wallace, located three miles south of York on the old Pickney Road.

Representatives. He filled the positions with marked ability and left to his family the proud heritage of an unsullied name. A good citizen, a consistent Christian, a friend of the poor, His deeds will not be forgotten."

The small turnout for the Republican rally in October seemed to confirm the Democrats' delusion that Radicalism was dying. Mr. Grist boasted, "The indications are that Radicalism in York District is on its last legs, and before many months have elapsed, it will, doubtless, only be remembered as a thing of the past. Rumors are current that many of the freedmen who have heretofore acted with the Radical party are deserting it, having become satisfied that their true interest is identical with that of the respectable white man of the country."[65] Following the Republican gathering, Democrats on Kings and Buffalo creeks in extreme western York County held a meeting at the Bascion School House on the 17th. Judge Beatty and Colonel Wilson were guest speakers for the event.[66]

On the evening of Thursday, October 21, excitement beginning at the train depot spread over Yorkville when a company of the Eighth United States Infantry Regiment disembarked. About 40 men under the command of Brevet Major W. S. Worth had been dispatched to York County by General George G. Meade, head of the Department of the South that had superseded the Second and Third Military Districts. The purpose of these federal troops was to repress any disturbance that might occur at the upcoming November election. The area populace was informed by the newspaper on the following day that they should put no political significance in their arrival because troops had been dispatched to Chester, Union, Laurens, Abbeville, Newberry, Edgefield, Beaufort, Georgetown and Darlington.[67]

As the election approached, newspaper editor Lewis Grist encouraged Democrats to go to the ballot boxes, warning that they must vote at the precinct where they were registered or else they would lose their vote. "The issue is plain and simple. Every one has an equal interest in the result. See to it that every man is at his place on Tuesday next. We are all tired of the abomination of radicalism."[68] "If radicalism is to be voted down in York District, every man must be at his own box or precinct. There will be no exception made in any case. You must vote at home or lose your vote. Remember you cannot vote at Yorkville unless you have registered at Yorkville. Explain to your neighbors, that all may understand."[69]

A week before the election, the newspaper was peppered with pleas for Democratic conservatives to participate in the election. "We desire that the full vote of the District be polled on Tuesday next.... See to it that all of your neighbors are out. If they cannot walk, haul them to the polls. If every man turns out, radicalism will go up in York District. If we do not turn out, strife and contest will be secured in the next election. Success will secure us peace and quiet in York District."[70] "We may or may not be able to elect a President at the approaching election. We certainly can elect the Hon. W. D. Simpson for Congress. We certainly can give [him] a large majority in York District. We can satisfy our colored people that they [can] live among Democrats. Success in the District will diminish the evil influence of carpet-baggers. Our people, white and colored, can agree and understand each other better. Such will be some of the fruits of success and a general vote. *Let us have peace.*"[71]

The polls opened at 6 o'clock A.M. on November 3, and a great number of blacks had already assembled and voted by 11 o'clock.[72] Although the *Yorkville Enquirer* reported there were no reports of disturbances at any of the voting places, testimony at the Klan trials suggests a far different story. Sometime prior to election day, the Klan met and agreed to go to the polls and "crowd off" Radical voters. At Rock Hill, Doctor Avery and other undisguised Klansmen stood in a ring around the polls and elbowed many black men away. As some black voters approached the polls, rough efforts were applied to convince them to vote the Democratic ticket; others were pushed away with an announcement they were not old enough to cast a ballot. When questioned at the Klan trials, R. P. Mayrant, constable of Rock Hill, denied that Avery challenged any voter, but a number of blacks contradicted his testimony.[73] The exact truth may never be known, but the results of the York County election were decidedly in favor of the Democrats:

Congressional		Presidential	
Simpson (D)	Wallace (R)	Seymour (D)	Grant (R)
2,039	1,537	2,043	1,543

Congress, however, overturned the election months later when enough evidence about fraudulent or illegal voting practices had been presented to initiate such an action. A. S. Wallace, the loser in the election, went to Washington as a legislator to serve with the administration of President Grant.[74] Before York voters learned their ballots would be discounted, they experienced other happenings that caused grave concern. On the heels of murders in Laurens and Newberry counties, on November 19 at the depot in Columbia, black radicals killed James Minor, the black Democrat who had spoken at the mass meeting in Yorkville in September. The following day, Governor Robert K. Scott charged the counties of Abbeville, Anderson, Edgefield, Lexington, Newberry, Chester, Laurens, Union, York and Darlington "with violating the laws, and [that] the officers of the law [are] set at defiance; that the peaceful citizens are murdered in cold blood, and the murderers not only permitted but assisted to escape from justice; that families have been forced to abandon their homes from fear of violence, and [that] the utterance of political opinions [are] stifled by threats of violence, &c; and that to carry out these principles, large quantities of firearms, of the most improved patterns have been secretly brought into the State and distributed."[75] The peace many thought was at hand was in reality far from them; in fact, one of the most violent and disruptive eras York County would ever know was already breaking upon the scene.

2

Advent of the Ku Klux Klan

"Them ... Missouri Soldiers..."

Some fifty years after Reconstruction and the reign of the Ku Klux Klan,[1] Milus Smith Carroll, a convicted York County Klansman who took part in the raid on black militia Captain Jim Williams, penned a recollection of the period:

> From the close of the Civil War in April 1865 until 1876 was a period never to be forgotten by those who lived through it. A horde of Carpet Baggers from the North descended upon us, and they, in conjunction with the *meanest*, most detestable creatures that ever wore the skin of a white man; (I mean the Scalawags) Scamps, who turned traitor to their own people in order to rob.
>
> The Negroes, having been freed and given the right of suffrage, were easily the dupes of these scoundrels and were told that they were entitled to forty acres[2] of land and a mule[,] and if they could not get it any other way, to burn out the whites and take it by force, even to the killing of the Whites from the cradle to the grave. While I don't recall any murder committed, they did proceed to burn hundreds of dwellings, gin houses and barns.[3] Until about 1869 and 1870, there was scarcely a night passed without a fire in some direction.
>
> The people had become desperate under this state of affairs. Something must be done to protect themselves. This brought about what was, and is, known as the Ku Klux Klan. [It was] originated by General N. B. Forrest ... under his leadership thousands and tens of thousands of the best men of the South joined the Order, banded together by a solemn oath and led by wise men.

2. Advent of the Ku Klux Klan

The influence of the Order soon manifested itself by bringing about a wholesome change in the minds of the scoundrels who had been robbing us and they began seeking other climes until the memorable campaign under the Red Shirts and General Wade Hampton in 1876 forever redeemed South Carolina from the Carpet Bagger and Scalawag rule.[4]

Though Carroll sums up his feelings, and likely the attitude of numbers of other white residents of the Piedmont of South Carolina who recalled the Reconstruction years, his account actually tells little about the Klan organization or its activities in York County. J.D. McConnell, however, offers a few more details of the first organization:

The Constitutional Convention of 1868 was composed entirely of Negroes with a sprinkling of Northern Carpet Baggers and a few native scalawags and then began the days of the Negro rule. It was at this time, '68, that the first Ku Klux Klan was organized. I was one being sworn in with a terrible oath by Col. Avery and Dr. Rufus Bratton in the back room of what was May's Drugstore in York. This Klan was made up of ex–Confederate officers and we hoped to take the place of the patrol system used before the war to keep the slaves in order. There were only about thirty of us in the country and we went on no raids.[5]

Various Klan types of actions appear to have taken place in the Piedmont between mid 1865 and 1868, but the first public suggestion of the Ku Klux Klan's presence in York County is an anonymous advertisement published 2 April 1868. This notice ran in the *Yorkville Enquirer* only days before the spring election that would jolt white Democrats into political action.

K. K. K.

Dead-Man's Hollow, Southern Div.

Midnight, March 30.

General Order, No. 1

REMEMBER the hour appointed by our most Excellent Grand Captain-General. The dismal hour draws nigh for the meeting of our mystic Circle. The Shrouded-Knight will come with pick and spade; the Grand Chaplain will come with the ritual of the dead. The grave Yawneth, the lightnings flash althwart the heavens, the thunders roll, but the Past Grand Knight of the Sepulcher will recoil not.

By order of the Great Grand Centaur.

SULEYMAN, G. G. S.[6]

In the same issue of the *Yorkville Enquirer*, publisher Lewis Grist wrote:

> Our advertising columns contain a mysterious notice, which reached us through the mails, a day or two since, and which, contrary to the usual custom with anonymous advertisements, we insert in our present issue. The mystical characters—"K.K.K."—will perhaps be understood by those to whom the notice is addressed; but being among the uninitiated, we are at a loss to know what they mean, unless it be a message from that singularly secret and doubly mysterious and hideous organization know as the "Ku-Klux-Klan," which is rapidly spreading over the country.
>
> The "Ku-Klux-Klan" is a fantastical name assumed by the Conservatives in Tennessee, and the secrecy and caution under which it carries on its work, beats the Union Leagues all hollow. It has inspired no small degree of terror among certain classes in the West, and has become of sufficient importance to induce General Thomas, commanding the Tennessee Department, to send to Washington for more troops to suppress it.
>
> We believe no good can result from such organizations, and regret to hear of the K.K.K.'s in our midst.[7]

A week later, Grist, who obviously was being hypocritical in the above editorial, altered his published opinion and informed readers of the potential value of the Ku Klux Klan by reprinting an article from the *Memphis Ledger*:

> All this vague alarm manifested by certain carpet bag adventurers and office holders, who came here simply to plunder and impoverish people, will hardly suffer at the hand of the Ku Klux ... there will be no violation of law by the Ku Klux, and others who attempt wrongful acts may find a power interposing its authority which is only terrible to thieves and wrong-doers ... there surely can be little reason for the condemnation of a society which at worst is a counterpart of the Loyal Leagues.... [The Ku Klux Klan is] interested in the maintenance of order and good government, while Loyal Leaguers[8] have everything to gain by public wrongs and disorders.[9]

Then perhaps trying to distance himself slightly from any association with, or approval of, the organization, he published another reprint with a disclaimer, "the Richmond *Dispatch* is responsible for the following":

> The Ku Klux Klan are kalled upon to kastigate or kill any kolored kusses who may approve the konstitution being konkocted by the kontemptible karpetbaggers at the kapitol. Each Klan is kommanded by a karniverous kernel who kollects his komrades with the magnitude of the kause. Whenever konvened they must korrectly give four kountersigns. These are: Kill the kullered kuss. Klean out the karpetbaggers; krush the konvention; karry konservatism; konfusion to kongress; konfederates will konquer. Of kourse the Klan kreates konsiderable konsternation among the Kongos and their

kunning konductors, who kalkulate that their kareer may be kut short by katastrophies. Kowardly kurs, they kan't komplain.[10]

Although Grist wrote in somewhat apologetic tones about the *Dispatch* article, again saying that he had no knowledge of such an organization and suggesting that the county would not be improved by such a society, his veracity is extremely suspect. Certainly, it seems very unlikely that a man in his occupation and with his political and social connections would have been ignorant of the Klan's presence. In fact, the Klan existed in York County at the time Grist ran the KKK notice on April 2, and he in actuality was announcing its presence. As one scholar of the organization suggests, "There is abundant evidence that the primary role in spreading the Ku Klux Klan was played, not by General Forrest and his cohorts, but by the Southern Democratic newspaper press." Under the guise of reporting "news" and informing local citizens through reprinting inflammatory articles from distant newspapers, the *Yorkville Enquirer* may have acted as a tool for advancing the Klan's rise in York County. Grist in late April published a lengthy letter written to the editor of the *New York Herald*. It, like previously reprinted materials from other newspapers, portrayed the Klan as a necessary and useful organization, whose purpose was to battle the radical elements of society who wished to subjugate the Democratic Party "and to Africanize the South."

> The organization of the Ku Klux Klan originated from a necessity — the result of Radical legislation and the formation of the secret political orders of the "Loyal league" and the "Grand Army of the Republic," consequently the Ku Klux Klan is the effect of Radical despotism and injustice.... Until recently, however, the enemies of the Ku Klux Klan possessed the government and wielded its mighty powers. They possess it today, but only in name, not in reality. Let the tyrants of a mongrel and infamously corrupt party beware! Your part is but a shell. The castle of radicalism has been permeated and undermined by the white ant[11] of the Ku Klux. [The] sole object of which is to thwart Radicalism, arrest negro domination in the South ... perpetuate the Federal Union and preserve the Constitution as the fathers made it. And whoever asserts to the contrary utters falsehood. That the Ku Klux Klan have secrets unknown to the uninitiated is not denied; so have the ancient orders of Free Masonry, Odd Fellowship and other secret orders and societies....[12]

The Yorkville editor continued to run such articles while simultaneously proclaiming ignorance about the organization; he was not unique. In May 1868, a Chester correspondent wrote: [the] "Negroes have settled down after a scare of the KKK; but the scare was initiated from their own imagination and no such organization was in existence."[13] Regardless of denials about the group's presence in the spring of 1868, information presented at the Klan trials three years later verified that the organization was quite active in York, as well as in surrounding counties, by the late 1860s. At the same time the Democratic Conservative Clubs were bursting onto the scene, the Ku Klux Klan was developing in secret.

Dr. Charles Clawson purportedly brought the Klan to York County. Mrs. Jean Agee of Richburg (Chester County) relates that her grandfather Clawson heard about the group, went to Tennessee to learn about it, and organized the first area Klan upon his return.[14] Although Clawson may have introduced the Klan in York County after his visit to Tennessee, it is unlikely that the initial York County group was tied with the larger organization headquartered in Tennessee.[15] Historian Allen Trelease tells of a group in Chester, calling itself the Chester Conservative Clan, that in June of 1868 "permitted ten residents of neighboring York County to organize a branch.... One of the ten, a young Confederate veteran at Rock Hill named Iredell Jones, was soon to become Grand Scribe of the county's Ku Klux organization which bore the name of the Invisible Empire."[16] Stanley F. Horn in *The Invisible Empire* relates that the Klan was not regularly organized in South Carolina until the summer of 1868, when the Grand Dragon of Tennessee sent R. J. Brunson to Rock Hill with a supply of printed rituals, and with orders to formalize the Klan organization in the state. (Samuel G. Brown testified to being told by Albertus Hope[17] in 1868 or early 1869 that he had a copy of the constitution and bylaws of the K. K. K.) While Clawson may have brought the idea to York County,[18] it was Brunson who apparently organized several dens before returning to Tennessee.[19]

In 1933 S. B. Lathan told still another account on the organization of the first Klan. He related that while walking with John A. Barron one evening in Yorkville, he and Barron went into the law offices of George W. Williams and Sons which was located next door to the office of Doctor Jackson. Inside were Tom Bell, John Tomlinson, Frank Harris and several others who were discussing the particulars of organizing a Klan. According to Lathan, one of the men "had been out west and knew how to organize." Lathan said he did not join but recalled a question as to whether Probate Judge Frank Harris should join since he had only one arm. Tom Bell thought it was not a real handicap since it took only one hand to shoot a pistol.

Some writers have contended that the Klan arrived without any political character or ambitions[20]—that its only interest was to insure some kind of protection from abuse by freedmen and radical elements of the Republican Party. Others rightly have argued that the organization initially was political and resorted quickly to intimidation, if not violence. No matter which position one accepts, all researchers agree that the Klan's

2. Advent of the Ku Klux Klan

York County Court House as it appeared during Reconstruction.

activities became more noticeable following the 1868 spring election and the adoption of the new state constitution and black suffrage.[21]

The Klan first appears to have confined itself to threats and symbolic posturing throughout the spring and at least part of the summer. Lee Guyton, a black man who lived near Hickory Grove, related one of the Klan's pranks played on his younger brother, Henry. "Them ... Missouri soldiers [seemingly a local term referring to Klansmen] took Henry Guyton off. Stole him ... stole his mule. They was so mean. They found out when they shoot, the mule so scared it would throw Henry. They kept it up and laughed. Course it hurt Henry, liable to kill him. They say they making a Yankee soldier outen him that way." Following outrages supposedly committed by freedmen, and to correct perceived injustices and in retaliation for what was interpreted as the government's disregard for the lives and property of the white population, the Ku Klux Klan in York County increasingly went beyond symbolic actions and resorted to vigilante methods. Whippings (sometimes known as "cowhiding"), destruction of property, and even murder and rape became trademarks of the Klansmen.

Judging from reports appearing in the *Yorkville Enquirer*, the heaviest concentration of early Klan dens were probably in western York County. During the Klan trials, at least six dens were mentioned as being in operation there in 1868 — all under the direction of Klan chief John Whitley Mitchell. Five of these can be identified: John Mitchell's Klan, Robert Burris's Klan, Charley Byers' Klan, Alex Smith's Klan, and Madison Smarr's Klan.[22]

Klan dens can best be described as the rough vigilante arm of the Democratic Clubs; in fact, a Klansman in Abbeville County told that secret committees of the Democratic Clubs fostered the development of the Klan.[23] Klan dens do appear to differ from the Conservative Clubs in the age of their membership. The clubs were largely composed of older men whose average age was 55, while the Klan was generally filled with men 30 years of age or younger and from every level of social standing.[24] While western York County boasted a large membership in the Democratic Conservative Clubs, additional research may establish that a father-son relationship existed between some members of the clubs and the Klan in that part of the county.

Other researchers have concluded that men holding Klan membership were mostly of the poorer classes because they have been identified as "laborers." This categorization can be misleading, however, because many of these men were still living at home and working on the family farm they would later inherit. Certainly some Klan members exhibited wealth and position; both of Yorkville's constables (Rufus McLain and William Snyder) as well as the mayor were in a den. Major James W. Avery, an affluent merchant, was County Chief (probably Grand Giant), and Dr. J. Rufus Bratton was a Klan Chief (Grand Cyclops). Of the organization's membership, Reverend R. A. Holland of Warm Springs, North Carolina, remarked:

> Do not imagine that the Ku Klux were recruited from the criminal classes. Such I know is the prevalent northern idea, but is absolutely false. The members of the K. K. K. were gentlemen of fine education, struggling manfully to retain and sustain their manhood, and give to their children as a heritage of the war a higher civilization than perhaps they themselves had enjoyed. In many instances that was the only legacy they had to give, for all else had been swept away in the storm of shot and shell that for four years [had] been sweeping over the land.[25]

It would appear that membership in the local Klan was somewhat selective in its earliest days. By 1871, however, it seems that a sizable number of those enrolled consisted of lower-class individuals who were difficult to control. Samuel G. Brown, some time before he was arrested in October 1871 for conspiracy, advised his sons to separate from the organization as it had been infiltrated by an undesirable element.

2. Advent of the Ku Klux Klan

J.D. McConnell substantiates Brown's belief that change in membership had begun to take place during the early part of 1871:

> Political conditions grew much worse and in 1871 the Ku Klux Klan was reorganized. At that time, nearly every white man was taken into it, but I refused to join, telling my friends, "What we are thinking of is treason against the U. S. Government and when I go into anything as serious as that, I want to know *exactly* who is in with me. Some weak fellow will give the whole thing away." So I had nothing further to do with the Klan though I knew all their grips, signs, etc.[26]

One noted researcher, Allen Trelease, suspects that sworn membership in the York County Klan eventually numbered between 1,800 and 2,300,[27] and involved more than 45 dens with ten or more members. Perhaps as many as 12 Klan dens were in the town of Yorkville alone.[28] Trelease likely overstates the number of individuals involved, as well as dens, to prove his position. As Robert Drew Loftis suggests, large Klans were divided into small units, thus allowing hit-and-run types of operations to trail across the country; this explains the large number of dens sited in Yorkville alone. Such an arrangement undoubtedly made it easy for members of one den to offer alibis for members of another. Based on the correspondence of Major Lewis Merrill, prominently mentioned later in this study, Loftis suggests that only about 18 Klan dens, excluding those in Yorkville, existed within the county, rather than the 33 offered by Trelease.[29] Further, Loftis quotes part of a letter appearing in the Columbia *Phoenix* written under the nom de plume of "Brutus" telling that the number of Klansmen in Union county was over 1000.[30] Even so, this number is considerably below the membership given by Trelease for adjacent York County. The actual number of Klan members in York County was probably less than 1,400.

Some of the more prominent men who participated in the Klan publicly disapproved of its activities while simultaneously ordering the actions of the rank and file membership. Many of the organization's middle class, who led a somewhat less conspicuous life than their wealthy counterparts, were usually among those responsible for the majority of the violence.[31] Various other community members played a role in Klan activities without directly taking part in the raids. Some were not allowed to participate in the nighttime assaults since they might be readily identified, such as William Cloud Hicklin of Chester County, who had lost an arm in the Civil War. He chose to work undercover for the Klan. According to a number of local family traditions, women occasionally volunteered as couriers to carry messages from one den to another and they provided support services such as sewing costumes, preparing meals at odd hours, hiding sought Klansmen, and concocting alibis.

Though some white Democrats chose to speak against the violence of the organization, most believed the Ku Klux Klan was a necessary last-ditch effort to gain political supremacy, chase out the Radicals and "put the Negro in his place." On the whole, Democrats generally condoned the Klan's activities. Of those that opposed the organization, few dared to openly oppose its goals, and any criticism had to be amended by a concession that it had done some good by forcing blacks to behave. Johnston Jones, editor of the *Lantern,* a Rock Hill based newspaper, voiced a typical allowance: "Ku Kluxism is wrong, morally and politically.... It [is] a horrible remedy for terrible evils. It ought not to have been done. But the provocations which the white people ... were subjected to ... were great — such as no people under the sun would have borne patiently.... Ku Klux-ism was wrong, and cannot be justified; but it has its palliations which every fair-minded observer must admit, and which every impartial judge, and every unprejudiced jury, would regard in a Court of Law."

Not only did the Klan attempt to "put the Negro in his place," it also kept the whites within acceptable behavioral boundaries through intimidation. Though most Klan members were willing participants, a number testified they had been compelled under threats of violence to enlist in a local den. Compelling individuals to join the Klan, or to perform certain work assigned its members, was a way of establishing control over some of the whites. Sherrod Childers, age 23, told he unwillingly enrolled after it was discovered he had voted the "Radical Ticket," and Elias Ramsey said he was forced into the organization after an incident of selling liquor to blacks. William, another member of the Ramsey family, testified, "We did not unite and resist them because we did not have sense enough; but I know a good many didn't join voluntarily; it seems to me that men who had good learning and knowledge ought to have teached us better." Yet others testified to being "told" or "instructed" that they had to go on one raid or another, even though such action was against their better judgment. However, certain individuals among those arrested claimed they joined the Klan as a means of protecting the blacks within their employment in case of threat; still other farmers stated that knowledge of their membership in the Klan enabled them, through fear imparted, to retain a necessary labor force on their plantations. This latter position, as Allen Trelease suggests, probably "did much more to drive off labor and disrupt economic life. It was on this point that many landowners eventually became disenchanted with the Klan, whether they dared express their feelings or not."

By the time of the election in April 1868, the men of the Union League had invented a way of ensuring their illiterate members the right to vote. Some days before the election, Union League runners traversed areas of the state reminding freedmen of the upcoming vote and telling them to assemble at some designated place where often ceremonial drilling and rifle volleys would be a feature.[32] This quasi-military style of gathering made black voters highly visible and audible, and effectively unnerved the white population. As blacks had evidently learned in the constitutional referendum of late 1867, casting a vote could be most nearly described as a jousting event where men pushed, shoved and elbowed the opposition. Since the ballots distributed were so visibly marked, it was no secret for which party the voters were casting their ballots. Not only was the voter a target for physical confrontation, the agent who distributed the ballots was equally fair game. While the military style gathering used by blacks was an effective propaganda program that helped them overcome intimidation, their main object was to occupy the polls early and monopolize the precincts for most of the day. Although the *Yorkville Enquirer* editorialized that whites had exhibited much indifference at the election of April 1868, it would appear they were really affected by blacks monopolizing the polls the first day and extremely bad weather that followed. Heavy rains had indeed kept many whites from the polls during most of the three days of the April 1868 election; but the blacks had voted en masse the first day, a Tuesday, before streams became too swollen to cross.

The tally of votes, which the newspaper had "much difficulty in procuring" and was thus unable to post until 23 April, brought the Democrats face to face with their worst fears—the Radicals had won every position on the ballot. Not only had the new constitution been accepted, all the Republican nominees had been elected to Congress.

Candidate	Votes by Regimental Precincts			
	1st	2nd	3rd	Total
		Senate		
J. H. Adams (D)	883	313	499	1,695
W. E. Rose (R)	847	321	593	1,761
		House of Representatives		
John Smith (D)	870	309	496	1,675
J. B. Williamson (D)	846	300	497	1,643
A. P. Campbell (D)	883	315	497	1,695
Peter Garrison (D)	881	313	496	1,690
John W. Mead (R)	841	314	592	1,747
J. H. White (R)	860	317	592	1,769
J. L. Neagle (R)	836	315	593	1,744
P. J. O'Connell (R)	848	318	596	1,762

Although bad weather and indifference had prevented numbers of whites from casting ballots, white Democrats had underestimated the power of en masse voting by black registered voters. Indifference reported by the local newspaper is likewise revealed in a report by Louis V. Caziarc, whose tabulation of registered voters and those not voting in York and surrounding counties, originally printed in the Charleston newspapers, is reproduced below.

District	Registered Voters	Not Voting	% Not Voting
York	4,233	724	17
Union	3,383	1,122	33
Spartanburg	4,449	1,036	23
Chester	3,471	740	21

3

A Threat of Violence

"Kill all the damn white Republicans first..."

By the summer of 1868, only a few months after the arrival of the Ku Klux Klan, leaders of the Republican Party were convinced that the Klan was a threat to the peace of the upcountry. A fair election in November was thought impossible, and many were urging Governor Scott to place armed militia units throughout the region. Scott was reluctant, however, believing that arming blacks would only increase tensions and possibly cause the outbreak of a racial war. A letter from Union County had warned Scott that a conflict was eagerly anticipated and "all that wonts to see the Negroes and Rebels fight can com up here[,] they say that war has to start."[1]

As the summer progressed, articles on the Klan diminished and then abruptly disappeared from the pages of the *Yorkville Enquirer* and more than a year passed before the subject was broached anew. Editor Grist's actions were typical and reflected the earlier position that Southern Democratic newspapers—including the *Yorkville Enquirer*—had taken. Initially, in 1868, "...favorable coverage lasted until the Klan began to commit acts of violence and the authorities took steps to suppress it. Then Democratic editors became more cautious, either denying that outrages had been committed or pretending that the Klan was nothing but a hoax. The very same paper which in March reported the Klan's expansion and in April invited its readers to form dens themselves was sometimes claiming by

June [1868] that the Ku Klux were only figments of disordered Republican imaginations. The next step was to ignore the Klan altogether...."[2]

Although Grist claimed the Klan was only a figment of Republican imagination, Richard M. Jolly of northwest Cherokee Township made a counterclaim in his reminiscences printed in 1924. Jolly relates what he believed was the "first work of the Ku Klux Klan in that vicinity":

> In that year [1868] I had an escapade with a negro who had risen above her station at a sale of my mother-in-law's. She told some one in their smart set that my mother had told a lie. When I heard it I could not contain my wrath. I asked if she had said it. The woman replied that she had. Whereupon I knocked her down and was on the point of using a chair to finish the job when she scrambled up and ran for her life. I attempted to get a gun but was stopped by James Phillips, who reminded me that night would come.
>
> One night in June mother told me that I should not go home because I had been reported to the Yankees by the negroes. Then was I wrath. I determined to kill, and told my brother, C. M., to ask Gilbert Surratt to send me Old Mike, a mule, but not to ask questions. He returned with the mule and off we put to gather some companions. The chickens were crowing for day when we tolled the wench off into the woods by getting her to show us the way to my house. Another fellow and I brought up the rear. The wench did not go far before she began to suspect a trap, and stopped still. She started to run, but I caught her as she went behind a tree. She began yelling murder. I stopped that with my hands and jerked a switch from a nearby tree which I laid upon her. My companion rushed up and insisted that I had killed her. In a little while she revived. As she arose both of us hitting at the same time knocked her down the hill to a man who had come in answer to her cries with a light, a gun, and dogs which he was sicing on. Then we went up the hill where the others were supposed to be to await for the man and to have it out with him. They, however, much to my surprise, had become frightened and left. The man did not come to us but took the negro back to his house.
>
> We then went back to our horses before any one was up. That is so far as I know [was] the first work of the Ku Klux Klan in that vicinity.[3]

Allen Trelease's analysis of the Ku Klux Klan nearly outlines Grist's pattern of reporting, for he makes almost no mention whatever of the Klan in 1869 and continues to deny its existence into the 1870s. The absence of such material may have been directly related to Governor Scott's proclamation issued 31 August 1868, in which he condemned the secret organization, saying that unless its activities were curbed a civil war would result. The Governor declared:

> It is alleged that armed organizations exist, which are regularly officered and drilled, and pretending to act by authority. There is not only no authority for armed or military organizations in South Carolina, but they are in

3. A Threat of Violence

direct violation of the laws of the United States. They must, therefore be at once disbanded.

I have been informed of the surreptitious introduction into the State of firearms and ammunition of the most improved description ... to be used for partisan purposes. Although not so openly in conflict with the laws, this is equally dangerous and threatening to the public peace. Deadly weapons in the hands of inconsiderate persons, inflamed by political excitement, may lead to the most deplorable results and all good citizens who can foresee the frightful consequences of a collision should earnestly and promptly throw the whole weight of their moral influence against a policy which would place life and property at the mercy of a mob.

...Inflammatory and threatening language at public meetings, and in the newspapers, should be avoided and discountenanced, because it unnecessarily aggravates the excitement incident to the present political canvass. The right of every voter to ... support such candidates as commend themselves ... must be secured to him without restraint or intimidation.[4]

The Governor also warned Wade Hampton, a member of the Democratic State Committee, that violence would beget violence, and that he would allow the blacks to retaliate unless Hampton publicly tried to stem the disorder. Being politically savvy, Hampton knew that a racial clash would produce nothing fruitful for white Democrats and might even bring federal intervention. In October he addressed the state's Democrats through local newspapers urging an end to the violence.[5] The moratorium he advocated lasted for nearly 1½ years and there were no reported violent Klan raids until the early part of 1870.

This does not mean the Klan was inactive through the moratorium, however. In the fall, reports began to surface that Democrats throughout the upcountry were raising money to arm themselves with the latest weapons in preparation for gaining political control. In October 1868, Iredell Jones of Rock Hill told A. B. Springs that he had $50 allotted by the State Central (Democratic) Club to buy rifles for his district. Later in the month James Pagan notified Springs that a shipment of rifles was being smuggled in; Pagan assured Springs that "no American citizen of African descent could stand up against such arms."[6]

Whether Scott's threats of retaliation reacted negatively on the whites cannot be determined; perhaps it was because the majority of whites believed their interests were completely ignored by the state government that they decided their only recourse was to secure arms for themselves. One can only believe that had the South Carolina government given equal concern for all its citizens—black and white, Democrat and Republican—white Democrats might not have initiated an arms race, and bloodshed might never have been experienced. John S. Reynolds describes the no-recourse position the white population believed itself to be facing: "The

State Government was in fact hostile to the white race, and that government, without reference to its personnel — with reference to the character of its agents — was doggedly backed by the military power of the United States."[7]

Although the countryside was relatively quiet during the month before the November elections, white Democrats (including Klan members) kept a watchful eye on all social and political events. Reports of Klan activities in York County up to the time of the congressional and presidential election in November 1868 are limited, but the organization's presence diminished the black vote and gave the election to county Democrats.[8] During the voting, several men having no official capacity sat at a desk at one poll in York County and recorded the names of every man who voted Republican.[9] Election Commissioner John L. Watson reported that many blacks had been so intimidated by the Klan the night prior, they refused to leave their houses on election day to cast ballots.[10] Such tactics insured Democrats a victory in the congressional race.

During the moratorium, Congress repealed part of the Reconstruction Act of March 1867 that restricted the southern states from having standing militias. Sensing an opportunity to gain political allies by organizing peacekeeping military units, Governor Scott began reconsidering his position regarding militia units. On 16 March 1869, he signed a militia bill into law by which all males (both black and white) between the ages of 18 and 45 were eligible for paid service.[11] It was not until January 1870, however, when violence seemed inevitable that Scott would use this bill to place armed units in the Piedmont.

In April 1869 an assassination attempt was made on County Commissioner M. O'Connell, a Republican from Fort Mill. The *Yorkville Enquirer* doubted the incident and scoffed at Governor Scott's reward of $1,000 to anyone finding a man with black whiskers and wearing a blue jean frock coat.[12] Although the newspaper editor did not credit the Klan with the attempt, it seems likely that it was the work of that organization. If so, it was the earliest reported act of violence in the county.

With the ideology of the two political factions in direct opposition, every incident seemingly inflamed the imaginations of both parties, and each blamed the other for various outrages. An example focuses on a Chester County church. The *Yorkville Enquirer* on 9 September 1869 reported the destruction of the Pilgrim Church located in northwestern Chester County.[13] The building, situated near the residence of Major John Sanders, was home to a black congregation when it burned to the ground. The newspaper decried it as a "mean, cowardly, dastardly act." Regardless of who the arsonist may have been, the article clearly suggests that at least some believed the Ku Klux Klan was involved. Soon thereafter, it was

3. A Threat of Violence

learned the church had been experiencing internal problems, and speculation arose that the fire had been set by one of its members. While local Democrats may have comforted themselves by believing whites had not perpetrated the destruction, they were positive that Republican state officials would believe otherwise. Many believed that "Governor Scott [had] already entered it upon his memorandum as a great Ku Klux outrage, and that it [would] duly appear in the next swearing he does about the condition of the up-country."[14]

The conflict at Pilgrim Church centered on its pastor, Sancho Sanders,[15] who had been Pilgrim's leader for several years except for time spent at the Constitutional Convention of 1868 and subsequently in the House of Representatives. His powerful political and religious influence on the black people of the area continued until rumors arose of his "stupidity in the House, of his employing his time while a legislator in learning to write and many other things unbecoming a man whose wisdom they had entertained."[16] When he lost prestige as a legislator, he also lost influence in the church. The pastor was ousted from the pulpit and replaced with Lee Sanders, whose relationship, if any, to Sancho Sanders is unknown. Factions that had formed within the church met each other on several occasions, and physical assaults at these encounters even progressed to the point of brandishing firearms.

Although the Pilgrim Church incident initially generated fear of widespread conflict, the rest of 1869 in York and Chester counties passed without any reported incidents. However, as political campaigns commenced early in 1870 in preparation for the spring elections, violence erupted across the Piedmont as if by some unheard command. The state's Chief Constable J. B. Hubbard received word that armed groups of whites were roving the upper Piedmont intimidating blacks and promising to kill "all the damned *white* Republicans first."[17] Newberry and Chester as well as other upcountry areas reported bands of heavily armed men making threats. The Republican state government reacted by making preparations to form several militia companies in York, Fairfield, Chester, Union and Spartanburg counties.[18]

The first reported act of brutality in York County after a 1½ year moratorium occurred near the Antioch Community in the county's northwest corner (now Cherokee County)[19]; this event signaled the adoption of forceful methods by the organization. In January 1870, Klan members arrived at the farm of Henry J. Hullender, near Wear Muster Ground. Their purpose was to intimidate and perhaps physically harm Billy Wright, a black living there and "keeping a young white girl as his concubine."[20] Although Wright may have eluded the Klan, they burned his house that stood just 400 yards from Hullender's home, and made threatening demonstrations toward Hullender for allowing Wright to reside there. A grand jury report presented two months after the raid claimed that Wright earlier had been charged with horse stealing in Cleveland County, North Carolina, and then had moved to Hullender's to escape threatening neighbors.[21]

Hugh K. Roberts, a magistrate living near the Antioch post office, wrote Governor Scott two days after the incident:

> Sir, I say to you that there is an organization in the upper part of this County and in parts of N. C. who is a Doing damages to the Citizens of both States and on the night of the 12 there was about twenty passed my house in Disguise as well as I could tell by moon light they went about 3 miles and burnt a mans house to the ground and then went to a good Citizens house by the name of H. J. Hullender and threatened to burn his house if he did not run wright off of his land and fired some 15 shots they went past our N. C. line and hurt a man by the name of Edward Patterson Colored. I am afraid to start proceedings against them if I know them. Some think they can Swear to George Cellers a citizen of N. C. and I think if the matter was investigated you might gits some boss of the organization. I feel that the property and lives of citizens about here is insecure therfor I request you to send a guarrison in this parts of the State and I would be pleased if you would send Capt Yokum I will Direct this letter to J. L. Neagle as I am affraid to write to you.[22]

Even though the local newspaper argued that it was Hullender who ignored local law enforcement officials and made application directly to Governor Robert K. Scott for protection, there is no proof he did so. The paper likely referred to Magistrate Roberts' letter. Hullender also supposedly consulted with House Representative John L. Neagle in Columbia, thereby irritating other York County legislators by neglecting to confer with them. It matters little which communication had the desired effect; Governor Scott soon took steps to secure the safety of citizens in the area.

Six state constables under the command of Deputy Constable William Littlefield were sent to Hullender's house to investigate the incident. On Monday, January 24, Littlefield reported to Captain J. B. Hubbard, chief of the constabulary in Columbia, from his temporary camp at Hullender's farm:

> We got here Sunday about 12 o'clock. Had to walk most of the way over very bad roads. Things look rather rough. We are right on the North Carolina line. Will have a company of thirty white men by Wednesday; have eighteen names now. Can not say whether we will have any trouble or not. Many threats have been made also many outrages committed but the perpetrators

are unknown. After the company is organized and all things quiet I will propose to leave three men and return home if not otherwise ordered. Any communications addressed to me will be received if addressing me at Yorkville, S. C. Be careful what you write....[23]

Littlefield

A Kings Mountain Township resident reported that the constables came to York County with several boxes of Winchester rifles, began recruiting a peacekeeping force from local residents four days after their arrival,[24] and organized a troop of 32 men. John R. Faris[25] was elected captain, with Hugh K. Roberts serving as his lieutenant.[26] The Kings Mountain correspondent's report appearing in the *Yorkville Enquirer* suggests that most of the recruits were white, though it stated that "several persons of color have enlisted." He further mentioned that a number of these blacks earlier had made farming contracts with local white farmers, and their enlistment was "embarrassing ... their former employers."[27]

In the February 10 issue of the *Yorkville Enquirer*, Grist went to some lengths to scoff at the Republican government that formed the militia in Cherokee Township:

> The State constables have gone back to Columbia, leaving the task of protecting the border against Ku Klux raids in the hands of the new made warriors. As there is nothing for these to do but to draw pay, we feel assured their duties will be nobly done.
>
> Outside the immediate neighborhood of this alleged Ku Klux raid, there has been little interest expressed. The people generally regard the whole thing as a political trick, which was to be expected and could not be prevented by anything they could say or do. They do not, therefore, feel disposed to indulge in useless whining, on the one hand or to magnify the evil by becoming exasperated on the other.
>
> While unable to speak with certainty as to the origin of the reported outrage, we are disposed to doubt that there were any Ku Klux dem-onstrations at all. A house was burnt, and Hullender seems to be the only man who can give any account of the burning. Deputy Constable Littlefield reported that he found the country in the hands of armed bands of desperadoes, a statement which we pronounce false. There are ten townships in this country, and he garrisoned but one of these. We do not believe he found any armed bands in that one; for he says himself that he could not get evidence to justify him in making any arrests, a state of affairs which would have been utterly impossible, had the county been in the conditions he said it was. The "desperados" must be of a remarkably timid class, if they subsided so quietly upon the approach of six constables.
>
> The truth is, the county is in the hands of our civil officers, who have never had any difficulty in making arrests or preserving the peace, when

called upon. Littlefield lets the cat out of the wallet when he says he "immediately organized a military company, and gave them arms agreeably to his instructions." That's the whole secret. His instructions were to form a military company first, and trump up some excuse for it afterwards. And here is his excuse. A conversation was overheard between two supposed "desperadoes," one of whom said to the other, "We will continue these outrages until the elections and if it does not intimidate these Radicals so that they will stay away from the polls, we will then take forcible possession of them, and carry the election next fall at all hazards."

In an editorial, Grist asked the questions he believed the people of York County were asking. Why had Littlefield not arrested the two men and confronted them with their accusers? It was his duty and after all, he supposedly had the evidence he wanted. Grist claimed that it was all a ruse to place a body of law enforcement in the county and that any move to arrest the two would result in damage to Governor Scott. "The result will be damaging to Governor Scott also who abuses the power entrusted to him by keeping up a show of preserving order by force, when he must be convinced, if he pays any regard to evidence, that it is more calculated to promote than to prevent disturbance. So far as political effect is concerned, the Governor has taken this wrong method to radicalize York. Take care of the rebound, Governor, when this matter is discussed next summer."[28]

In another article, Grist claimed that Governor Scott was on a witch-hunting expedition in sending a constabulary force into York County, merely in the hope of finding some proof of an organization of terrorists. The editor predicted the effort would be fruitless, as there was no such group anywhere in the county. Grist capitalized on the chief constable's name using a well known nursery rhyme to exemplify Hubbard's work for Scott[29]:

> Old Mother Hubbard went to the cupboard,
> To get the poor dog a bone.
> But when she went there, the cupboard was bare,
> And so the poor dog got none.

Residents of the northwest corner of York County[30] had reasons to believe that the men who had committed certain outrages were from North Carolina rather than from York County. A number of Cherokee Township citizens accordingly petitioned Governor Scott on February 10 endeavoring to show that a garrison in York County was unwarranted because "the evidence is almost conclusive that the trespassers were, in every instance, from the State of North Carolina."[31] After mentioning the incident at Hullender's farm, they told of a similar situation involving a

3. A Threat of Violence

"Miss Dover ... [who had] taken up with a colored man." She, like Wright, had been driven out of North Carolina, moved across the state line, and established residence about a mile inside South Carolina. Dover was followed "by persons in disguise — her household furniture carefully removed, and the house thrown down — the party failing to apprehend the Negro." The petition continued: "It is also reported that the North Carolina Ku Klux, whipped Tony McGill (p.c.) who is said to have struck a small boy, the son of a widow Falls, and grossly abused the Widow herself."

They concluded:

> We therefore ... pray your Excellency to disband, or remove, the State Militia organized in this Township — it being utterly inefficient to accomplish the ends desired; and whilst we have confidence in our own citizens, that they would not be obnoxious to the charge of being disturbers of the peace, if left to themselves.
>
> Whilst the military cannot sufficiently guard our frontier boundary, without greatly increasing the force, and consequently the <u>tax</u> to such a degree, that our citizens have not the means to meet it. And whilst we would pray your Excellency to disband, or remove them, we would respectfully ask your Excellency to use all the civil means given you — the law and its officers — in preserving the peace, and protecting the citizens of this section. If your Excellency deems it necessary to use a strong Constabulary force here, we pledge ourselves to give to them, and to you, our undivided support in sustaining the laws, and maintaining the peace of the country. That whilst we object to the Military on account of its <u>inexpediency</u>, and <u>expensiveness</u>, we have no objections to, but rather prefer that the civil force be increased to any extent Your Excellency may deem necessary for the protection of the country.

Sixty-five prominent men of Yorkville added their names to an attachment to the petition stating they "heartily concur with the citizens of Cherokee Township, praying for the removal of the armed militia." While most of these appear to have been Democrats, some few had alliances with the Republican Party. The petition might be construed as an attempt to wrestle control from the state government and give it to county authorities.

Captain Faris divided his troops into three companies to patrol a wider area. One of these patrols remained at the headquarters near Hullender's, another was positioned near the residence of a Mrs. Hambright and ordered to picket the North Carolina line in that area, and the third was assigned to picket the Shelby Road.

From an incident occurring in Cherokee Township (eventually reported in the *Yorkville Enquirer*), it appears the local Klan was not altogether intimidated by the presence of the militia. On the night of

February 13, one of the patrols on duty claimed to hear the sound of two cow bells coming from the direction of the Kings Mountain battleground. The commanding officer sent out a detail of five men who reported finding horse and mule tracks but no "desperadoes." The Yorkville publisher seemed to relish the incident, declaring that "no reasonable man can doubt that the alarm was caused by *bona fide* Ku Klux, who are well known to possess the power of making any sort of noises or tracks they choose...."

On yet another February night, the 17th, a store belonging to John McGill located near the New House Post Office and the militia camp, was entered and robbed. This incident at first seemed to be an isolated occurrence. Then another store ten miles away on Clark's Fork and also belonging to John McGill, burned to the ground in early March. When it was discovered that Captain Faris had left his post and the county on the morning of the fire, suspicion immediately turned to the militia. Seven days earlier, more than 150 petitioners from Cherokee Township had requested the removal of the military company; the McGill store fires obviously intensified the pressure for troop removal. The Governor responded by reducing the patrol to 15 and instructed them to act only as a peacekeeping force.

State Constable S. F. Noyes offered his services to McGill to apprehend the robbers and arsonists. He went to Captain Faris's camp and requested a detachment of men, but the request was either denied or not communicated to the captain. Noyes, without Faris's knowledge, then ordered a group from the company to picket the road leading to the burned store; they soon deserted their post. On March 8, Constable Noyes, aided by 40 or 50 men, arrested James Berry and Thomas Berry on charges of robbery and arson, and John D. Pursley and William B. Stewart (both members of Faris's company) for abetting.

Noyes had violated his authority by crossing into North Carolina to make the arrests, and he soon thereafter was relieved of his position by Chief Hubbard. Hoping to be reinstated, Noyes contended in a letter to Governor Scott that he "had chased the criminals for 8 days and nights" before entering into North Carolina and would have lost the pursuit had he not done so. Pleading his case, he informed the Governor that the people of Cleveland County, North Carolina, were pleased that the criminals were returned to York County. Noyes was not reinstated as he hoped; he apparently had fallen from Governor Scott's favor after signing a petition circulated by Democrats that was somewhat less than flattering to Scott and the Republican Party. In his plea, Noyes tried to reassure the governor saying that he was "pumping some democrats in reference to our party and I had to sign so as to bluff them."

Those charged with the McGill store robbery and fires came before

3. *A Threat of Violence*

the grand jury in late March, composed of H. H. Drennan (foreman), John S. Bratton, S. G. Hemphill, M. L. Tate, J. D. Johnston, John McCants, William Bolivar Byers, W. M. Horton, W. G. Dowdle, Russell L. Hope, J. H. Roddy, Allen Beatty, Alex Gunn, Mingo Armstrong, Robert Mason, Green Avery, Sam Byrd and Jefferson Adickes. They questioned the captain to discover why he had gone to Columbia on the morning of the McGill store fire. Faris explained his departure had nothing to do with the arson. He admitted seeing a bright light on the horizon while boarding a train to Columbia and confessed he thought it might be McGill's store, yet Faris claimed he did not hear of the fires until three days later during his stay in Columbia.

Reports following the McGill store fires were limited, though any number of minor occurrences may have taken place. The next incident reported by the *Yorkville Enquirer* occurred on March 18 on the east side of the county near Ebenezerville. There, a barn on the Harris plantation owned by Dr. Edward T. Avery was burned to the ground. Avery reported that five or six hundred bushels of corn were destroyed along with a large amount of forage. Suspicion of arson immediately arose, and a black man was arrested and taken to the county jail.

The events of early 1870 were indications of the escalating violence within York County. Governor Scott's fear that Republican voters might be threatened or actually endangered by the time of the November elections was also escalating. The militia offered some promise of at least moderating the threat by Klansmen. Perhaps before the petition from Cherokee Township concerning removal of the troops reached Governor Scott's desk, he was questioned during a February newspaper interview about his wisdom in creating an armed militia in parts of the upcountry. Speaking specifically of York County, Scott claimed that the Klan had been organized there, and that the group was beating black Republicans and destroying property. He defended his authorization by referring to the 1869 act passed by the Legislature providing for the organization of a state militia, and Scott stated his determination to see an effective militia raised. He claimed to care little whether a Confederate or a Federal commanded them—so long as the commander was trustworthy. Naturally, no white Democrat believed his statement.

From the outset of placing an armed force in the county, many viewed the action as a political ploy on Scott's part to ensure a Republican victory at the fall elections in York County as well as other Piedmont counties. A newspaper reporter went so far as to suggest that the governor hoped the presence of troops at an upcoming election might provoke a disturbance or bloodshed. Scott rebuffed the reporter, "You may rest assured that after the next election, the Republican party will never go before Congress stating that its voters were intimidated or prevented from voting by Democrats, Ku Klux or any organization whatever. The Republicans want to have peace and order during the next election, and if possible they will have it. If the Democrats can beat us fairly we will submit; but we will not be driven from the State, as some propose. We from the North have come here to stay and intend to do so. If the Democrats choose to practice their old tricks of murder and intimidation, the result will be terrible to them and to the State."

Grist of the *Yorkville Enquirer* took exception to the governor's remarks and denied the existence of any secret organization other than the Union League. He challenged Governor Scott, demanding that he support his charges about outrages. Grist insisted that if "…there is any evidence to prove it, it is time to bring it forth." Scott gave little attention to Grist's demand for proof of Klan activities or even the Klan itself; he sought bigger platforms for his positions than the *Yorkville Enquirer* or other Piedmont newspapers. Attending a mass Republican meeting in Washington in March 1870, Governor Scott spoke to the convention on the 22nd:

> It is time that weak-kneed men in Congress, who feel that they are carrying legislation a little too far, should make up their minds to recognize the Southern Confederacy, and leave us to do the best we can for ourselves …

Yorkville home of L. M. Grist, owner and publisher of the Yorkville Enquirer.

3. A Threat of Violence 57

as for South Carolina, no Republican will ever go to the doors of Congress again and knock for admission with a majority against him, because his friends have been prohibited by intimidation and murder from voting. Unless this thing stops here, I tell you that the next class of men that comes here will be the rebel element of that country, asking for protection.... I say to the members of the Legislature of Georgia, when you go home pass such laws as will give your Governor power to arm every man in the State. Make an appropriation to enable him to buy all the Winchester rifles that he can, and one hundred rounds of ammunition for each man, and then demand a fair election. Let every man vote as he pleases. Coerce no man; keep no man away; but let him go up and vote, and you yourselves demand the same right. I tell you, the Winchester rifle is the best law that you can have there!

In April 1870, with a municipal election in view for Columbia, Scott attended a meeting of Radicals in that city and took the opportunity to inflame specifically the Democrats of York County. Attacking its grand jury, he declared,

I have in my pocket a newspaper roll of a militia company of native white men of York County whom I was compelled to organize for the protection of their own lives and property. Men were taken out, tied, whipped, and some beaten to death, while their dwellings were burning. I have in my hand the *Yorkville Enquirer* containing a copy of the presentment of the Grand Jury of York County, in which they present as a nuisance the militia company I organized there. I would like some gentlemen here to show me a newspaper with a presentment of a Grand Jury, setting forth as a nuisance the acts of those parties who destroyed the property of Republicans or good and peaceable citizens. I would like to see where a Grand Jury has presented as a nuisance any of those organizations banded together for the purpose of blood and arson, and of disturbing the public peace. When our opponents want to claim all that good citizens are entitled to claim, let them present and show up some of these wrong-doers. When they do that, then we shall have faith in what they say. Until then we must regard them as the accomplices of bad men, if not actual participants in their crimes.

In contrast to Scott's assertions, the *Yorkville Enquirer* persisted in its denial of the existence of the Ku Klux Klan. The paper claimed that the jury did not charge any organization with murder and arson because there was no evidence that any such group existed. Grist disputed Scott's statement about being compelled to organize the militia in the county to keep the peace, arguing that he actually put the peace of the county in jeopardy by doing so.

Several books on the Ku Klux Klan of South Carolina mention that three militia units were raised in York County in January 1870; it appears, however, that only one was formed that early in the year. The other two units were raised later. A review of the *Yorkville Enquirer* and Governor Scott's statements supports this conclusion. In February, the only militia mentioned is that in Cherokee Township formed by Littlefield.[32] Even as late as April, Governor Scott referred to only one company in place in the county.[33] The remaining companies evidently were not formed until sometime during the summer. When they were formed, it appears that the first unit had either been disbanded earlier or was moved closer and bivouacked just north of Yorkville. Another was located in Rock Hill, and the third on a hill somewhere near "Forest Hall,"[34] John S. Bratton's home near present-day McConnells. The unit near McConnellsville was commanded by Captain Jim Williams,[35] a black man who lived in the area and later was murdered. When the first company was raised in Cherokee Township, petitions were collected requesting its removal. No petitions have been discovered, however, that discuss the other companies. Since there appears to be no evidence of a public outcry when these militia units were placed within the county, their presence perhaps had become more accepted, albeit unappreciated. The first company remained for a year and the others for no more than six or seven months, before Scott realized that these units were not bringing peace; they instead were driving the county to the brink of a racial war. He disbanded these black militias at the end of January 1871.

County residents (as well as persons across the entire upper Piedmont) made the presence of the all-black militia units and Governor Scott's refusal to form white companies a major issue. Sometime after the integrated force was organized in the Cherokee Township, whites apparently left the ranks; their abandonment may have resulted from the Ku Klux Klan exerting pressure on them to resign. The vacancies left were filled by blacks loyal to the Republican government. Although it was never intended that this unit, or any other subsequently placed in the county, be all black, Governor Scott had little choice but to allow it to become so. Few whites volunteered to serve in the militia; integrated units violated Southern racial attitudes, and most whites were unwilling to declare themselves loyal to the state government. Any white enlisting risked being viewed as a traitor to his race and country. Blacks quickly filled the ranks for self-protection, loyalty to the Republican Party, or financial gain.

For nearly a hundred years prior, the arming of the African-American population — slave or freedmen — had struck fear into the heart of the whites constantly disquieted by the suspicion that blacks were plotting a bloody insurrection.[36] In short, guns were for white men only. The potential for any armed black to be an assassin resulted in paranoia among York County whites.[37] James Long, a laborer born in Fairfield County and living in York County, told at the Klan trials that "folks were pretty much scared" not knowing "but what the niggers might come with their arms and kill them."[38] Charles W. Foster of the Bullock's Creek area, offering testimony at the trials, claimed that he had nothing to be afraid in the black militia; but he then told about the many rumors of potential danger from the blacks. Foster claimed he eventually was persuaded to join the Klan for protection.[39]

By late summer 1870, 10,000 rounds of ammunition reached Union County and were consigned to June Mobley, a black member of the Legislature from that county.[40] At a rally of about 60 people held at Boydton in western York County[41] on 10 September 1870, the crowd was evenly divided between blacks and whites. According to the *Yorkville Enquirer*, only six were known Radicals.[42] Major B. F. Briggs,[43] Captain J. W. Anderson, Samuel B. Hall[44] and Miles Johnson[45] addressed the crowd.[46] Samuel B. Hall in *A Shell in the Radical Camp* relates that Representative John Hannibal White[47] of the South Carolina General Assembly was on hand and spoke to the gathering.[48] He also said that when P. J. O'Connell[49] addressed the freedmen he told them that enough arms had been shipped into the county to equip several companies. Assuring the freedmen, he said, "These guns, my friends, will protect you, and your liberty at the ballot box will be sustained, as these glittering bayonets will put a cold chill upon your enemies wherever they come in contact with their eyes...."[50] Such comments obviously caused concern among the white population.

Arms Distributed to the Black Militias of the 14th Regiment[51]			
No Date	Capt. Jim Williams	96	Rifle-Muskets
No Date	Chief Constable J. B. Hubbard	430	Winchester Rifles
October 25	Chief Constable J. B. Hubbard	2	Winchester Rifles
No Date	Chief Constable J. B. Hubbard	8,150	Rounds Ammunition
June 10	Capt. Henry Johnson	96	Rifle-Muskets
June 17	Capt. James H. Cook	96	Rifle-Muskets
June 23	Capt. John Lee	96	Rifle-Muskets
No Date	Capt. George Adams	96	Rifle-Muskets
June 23	Capt. Andy Walker	96	Rifle-Muskets
June 24	Capt. Andrew Stewart	96	Rifle-Muskets
June 25	Capt W. L. Kee	96	Rifle-Muskets
July 9	Capt. Thomas Moore	96	Rifle-Muskets
September 6	Capt. Jacob Moore	96	Rifle-Muskets

The *Yorkville Enquirer* called for the people of York County to control themselves as Scott would be looking for any reason to declare martial law on the area. The *Charleston Courier* earlier reported in August that Scott was still arming the black militia units while refusing to accept the lists of white militia units tendered to him. Union County presented

Governor Scott with enough names of white men to form two regiments; the governor rejected them.[52] In York County, while calling for restraint, the newspaper as well as the grand jury advocated the formation of a white militia company of 30 armed men within each of the ten townships. These companies, it was reasoned, would counterbalance the black companies, constrain them from recklessness that might lead to general disorder, and cool the ardor of those that might try to use the black forces to terrify "a peaceful and unoffending population." The appeal to Governor Scott, which suggested that companies could be combined to form three full companies "whose services can be tendered to the Governor," obviously had a hidden agenda.[53] A few days later the *Charleston Republican* reprinted the *Enquirer*'s demand for a white militia, but added,

> The *Yorkville Enquirer* says, in substance: Let the whites arm themselves so as to be prepared for making peace. It is as if a man should say: I will make myself a set of burglar's tools, so as to prevent thieves from breaking into my house. People provide instruments for the purpose of using them.

Scott would have agreed with the *Republican*; he was afraid with good cause that the proposed white militias would be used to confront the black militia men and create a race war in the upcountry. In response to the *Republican*, Grist argued that the whites of York County had no choice in the situation. He explained that the county residents "would have preferred to leave the protection of civil rights in the hands of the constituted civil authorities, where the law places it; but if it is decreed otherwise, they must take care of themselves the best way they can." Republican John L. Neagle of Yorkville expressed his surprise that the *Enquirer* would recommend the formation of white companies. Considering the good feeling between the two races that Neagle said existed, he professed not to understand the concern of some. Neagle claimed he felt perfectly secure with an armed guard of black men and "could sleep serenely with a colored guard around him."[54] The *Enquirer* responded, "The argument of good feeling applies as well in one case as the other, and we see no reason why the Doctor should not be willing to sleep in the care of a white as of a colored company."[55]

It is doubtful the black militia's presence had any effect—other than assuring that no Republican's right to vote was violated and in securing the November 1870 elections for continued Radical rule in South Carolina. Governor Scott easily won another term, and the Republicans retained a majority in the General Assembly. First reports showed the Senate would be composed of 26 Radical Republicans and five Democrats; the House would contain 104 Republicans and 26 Democrats.[56] Certainly the Democrats were not pleased with the election results, which

3. A Threat of Violence

unquestionably incited the increase in violence that marked the last months of 1870 and the first half of 1871 as the most violent period in South Carolina's history since the Civil War. The day following the November election, a riot broke out in Laurens County; at least nine Republicans were killed and the town of Laurensville was under guard by more than 2,000 armed white men. Governor Scott recognized that the armed, black militia units had only intensified the potential conflict; he therefore ordered all militia units in the county to surrender their arms and return them to Columbia. He then declared martial law in Laurens, Union, Newberry and Spartanburg counties.[57]

Violence continued to spread throughout the upcountry; outrages and brutal acts became common. About 200 blacks fled Union County in late 1870 as a result of outrages committed against them following the murder of a Republican justice of the peace.[58] In York County, following a death order by Klan leader and former legislator William C. Black, 50 to 75 robed Klansmen rode toward the Antioch community in the county's northwest corner on December 2. About midnight they surrounded the home of a "bad Negro," Thomas Black, alias Thomas Roundtree. They fired numerous rounds into the house and called out for the freedman. Roundtree hid in the loft, but the horsemen fired on the house until he climbed out of a window. He was shot down after running about 30 steps, and one of the horsemen dismounted and cut his throat from ear to ear.[59] Coroner J. H. Fayssoux reported that he examined the body on Monday, the 5th, and found about 30 bullet wounds as well as a cut throat. He and Constable J. G. Barber arrested Mack Byers the following day and issued warrants for John Hicks who, they assumed, had fled to North Carolina. When Harriet Roundtree identified several of the raiders, they were also arrested. Klansman Black organized their defense and produced alibis that freed them. Roundtree's widow and children were soon driven from their home.[60]

County resident, John L. Watson,[61] addressed the Governor about the Roundtree murder and offered a plan to break up the outrages. He suggested secretly hiring a detective with authority to arrest anyone "suspect of being concerned or knowing anything leading to the Conviction of the Mob Clan." Watson then suggested William Kerr, "an old Constable of York who has been very skillful in the way of catching murderers and villains," as the man to assume the job. "Kerr is well known as a fearless dare devil," and one whose motto was "Secrecy is the Secret of Success." No record has been discovered that indicates Kerr was hired. In the same communication, Watson reported another murder that had taken place in Rock Hill, where Republican freeman Tim Black had been shot 18 times and had had his throat slit.

Magistrate Hugh K. Roberts, terrified by the attack on Roundtree, wrote to Governor Scott reporting the murder and asking him to send "U.S. Soldiers." Roberts pleaded, "…there must be something don and that quick too for I do believe they entend to beat & kill out the Radical party in the upper Counties of the State where the vote is close." Roberts' opinion of the fate of Radicals seems to have been the general consensus shared by many living in the county. Years later, a black man told of an incident concerning a northern Republican, one Alfred Owens, who operated a tanyard in western York county. "He seemed all right, but he was a Republican. He said he was not afraid. He run a tanyard and kept a heap of guns in a big room. They all loaded. He married a Southern woman. Her husband either died or was killed. She had a son living with them. The Ku Klux was called Upper League." When Klansmen arrived at his home and ordered him to surrender, Owens insisted he had no loaded guns, "but the Ku Klux shot in the houses and shot him up like lacework…. The Ku Klux sure run them outen their country. They say they not going to have them round, and they sure run them out, where they came from."

By the beginning of 1871 Governor Scott was suffering extreme ill will from his own political party. For three years he had successfully remained aloof from the troubles in upper South Carolina, but gradually he had become the focus of blame. Many were calling for federal intervention. Though Scott had been in contact with various officials including President Grant regarding assistance, he was reluctant to form any militia units on his own, believing it would bring about a mini Civil War. However, many Radical members of the Legislature considered violence in both Union and Spartanburg counties to be out of control. They bitterly denounced the governor and threatened him with impeachment because he had not declared martial law and protected these two "counties with negro militia." Congressman Elliott, a black member of the Legislature, declared in a caucus that Scott was "criminally guilty, and should be dealt with accordingly." Elliott then argued the governor should accept blame for not organizing additional militia units in the two violence-ridden counties and for rejecting companies already assembled, considering that these companies were presented to him. Supposedly only a few of the governor's closest friends agreed with his feeling that sending troops into Union and Spartanburg counties would "only have the effect to add fuel to the flame…." Determined to end the violence, Radical legislators introduced a bill on January 11 to place armed militia units in these counties to check outrages. Radical members also demanded the raising of additional taxes for the militia's support, and required that martial law be put into effect.

3. A Threat of Violence

Blacks in York County were faring no better than those in the neighboring counties commanding the attention of the legislature. On 9 January 1871, five blacks were whipped at Howell's Ferry by a body of 20 Klansmen. Presley Thompson was beaten for boasting of his plans to be buried with the white people at Salem Cemetery (now Cherokee County); Jerry Thompson was scourged for saying he would kick an old soldier's hind parts. For attending a Union League meeting and for refusing to vote the Democratic ticket, Charley Good was beaten and murdered. Lee Guyton related that when Good, a blacksmith, was apprehended by the Klan, he was tied to a tree with his own suspenders, shot in the face with buckshot, and left to suffer. After several days his attackers returned and beat him over the head with guns until he died.

In 1933, Mrs. Lucy Zipporah Smith Howell, wife of Darvin G. "Dock" Howell, told the *Yorkville Enquirer* that she believed Good had made himself "obnoxious to the Ku Kluxers" by putting markings on the shoes of mules and horses in order to identify them at the scene of crimes. Planning to dispose of the body in the Broad River, they made several unsuccessful attempts to sink it to the bottom. After a week, Klansmen Joe Smith and Pinckney Caldwell were chosen to deal with the situation. They tied the body to a bateau and carried it to a deep place in the river, loaded the vessel down with plowshares, and cut it loose. Not long after that Joe Smith fled from York County to Paris, Texas, and then to Oregon — his family never heard of him after that.[62]

4

The Klan Wars

"They are going to make the Negroes give up the guns…"

Violence was hardly limited to victims of Klan activity. Reports in late 1870 and into 1871 of nighttime arsons in York as well as surrounding counties were common.[1] Diarist Mary Davis Brown commented about one such fire: "…some ones tryed to burn up ould Dr Allison last night; set his shuck house affire and thougt it would burn up the barn, horses and all. Burnt up his gin house and seven bags of cotton and his saw mill. The incendiaryes is coming nearer home. Lawson [Brown's] meat house was burnt up last night but the house was providentialy saved; there was no one theire[.] the fire burnt with in a few steps of the house and died out."[2] Several fires in western York County lit the night sky of 24 January 1871. At Blairsville, the gin and gin house of Dennis Crosby was burned, destroying 600 pounds of cotton and 1,400 bushels of cotton seed. A barn on Hiram C. Thomasson's plantation three miles north of Yorkville was lost to fire, along with 4,000 bundles of fodder, a wheat thresher and fan. Two hours prior, his straw-house, located at the R. W. Shaw home, was destroyed. A relative of Thomasson's recorded that the burning of his barn "…was a great loss to him — came near having his horses burnt up too in the flames but he got theire in time to save them."[3] At eleven o'clock that evening a fire was discovered on the farm of S. N. Miller, who lived six miles southeast of Yorkville. He lost his gin, gin house, a wheat thresher, a large quantity of cotton seed, four bales of cotton and several young calves. On the same

4. The Klan Wars

night, the gin house of Hugh Warren was destroyed. Mrs. Jane Thomasson's gin house along with her cotton gin, wheat thrasher, cotton and 300 bushels of cotton seed, was burned several nights later. The home of William Wood, who lived about a half mile from Mrs. Thomasson, was fired upon that night by unseen riflemen.[4] During January and February more than a dozen farm buildings went up in flames; two dozen were burned by the summer. The Klan blamed the fires on black incendiaries who had been incited by Republican leaders.[5] One York County resident and comptroller, John L. Neagle, along with county treasurer, Edward M. Rose, were suspected of supplying direction.[6]

On January 22 the Klan had posted notices around the county threatening to execute ten leading blacks along with two leading white sympathizers unless the fires ended.[7] Since it was common knowledge that Governor Scott believed any intervention by federal troops might enrage the whites to the point of civil war, this open threat by the Klan may have been intended to give credibility to his concerns. The Klan also threatened officers of the black militia with execution if they continued to patrol the roads, and promised to thoroughly punish anyone who spoke of arson.[8] A combination of these threats and increased raids made the blacks around Yorkville fearful of a massive nighttime attack. A nearby militia unit was moved into town to afford protection, and the Rose Hotel became its headquarters. While the incendiaries were acting at night, the black troops were growing increasingly bold in their harassment of the whites during the day. Militiamen patrolled the streets of Yorkville and the country roads, firing their weapons and frightening white residents. Men traveling to and from the county seat were stopped, questioned and

The Rose Hotel, Yorkville, SC. Built in 1852 and reported to be one of the finest hotels in upstate South Carolina.

threatened. White Democrats claimed they frequently were jostled off the sidewalks.⁹ Although the part of the county involved is not reported (it was probably the McConnellsville area), at least one white man was illegally seized, and some men sent their wives and children away for safety.¹⁰

Some blacks purportedly threatened to burn Yorkville to the ground. This and other rumors intensified the fears of the townspeople and kept them on constant vigilance. On the night of January 25 several shots were fired from a window of the Rose Hotel, and three gin houses, a mill and a barn simultaneously burst into flames on the town's outskirts.¹¹ Word spread over the county that the blacks had taken over the town and were threatening to burn it, and that the white people were afraid to come out of their houses. The Klan issued a call for help, and the response came from Cleveland and Gaston counties in North Carolina, as well as from Spartanburg County in South Carolina.¹² Although Grist of the *Yorkville Enquirer* labeled the threats of burning Yorkville as "vague,"¹³ area diaries reveal they were taken seriously. Mary D. Brown wrote, "Theire is great excitement to day, the negroes have threattend to burn York up to night and the men has most all gone to York and they are going to make the negroes give up the guns that Governer Scott gave them...."¹⁴

Locally armed white men, as well as a number from North Carolina, continued to patrol the town for several days while the black militia picketed the roads into town. On Saturday, January 29, a drunken black militiaman confronted Dr. Horace D. Thomasson on a Yorkville street. When the doctor mentioned the militia picketing the roads, the soldier cursed Thomasson and made motions of thrusting him with his bayonet. Thomasson knocked the man down and disarmed him. An embellished report telling that Dr. Thomasson had killed a black soldier quickly reached a meeting in progress at the black church south of town. A number of men, some of whom were in the militia, left the church and stopped by the Rose Hotel to gather their arms before proceeding down the street. Colonel Asbury Coward, Major James W. Avery¹⁵ and Dr. John F. Lindsey met the mob and explained the incident and temporarily headed off a collision.

Throughout the night and into the next day, tempers continued to smolder and a racial war seemed about to commence. In a determined effort to disarm the black militia, Klansmen were sent out to block all the roads leading into Yorkville, thus closing any route of escape.¹⁶ The Governor was notified of the situation, and he dispatched Major General C. L. Anderson, commander of the State Militia, to Yorkville with orders to disarm the black troops.¹⁷ That evening a tremendous crowd, black and white, from various parts of the county gathered in the streets. Both sides were seeking a fight since each faction was dissatisfied with the previous night's events. Just as the crowd was on the verge of exploding, Anderson

4. The Klan Wars

arrived accompanied by Senator W. E. Rose[18] and Representative J. Hannibal White.

A committee of some of the town's leading citizens was soon formed to speak with Anderson concerning the escalating troubles in the county, which most believed were attributable to the militia. Anderson explained that Governor Scott had sent him to investigate the situation and to determine if the troops needed to be disarmed. After Colonel Coward and the sheriff spoke to the crowds in the street assuring them the situation would be settled satisfactorily, the throng dispersed and the potential outbreak was avoided. As Mary D. Brown described the evening: "General Anterson [sic] came up that night [January 30] and said that he would have the guns all brought in the next day. They set one house a fire that night but it was soon put out and they had stirring times fore a while; but they all got cooled down after while[,] and I set up till John and Lawson came home about one oclock in the night."[19]

The following morning, Tuesday, Anderson met with a large cross-section of the townspeople who openly and candidly voiced the tensions between the blacks and whites. The numerous representatives restated some of their sentiments expressed the past evening. They again emphasized that the whole problem was rooted in the governor's policy of organizing and arming military companies within the county that were composed entirely of blacks, and his refusal to place white militia companies on the same footing. General Anderson was also told that the black companies were the origin of the many cases of arson, and that the officers of the units did not affect proper discipline over the troops. Anderson subsequently gave an order to Captain George Adams, commander of the militia unit that had moved into town, to turn in the company's weapons. Speaking to the black troops, Anderson told them how foolish it would be to get into a row with the whites who wanted no more trouble. He further warned that they likely would be the losers if a conflict developed. On Tuesday afternoon, Anderson issued the order for the militia unit to surrender arms,[20] thereby initiating the disbandment of the York County black militia units.

Headquarters, N. G., S. C.

Yorkville, S. C., January 31, 1871

By direction of C. L. Anderson, Maj. Gen. Commanding, it is hereby ordered that the guns, accouterments and ammunition of Captain George Adams' Company, National Guard, State of South Carolina, be turned over forthwith to R. H. Glenn, Sheriff of York County, for storage and custody.

GEORGE ADAMS,
Capt. Co.—14th Regt. N. G. [National Guard] State of S. C.

While General Anderson was in Yorkville, a Columbia-based South Carolina newspaper, *The Union*, reported:

> Rumors of Ku Kluxing in York County were rife on the street last night. Letters have been received by prominent persons, stating that barns and gin-houses have been burned, and that forty colored men have been whipped. It is stated that fears are entertained of rash measures, the white citizens guarding the town nightly, and that Ku Klux notices have been posted about, stating that in case of incendiarism, ten prominent colored men and two white men will be shot, and in case armed bands patrol the road, the officer in command will be executed, and that considerable excitement exists there.[21]

Taking his usual stance, Grist denounced the statement concerning 40 blacks having been whipped as "a groundless fabrication." He denied that Ku Klux notices were posted, or that there were threats to kill blacks or whites in retaliation for incidents of arson.

Less than two weeks later — at eleven o'clock on Friday evening, February 10 — a party of 40 to 50 Klansmen arrived at the home of John R. Faris. Word had been received by the Klan that he still had in his possession a number of Winchester rifles belonging to the militia company that once existed there. The disguised horseman demanded and received the rifles, without hesitation on Faris's part, along with four pistols belonging to his family. Offering no explanation, Faris left Yorkville the following Monday on the train to Columbia.[22] Suspicion arose among white conservatives as memories resurfaced of his exit from the county almost exactly a year earlier when McGill's store was burned. After hearing that the Klan had visited Faris, many reasoned he had been threatened with another, less cordial visit if he breathed a word. Such a tactic would not have been unusual.[23]

On the day of Faris's arrival in Columbia, Governor Scott, under pressure from state legislators, wrote the president requesting federal military intervention because he was afraid of a heavy loss of loyal Republicans if he called out the State Militia. The General Assembly also sent representatives to Washington to meet with the president regarding the situation, and Congressman A. S. Wallace on February 22 had a secret meeting with the president concerning sending troops into the upper part of the state. On the 24th, Grant ordered four companies of infantry and cavalry to proceed to South Carolina, and promised Wallace that eight more companies each of infantry and of cavalry would be dispatched to the state and to North Carolina. Wallace voiced his hopes "that the cavalry coming unexpectedly upon the scene, would catch the marauders in their work unaware."[24]

4. The Klan Wars

About this same time, a Rock Hill Klan unit made raids on the homes of a black trial justice and a lieutenant who was in charge of a militia based in that town. Ex-Confederate Clark R. Starnes told of these raids:

> I did everything in my power to redeem South Carolina from the Republican and "Carpet Bagger" rule. I was a member of the Ku Klux Clan. I helped do some fine work in Rock Hill and York County. We had a Negro trial judge in Rock Hill. All white people had to appear before him for a trial. I, and a few of my friends called on him one night and what we did for him was a plenty. He was never known to hold another court in Rock Hill. We silenced his court for him. There was a tall, yellow lieutenant who drilled his company here. We went down to see him one night. I went into his house and caught him by one ear and brought him out across the railroad. We took our ramrods for our guns and gave him a good beating. I don't think you could have twisted them up any more around a tree. That dispersed his company immediately.[25]

After two of the three black militias in York County had turned in their armaments, some of their guns and ammunition were stored in Sheriff Glenn's office. Not having enough room for all the ammunition, Glenn inquired of Probate Judge Samuel B. Hall if several boxes of cartridges might be kept in his office. Hall agreed only when he was assured the boxes would be removed as soon as Glenn heard from Governor Scott concerning their disposition. Scott's decision about the guns and ammunition evidently was delayed, and Hall soon became uneasy as numbers of visitors to his office commented on the cartridges. The probate judge was told by Glenn that everything was to be shipped out by train the following morning. In order to pacify Hall further, Glenn agreed to stay in the office that night. He was given the keys and admonished not to let anyone have them. Later that evening as Sheriff Glenn was leaving for a short while, Hall's secretary came to him seeking the keys. He offered the pretense of having some work in need of immediate attention. Despite strict orders from Hall, Sheriff Glenn acquiesced.[26] The next morning, the office was discovered broken into and one of the boxes of cartridges missing.[27] The empty box was found about 300 feet from the courthouse on the steps of the Presbyterian Church. On it was written, "When do you commence your war, Pat. Bushwacker."[28] Hoping to avoid another incident, the remainder of the ammunition along with the guns was shipped to Columbia on the next train.[29]

Some miles away in Rock Hill, 50 to 100 Klansmen made a raid on the depot where the weapons of another of the disarmed militia were stored.[30] Approximately 75 guns were either damaged or stolen, and broken fragments were scattered around the depot and along the road leading out of town. Colonel C. J. Pride, a newly appointed magistrate, immediately requested permission from Governor Scott to ship to Columbia 25 stands of guns overlooked by the thieves.[31]

A few days later, Edward Rose told Probate Judge Hall, in confidence, that Republicans W. K. Owens, Rufus McClain, Ed McCaffrey (silversmith) and an old man named Bloodworth had stolen the cartridge box in York anticipating that the theft would appear to be aided by Sheriff Glenn. Glenn's membership in a Yorkville Klan apparently had been discovered, and the thieves planned for the robbery to appear to be a Klan act abetted by the Sheriff, thus exposing his duplicity. After Hall's secretary borrowed the key from Glenn, he took it to the silversmith who made a duplicate. The men originally had hoped to enter the office without any sign of damage. When the key broke off in the lock, however, they had to force the door open.[32]

Fear of arson and black uprisings remained strong in York County. Probably in mid February, the Yorkville residents again convinced themselves that disaster was at hand. Major James Avery called for Klan aid from nearby groups in North Carolina, and almost 300 men from Cleveland County responded. The crisis was short-lived, and the men soon returned home.[33] However, arson continued in York County, even after the area black militias were officially disbanded in early February; Captain James Williams and his men were likely suspects. Contrary to Major General Anderson's orders, Williams refused to turn in his unit's arms and disband the troop.[34] On Saturday night (February 18) near Bethany, Samuel McCarter's barn along with provender and several calves were destroyed by fire, and his house and outbuilding were broken into. Though nothing was taken from the home, a quantity of meat was stolen from the smokehouse. A strawfield along the Kings Mountain Road and in front of the residence of A. L. Smith was set afire the next night. Evidently this was a diversionary tactic, for about 30 minutes later his barns and stables were found ablaze. Set afire on Wednesday the 22nd was a corncrib of two unmarried sisters, the Misses Alcorn, living about seven miles northeast of Yorkville. The flames spread from the corncrib to the kitchen and then to the house. It ultimately destroyed every building on the place and nearly all the furniture and other property.[35]

Probably in retaliation, "a band of unknown men" surrounded and entered the home of County Commissioner Hugh K. Roberts two days later and demanded his presence. When his wife told the Klansmen that the commissioner was absent from home, they instructed her to inform Roberts that he had ten days to get out of the county. In a letter to Sheriff Glenn dated 6 March 1871, Roberts requested "a Deputy be furnished ... with power to call out a posse in case of necessity" to serve as his personal bodyguard. The following day Sheriff Glenn responded that he would

4. The Klan Wars

"detail an impartial and efficient deputy" to protect him during his office hours. Evidently wanting round-the-clock protection, Roberts remained dissatisfied. Fearing that both he and the guard might be killed, Roberts told Glenn he was "determined to leave if ... not protected satisfactorily."[36] The lynching of Militia Captain James Williams on March 7 may also have been carried out in retaliation for the arson attacks. Williams' troops had caused considerable trouble in the lower part of the county, and Williams had earlier said on several occasions that his intent was to "kill from the cradle to the grave" should there be significant trouble in the area.[37]

The morning following the hanging of Jim Williams, the coroner from Yorkville arrived at Brattonsville to perform an inquest. Upon his arrival, Williams' militia and other blacks numbering in total about 70 surrounded the still-hanging body and made threats of revenge. The body was cut down and taken to a nearby store belonging to Napoleon Bratton, a brother of John and Rufus Bratton, where the inquest was held. The undispersed blacks continued to be excited and spoke of killing every white in the neighborhood. Most of the whites either left the scene out of fear or kept out of sight. Fearing a bloodbath, John Bratton and Edward A. Crawford sent a note to Klan chief Major James Avery requesting that he send some men to protect them during the night; 15 or 20 men came later in response to the plea. A black lieutenant who took command of the militia unit in the southern part of the county after Williams' death arrived next ... told Avery he was afraid he could not control his men and asked the major to take their guns and deliver them to the sheriff. At first Avery refused, but acquiesced following the lieutenant's insistence, and collected 15 or 20 rifles. The Brattons gathered all their family into one of their homes and kept vigilance with the Klansmen through the night. The night passed without violence, and Avery and his men returned to York the next morning only to be arrested by Captain John Christopher.[38]

As the Klan increased its control over the county, a series of violent attacks on blacks began. On 25 February 1871, the Klan sought out Anderson Brown, a black man suspected of arson and known to have incited others with his political speeches. He was dragged from his house and shot several times—once in the head. Two other blacks were shot within the week.[39] The Klan then made plans for a raid on Yorkville and particularly the Rose Hotel. They intended to hang Edward Rose. Their plot was complicated slightly when word was received that Captain Christopher[40] along with a company of United States troops had reached Chesterville on Saturday, February 25. The troops were sent on order of General Alfred Terry and General William Tecumseh Sherman because they believed groups such as the Klan were gaining control of the state.[41] The men were slated to arrive in York County on Sunday by a special train sent out from Yorkville,[42] but during Saturday night the tracks on the line from Chesterville were torn up about a mile from Yorkville. Leaving town the next day, the engineer soon discovered the damage and returned by backing the distance. Several Republican leaders surmised the Klan was about to make a raid on Yorkville and quickly sought refuge some distance away. Although Miles Johnson, Edward Rose and David S. Russell[43] (all Radicals and officeholders) "smelled a rat," they remained at Rose's Hotel.[44] Some time around 1 o'clock on Monday morning, February 27, about 20 members of the Klan — amid gunshots, shouts, and general pandemonium — raided the living quarters of Edward M. Rose at his hotel in hopes of capturing and hanging him. The county treasurer escaped and appeared two days later at a nearby military camp being established by Captain Christopher.

Someone fired into the camp at night during Rose's stay there, and Christopher sent for Sheriff Glenn. After the law officer ascertained that Rose was the guilty party, the captain ordered him out of the camp that night. Rose disguised himself as a soldier and fled to Columbia.[45] The *Phoenix*, a Columbia newspaper, published a letter purportedly written by Rose to his father:

> Dear Father: The K. K. K. made a raid on me Saturday night, but I got out of the way. They destroyed all of my papers, but left the tax duplicate. The troops arrived yesterday. I came in last night. Russell's liquors and the record of the county commissioners were all destroyed. They have broken everything that they could — doors, etc., and took out of the safe about $1000, it may be less, but I cannot tell yet. They fired about one hundred and fifty shots at me as I was running.
>
> Your son,
> E.

Those who had investigated the premises flatly denied every element of his claim. They insinuated the letter had been sent to the newspaper as a ploy by Rose to cover his embezzlement of public funds. Men of some position within the county investigated Rose's office at the hotel after the raid and found all records and tax books undisturbed. When a survey of damages was made, it was estimated that less than $20 for repairs would be needed. The chairman of the county board of commissioners reported liquor from the hotel barroom and the commissioner's records intact as well. Three witnesses who testified that the safe was untouched by anyone involved in the raid supported the Klan's accusation that Rose absconded with $12,000 in county funds. Fearful of remaining in South

4. The Klan Wars

Carolina, Rose fled to Canada. He stayed there until the Radical-controlled Legislature passed an act on 4 March 1872 releasing him and his bondsmen (William E. Rose, James Windsor and John L. Watson) from any liability or accountability for the missing funds.

A particularly bloody skirmish with one of the Chester County black militia units took place in the boulder-strewn area of Carmel Hill Church (at Wilkesburg in northwestern Chester County) on 8 March 1871. This unit, commanded by Captain James Wilkes, was known as the "Carmel Hill Company," and contained a number of men from York County. The incident began when blacks (who were in the majority in Chester County) threatened to take over Chesterville and ultimately the entire county. The town's all black militia commanded by Captain John Lee called in the Carmel Hill Company to assist in the takeover. Fearful of a general uprising of blacks, a call for help was telegraphed to Rock Hill and Winnsboro. Ten or 12 white men from Rock Hill arrived, but because of a fire at Winnsboro only a few from that town responded. Conflict was averted that evening and the Carmel Hill company was convinced to return to their camp in western Chester County. A group of 50 to 60 armed white men coming from the town of Union and western York County met the militia who were blockading the road near the camp. The blacks opened fire; the whites under the leadership of Colonel Joseph F. Gist responded; the militia scattered. According to Dr. Samuel A. Smith, "it proved disastrous to the Negroes under arms—many were killed." Following the encounter, Dr. Addison Thomson, who owned a large plantation several miles south of the Bullock's Creek Church in York County, wrote his brother:

> We have just got through with Scott's Militia. Our boys met them at New Hope Church, nine miles this side of Chesterville — some killed, dispersed the rest. One young man was shot through the thigh, the bone was so shattered that it had to be amputated — he is doing well. Another had his horse killed and another was wounded. My neighbor boy, James Robison, says he was in many a hot place during the war, but never in a hotter one for a few seconds. The fight was on Wednesday morning. My boys, Joe and Billy Sims and Richard Thomson were out scouring the country disarming the Negroes till Friday night.[46]

Another mention of the incident appears in Mary Davis Brown's diary: "We have stirring times to day, oure men has been fighting the negroes down toward Chester; have killed some eight ore ten and taken about twenty to jaile. Oure men has all gone on to see if they need reinforcement but some of them has come back. Some gone on, they [the blacks] have got quiet again...."

The events in Chester quickly became known. When news of the battle reached Yorkville, Sheriff Glenn sent out a posse to intercept a number of fleeing "Carmel Hill" militiamen. Glenn met and arrested some of them before they could seek protection from the garrison located at Yorkville. Rather than being taken to jail as Mary Brown believed, they were escorted to the U.S. Army camp of Captain John Christopher and there given refuge. These men were:

Captain James Wilkes	Lee Sanders
Abner Hully	Wade Chalk
Warren Worthy	Wesley Simpson
John Hendrick	Rafe Gregory
Sylvanus Wilkes	Anderson Carter
Levi Berry	Martin Gage
Anthony Sanders	Aleck Skeal
Andrew Feemster	Harry Carter
Berry Wilkes	Frank Cahill
Green Sanders	Green Gore
Josh Mills	Vincent Wilkes

The militiamen were supplied with extra rations, and instructed to go to their homes and feed their families. In order not to attract additional attention, Christopher sent them out from the camp in small groups.

Writing from "Camp Sherman" (near Yorkville) ... Christopher informed Governor Scott of the details surrounding the affair.

> Hd. Qrts. Camp Sherman
> Yorkville. York Co. S. C.
> Mar. 12th 1871
>
> His Excellency
> R. K. Scott
> Governor of the State of South Carolina
>
> Sir.
>
> At the request of the Sheriff of this Co. and upon closer investigation in regard to the retreat of the "Carmel Hill" company of Militia upon this place. I make the following amendment to my letter of the 8th inst. as near as I can ascertain that company of militia were not fired upon in this county, but were closely trailed in this county, and judging from the condition of affairs in this county I believe they would have been murdered were there no U. S. Troops in this vicinity, the next morning after their capture a party of white citizens were disarmed by the Sheriff in the vicinity of my camp, some with public arms in their hands, a portion of this party were part of the *posse commitatus* [sic] that had been called out the evening previous to disarm and arrest the company of militia.
>
> I respectfully state that parties belonging to the secret organization in

4. The Klan Wars 75

existence in this county styled the "Ku Klux" or Council of Safety[47] which I have reason to believe have their Head Centre or Cheif [sic] in Yorkville, are in close communication with the sub chiefs [sic] in the townships of this county, and Union and Chester of this State, and of Cleveland and Gaston of the State of North Carolina, that this organization, I positively state[,] whip, murder, commit outrages and drive from their homes hundreds of families of this county, and are endeavoring to use their influence with the enlisted men of this command by encouraging desertion, purchasing arms, and facilitating their escape.

I respectfully call the attention of the Governor of this State to the case of H. K. Roberts, Esq. County Commissioner of this county, who resides near the North Carolina line, this gentleman has had his residence searched on two different occasions by this Council of Safety during his absence, and who notified his family that they would have him (if he did not leave the county) even were they compelled to place pickets at the forks of every road. Mr. Roberts has applied to the Sheriff of this county for security of person and property, he has written the two enclosed communications to the Sheriff of this county, and received the enclosed reply from him, and the only guarantee that he has received in regard thereto was that he could furnish him with a deputy, who would probably be murdered together with Mr. Roberts were he to accompany him, and informed Mr. Roberts that he had better remain here, and as near as I can ascertain the following outrages have been perpetrated since my arrival in York County.

The hanging of Capt. Williams (Colored) of the McConnellsville company of Militia at McConnellsville.

The shooting of Fred Williams (Colored) about two miles from this place.

The killing of Peter Boyce (Colored) in Cherokee Township.

The shooting of Lot Campbell, while at work in the fields, about six miles from this place.

The burning of a cotton gin and gin house belonging to Mr. Lowry about 13 miles from here.

And the interference with the family of a White man to which my attention was called by the Sheriff, but which I cannot now name.

Complaints come in to me daily from citizens of threats that have been made against their lives and property, which as a military officer of the army of the United States I am unable to take cognizance of, and which it seems civil law cannot reach while the Council of Safety is in existence.

I respectfully suggest that the Sheriff be directed to seize all the public arms in the hands of the Whites and Blacks, and especially those arms seized by the organization mentioned in this communication.

I respectfully state that the Council of Safety through its chief, ordered the rails of the Kings Mountain R. R. to be torn up to prevent my arrival in time to check any raid made upon the County Treasurer. I believe at the same time that the damage done to the R. R. was of not so serious a character but that any engineer or conductor that ever served in the Army could have repaired the damage in fifteen or twenty minutes were he disposed to do so. I was informed by the agent of the Charlotte R. R. at Chester that the conductor of the Kings Mountain R. R. received the telegram of the intended arrival of troops at Chester on Saturday, and had agreed to come for them on Sunday; it is claimed by this R. R. Company that one or two rails were carried off. I noticed myself on my trip along the road and on my arrival here material enough to repair the damage at once.

                        I am
                        Very Respectfully Your obt. Svt.
                        John Christopher
                        Capt. 18th U. S. Infty
                        Commd'g Camp Sherman

5

Federal Intervention

> "I think he is anxious for martial law.
> I think he is a very bad man."

In general, the atmosphere of violence during 1870 and into 1871 crippled the financial life of York County. The effects lasted for some time. In January 1872 the *Yorkville Enquirer* reported that "...the prosperity of the county is injured by the late difficulties [and this] cannot be truthfully denied. A feeling of uncertainty is connected with everything. This can be dispelled only by bravely going to work."[1] By the time the article appeared, the demand for laborers must have been intense. Numbers of males had left the county: whites to avoid arrest; blacks to avoid harassment or attack. From early winter 1870 through summer 1871, some of the black male population of select areas of the county slept in the woods out of concern for their personal safety; some deserted the plantations or left the county altogether, creating severe labor shortages.[2] Testimony during the Klan trials reveals part of the economic problem was caused by the nightriders. "Persons have lost a great deal on farms by the running off of the colored people, not being able to work them."[3] By April 1871, the Yorkville paper presented a depressing assessment of York's situation and attempted to put the blame on others:

> Seldom have the farmers had so many difficulties to encounter as have been put in their way during the last six months. The labors, in many instances were rendered useless by the circumstances.... If the powers that be will only

let the negro alone and not send him any more guns, or addle his brains about elections, things will do decidedly better.⁴

Agriculture was not the only segment of the economy to suffer. R. L. M. Camders of Philadelphia, and manager of the South Carolina Mining Company, complained that investments in a Bullock's Creek gold mine were in serious jeopardy. Dr. William H. Walling, an agent for the operation and "a Northern man," wrote:

> The cloud, which was no larger than a man's hand, is assuming high proportions — I mean in plain English the <u>Ku Klux Klan.</u> They are riding over the County, every night, whipping negroes, threatening people, and killing whoever opposes them. Thus far, they have not molested us; but they may be here some night; for I am, to use their words, "a <u>Damn Yankee.</u>" I hear their shooting, shouting, and blowing their horns every night, and I frankly tell you I do not like the looks of things.⁵

In addition, Republican merchants and craftsmen were often shunned by Democratic patrons. Such was the fate of the Higgins family in Spartanburg; 15-year-old Florence J. Higgins penned a request to Governor Scott for a loan of $1.00 "till we try to make a crop and will return it back in the fall." She reported that her father, a tailor and Republican, could not support his wife and large family since people denied him work because of his political persuasion.⁶

The winter violence of 1870 and 1871 had an even greater effect on the Radicals, causing a number to resign from office out of fear of the Klan; few other Republicans were willing to fill their positions. The Union Leagues were forced to recognize that their custom of meeting at night was instrumental in raising the suspicion of the white Democrats and thereby fanning the flames of violence. The Clay Hill League near Rock Hill resolved not to hold evening meetings and simultaneously condemned acts of violence committed by their race. The frenzied white Democrats evidently were not to be satisfied by "mere preambles and resolutions," and contended that nothing short of disbanding the league would restore order. In February 1871, one Democrat in a defiant tone declared, "So long as they keep up a secret organization ... it is probable that just so long will a counter organization exist...."⁷ All across the South, planters and farmers voiced the same sentiment by declaring that the existence of the league justified the Klan, even with its terror and violence.⁸ The Klan persisted in its efforts until it had battered the life out of the league. The destruction of the latter was one of the most dramatic political achievements of the Klan in York County.⁹

In late February and early March, several acts of violence portended things to come. First there was the murder of Anderson Brown who had been suspected of arson; then two other blacks, one suspected of arson and the other said to be living with two white women. Compounding these crimes were the murder of militia Captain James Williams on March 6,[10] and the Klan attack on the Chester black militia on March 8. Members of the state government obviously were concerned about the turn of events. Governor Scott, having been assured that a sufficient force of federal troops would be sent to South Carolina, met with a number of conservative men in the state on March 13th to seek their opinions. Two days before the meeting, General Alfred Terry, commander of the Department of the South in Louisville, Kentucky, telegraphed: "Have you power to proclaim martial law? If you have, I will enforce it with my whole command if necessary."[11] However, Scott was counseled by the conservatives to disperse the remaining state militia companies and advised against declaring martial law. He was also urged to replace some local officials.[12] Scott had little choice but to accept the conservatives' advice because the Klan was in a position to accomplish much of what it desired through force. Scott already had disbanded the militia in Union and York in January and February; the militia in Chester was disbanded after mid–March. He subsequently removed many blacks and corrupt whites from office, and then filled the positions with "respectable white men."[13] In return for his concessions, the conservatives promised they would do all within their power to restore peace.

Some scattered incidents occurred after Scott acted on the conservatives' recommendations, but Sheriff Glenn noted an alteration in the mood of the area's residents. He remarked to the governor: "...there is a marked change in the temper of the people of the County, and a growing disposition to maintain the Supremacy of the civil law.... A meeting of Citizens was held at this place today, at which resolutions were adopted looking to immediate concerted action throughout the county for accomplishing the purposes in view."[14] Captain John Christopher, commander of a company of United States troops that had arrived in late February, echoed Sheriff Glenn's view. There had been, he said, "a great change in the condition of the affairs in this County, acts of lawlessness and violence against all classes of citizens have ceased ... there seems to exist between the races a general sentiment of determination to check anarchy and confusion, and to sustain the Sheriff of the county in the enforcement of law and order without regard to political opinion."[15]

Scott's acquiescence was viewed as a positive move. When a grand Klan meeting was held in Spartanburg County by representatives from Spartanburg, York, Union and Chester counties and from some places in North Carolina, those present discussed plans for controlling local units of the Klans. Secrecy and the covert actions of the Klan were vital to the organization, and the chiefs were aware of deteriorating discipline. The leaders were little interested in dealing with petty misconduct of suspected blacks or in settling personal grievances, but many of the rank and file increasingly were becoming involved in such activities. The chiefs, who were of the opinion that these unauthorized raids were causing severe problems, discussed the situation. They determined to forbid any action without a specific order, and they established penalties for violations.[16] Grand Giant James W. Avery, a county chief representing York at the meeting, soon discovered little compliance with the mandate in his home county; he spent much of his time trying to curb the terror he had begun.

Though a cessation of violence seemed possible, the movement of troops into the area by the United States government was already in progress. Under federal orders, Colonel Lewis Merrill arrived in Columbia South Carolina, direct from Kansas, with three companies of the Seventh Cavalry.[17] One company was sent to Union and one to Spartanburg. Merrill arrived in Yorkville by rail, with a company numbering about 90 men and horses under the command of Captain Owen, on 16 March 1871 and assumed command from Captain Christopher.[18] On the 24th, General Alfred H. Terry informed Governor Scott that three companies of cavalry had left Louisville for Chester, York and Spartanburg, and that another would soon follow for Union.[19] Three days later Terry telegraphed the governor to relate that his present orders provided for garrisons at Columbia, Chester, York, Spartanburg and Union. He also inquired of Scott if "there are other places which you think should have troops."[20] Yet President Grant did not command them to take any major action, and they generally served as escorts for federal officials fearful of pursuing their duties.[21] Merrill's camp at Yorkville additionally served as a reception center for anyone fearing for their life. Some months later, a *New York Tribune* correspondent provided a scene of the military camp and of Yorkville under occupation; his description likely was little different from one that might have been written in the spring:

> As I walked up the long street from the depot to the hotel, the place had the look of a town in war time recently captured by an invading army. There were soldiers everywhere. An infantry camp of clean, white tents, arranged in regular rows, with the alleys between prettily shaded with arbors of green boughs, stood in an oak grove near the station. A squad of cavalry rode by; blue coats strolled up and down the street and lounged about the doors of the stores, in which seemed to be much talk and little traffic. Groups of countrymen in gray homespun stood upon the street corners and in the Court House yard, engaged in low and excited talk. Other men who appeared, by their dress, villagers, could be seen through the open doors of lawyers' and doctors' offices, or standing in knots of three or four upon the

sidewalks, absorbed in conversation on the one topic of the streets. Everybody but the negroes and soldiers had the look of excitement and despondency always observable in the inhabitants of a conquered town, and the people I met eyed me suspiciously, as if they feared I might have come to empty some new vial of Government wrath upon their devoted heads.[22]

Merrill discovered on his reaching Yorkville that a movement was already in progress to end the violence; citizens had hoped the effort would deter government intervention.[23] Immediately after his arrival he met with Captain Isaac D. Witherspoon, Dr. J. Rufus Bratton, Dr. John F. Lindsey and others. On what appeared to be a positive and agreeable note, Merrill told the gentlemen that he was satisfied the turmoil could be stopped with the people's support. Agreeing with the colonel, they authorized the preparation of a paper denouncing violence and calling for everyone to stand for law and order. The document was circulated through each of the ten townships and signed by many men and women.[24] Not all, however, were inclined to restore peace and harmony, no matter what efforts were being made by segments of the society. As is often the case, a certain element inevitably surfaces that will take advantage of a situation for their own benefit. A group of disguised black men, dressed as Ku Kluxers, stormed into the store of Thomas A. Douglas at Thorns Ferry, nine miles east of Yorkville, and robbed the clerk. These men had organized their own Klanlike group bound by an allegiance that required the death of any of their number who divulged their identity.[25]

Yorkville freight depot.

Probably as a reaction either to Klan Chief Avery's denouncement of violence earlier in March, or to the meeting between Colonel Merrill and prominent York County citizens, local men met in small caucuses across the county to consider the changing situation. Undoubtedly these caucuses took place under the watchful eye of the Klan and perhaps with its support. The *Yorkville Enquirer* reported one such meeting held at Hood's Store in Bullock's Creek Township. The group there resolved to cooperate with civil authorities and to suppress lawlessness in the area, but they pointed to the Legislature rather than to the Klan as the prime cause of lawlessness and violence. They further resolved to send two delegates to the Township Meeting at Yorkville on the following Saturday, March 25. J. P. Hood was appointed to represent whites and Moses Edwards to represent black constituents.[26]

As a result of the small attendance (attributed to short notice), the Township Meeting had to be postponed until Monday, April 1, a sale day. Even so, some business evidently was conducted on the Saturday since Cadwalder Jones, chairman, appointed a committee of men to represent their precincts at the meeting the following Monday. The all-white appointees were:

Bethel	John Adams, J. C. Phillips
Bethany	William McGill, A. P. Campbell
Buffalo	Jonathan Moore, Joseph G. Webber
Bullock's Creek	J. P. Hood, S. C. Youngblood
Clay Hill	W. B. Allison, David T. Partlow
Coat's Tavern	John R. Patton, Alexander Black
Fort Mill	J. H. Faulkner, Baxter Springs
Hickory Grove	D. C. McKinney, John W. Mitchell
King's Creek	W. W. Gaffney, W. C. Black
McConnellsville	J. P. Moore, K. P. Sadler
Pride's Old Mill	John S. Bratton, David Williams
Rock Hill	John Rattaree, F. H. Barber
Sharon	Samuel G. Brown, R. A. Ross
Yorkville	Walter B. Metts, J. Rufus Bratton

The blacks and whites held separate meetings on April 1, with Klan leader J. Rufus Bratton acting as secretary to both assemblies. At the meeting of the blacks, two men (supposedly under the prompting of Bratton) denounced the Republican Party for its deception of black men. Moses Edward, a black Republican from Bullock's Creek and a member of "Scott's Council," a chapter of the Union League, was one of three committeemen appointed to draft a resolution similar to the one published by the whites in his township. The resolution partly read: "...we the Colored people of the county, earnestly desiring the restoration of peace and harmony

5. Federal Intervention

through the country, and the perpetuation of kind feelings and true friendship among all classes—both white and black—do hereby request the members of the legislature ... Probate Judge, and the School Commissioner, to resign due to corruption and incompetency." When the resolution came up for discussion, Nelson Davis admitted to the corruption of the Legislature, extravagant spending of public money, and oppressive taxes, but he was under the impression that the meeting was called to condemn the Ku Klux Klan. Evidently the conversation became heated and the members could not reach an agreement on the best approach to curb the violence. General E. M. Law,[27] who was asked to offer some direction, told the three-member committee that the meetings were called to draft resolutions condemning the violence but without specifically naming the Klan. Law then gave his approval to the draft, which was promptly adopted by the black members.[28] These meetings, which sought to restore peace and harmony to the county, caused a number of blacks to renounce the Republican Party and quit politics entirely. Some placed a "card" or notice in the *Yorkville Enquirer* relating their intentions.[29] Frightened by the last few days' activities, they perhaps thought a renunciation would secure peace for themselves and their families.

At the time when some York County residents were investigating peace initiatives, Elias Hill suffered brutality at the hands of the Klan. Born into slavery in the Hill family residing in upper York County, he became crippled in an arm and leg at the age of seven. Hill's father purchased his own freedom about 1840, paying $150 to the Hill estate, and later purchased his wife's freedom. Elias also was freed in the latter transaction because he was crippled. He learned to read and write from white school children between 1830 and 1840 and then continued his studies without aid. Upon emancipation, he was prepared to step into a leadership role. Hill was soon licensed both to preach and teach, and he became a leader in a local chapter of the Union League.[30]

On 5 May 1871, Hill, then residing near Clay Hill, was torn from his bed by the Ku Klux Klan, thrown on the ground and beaten. Their blows were directed to his crippled limbs and were continued until he confessed to the false charges of burning several gin houses in order to save his life. His tormentors demanded that he stop preaching "political sermons" and receiving the *Charleston Republican*. The Klansmen also demanded to know the whereabouts of a letter from Republican Representative A. S. Wallace that supposedly answered Hill's inquiry about how freedmen might go to Liberia. After the Klansmen departed, his sister and brother-in-law carried Hill back to his bed. This encounter evidently congealed Hill's idea about leaving the area, and he subsequently spearheaded the Liberian emigration movement in York County. Under the auspices of the

American Colonization Society, 136 blacks from the Clay Hill area left in October 1871 to resettle in Liberia.

Perhaps by the mandate of the Klan leaders, many men in York County began declaring themselves on the side of law and order. On May 25, many men of the county made a lengthy statement denouncing violence and declaring their love of peace. In this declaration they claimed they were "...earnestly desiring the preservation of public peace, ... and urged ... every citizen to discourage all acts of violence ... pledging ... individual efforts and influence to prevent further acts of violence...."[31] More than 300 men attached their names to this open letter, some of whom later were arrested for their Ku Klux activities. The following week, a similar statement appeared in the local newspaper signed by men of the Bullock's Creek area.[32] Signatures of a group from Hickory Grove and Smyrna appeared in the next week's issue,[33] and yet another such statement from one additional section of the county appeared in the newspaper of June 15.[34] Such action apparently had some effect. The blacksmith in Company K of the Seventh Cavalry under Colonel Merrill reported on 11 June 1871 a rumor about the Klan massing that day for an evening assault on the troops at Yorkville. The following day, he recorded in disappointment: "The K.K.K. did not come as reported. Our Troop laid on their arms ready to receive them but they are too big of a coward [sic] to come and let us see them."[35] The times thereafter until he was mustered out of service in September were even less eventful.

Regardless of the relative peace settling on York County, federal authorities had already determined that extreme action — action far exceeding petitions and statements condemning violence — was going to be required to curb abuses in the South. In the weeks following the signing of the second Enforcement Act some months earlier in February, rumors circulated that the president would sign a third enforcement act and declare martial law in several up-country counties. Local citizens concluded that the arrival of Merrill's troops was part of a calculated plan to have the military in place when martial law was put into effect. Their concerns proved valid on 20 April 1871 when the "Ku Klux Klan Act" was signed. This law imposed heavy penalties on those who "shall conspire together, or go in disguise ... for the purpose ... of depriving any person or any class of persons of the equal protection of the laws, or of equal privileges or immunities under the laws."[36] Within weeks, the extent to which this act might apply to various York County complaints was under investigation.

In July, a three-man congressional subcommittee,[37] which already had held hearings in Columbia, Spartanburg and Union, came to Yorkville to hear testimony concerning Klan activities.[38] The York County unit of

5. Federal Intervention

the Klan apparently was in no mood for any further interference by the federal government; several days before the subcommittee's arrival, klansmen gathered and declared they would kill any member of theirs that divulged information. Soon after Colonel Merrill's arrival in Yorkville, he had applied a threat of retribution to Klan members and begun gathering information on their activities. Much of the testimony came from "Pukes," a title given to those who divulged secrets of the organization.[39] One locally infamous informant was William K. Owens,[40] an unscrupulous man who had been heard on several occasions claiming to know a great deal and anticipating the receipt of a considerable sum of money for information he might offer. When questioned before Merrill, Owens supplied the names of 18 men who allegedly were involved in the reported outrages. By the time of the subcommittee's arrival, Merrill had accumulated data about 11 murders, more than 600 whippings, and a variety of other outrages that had been committed in York County. Of these crimes, seven of the murders and 300 of the whippings had occurred during the fall and winter of 1870–71. A number of witnesses including Major James Avery and Dr. J. Rufus Bratton were called to testify before the visiting group. Amazed at the amount of documentation, the subcommittee chairman, Republican Senator John Scott of Pennsylvania, advised President Grant to declare martial law and use a military force to destroy the Klan.

Congressman Alexander S. Wallace had been instrumental in seeking and inducing witnesses to testify before the subcommittee. Although Wallace was a native of York County and owned a home several miles from Yorkville, hatred for the representative had all but made him a refugee in Washington. The Klan was well aware of his shadowy dealings with the president and his efforts to get Grant to sign the Ku Klux Act that resulted in the subcommittee's visit to South Carolina. Wallace was hissed and booed by the white adults and even followed and tormented by hooting children. In a corruption of his initials, "A. S.," the conservative Democrats often referred him to him as "Ass Wallace."[41] Wallace also acquired another nickname from an incident that occurred during the subcommittee's visit. While dining at Rawlinson's Hotel with several subcommittee members on the evening of their arrival, Wallace was subjected to an embarrassment that increased his ire. He had just sat down with Colonel Merrill, John L. Watson and Representative Job Stevenson of Ohio, when Major J. H. Berry picked up a pitcher of cream and attempted to toss it on Wallace. Mr. Rawlinson who was nearby serving a table interfered with Berry's throw, and most of the cream landed on Representative Stevenson. Both men leaped to their feet and reached into their pockets; the *Enquirer* claimed they were drawing pistols, but Wallace and Stevenson said they were reaching for handkerchiefs.[42] Shortly after Rawlinson had accompanied Berry out of the dining room, the major sent his apologies to representative Stevenson. Berry was arrested for assault and battery, but he became a local hero; Wallace became known as "Buttermilk" Wallace. This incident supposedly so infuriated Wallace that he and the others vowed to use all their influence to suspend habeas corpus in York County.[43]

Following dinner, the committee was entertained in front of the hotel by an all-black brass band. A number of Republican well-wishers had gathered there, as had a number of young white hecklers, and two constables who were dispatched to keep the sidewalks clear. After Constable William H. Snyder (a Klansman) attempted three times to move a black man, Tom Johnson, a scuffle ensued. Snyder's baton was jerked from his hand and he was knocked down. Snyder then drew his gun and shot Johnson five times, wounding him in the face, shoulder, hand, arms and back.[44] Colonel Merrill used his influence to prevent a fight by urging the blacks to disperse and go home. He also prevailed upon the mayor to do the same with the whites. The blacks were convinced that the incident was an effort to create a riot in which they would be slaughtered.[45] The congressional committee remained in Yorkville for six days hearing testimony along with the evidence that Merrill had accumulated since his arrival. The colonel reported that from December 1870 to 26 July 1871 there were 22 fires started by blacks in retaliation "for real snd supposed grievances. He went on to say, however, that three houses and several black schools and "about four or five" churches had been pulled down by the Klan, and that the Klan had committed since December of 1870 at least six murders and numerous other acts of violence against persons.[46] In addition to the subcommittee's findings, President Grant received and reviewed Merrill's personal report in late August. Attorney General Amos Ackerman was sent by the president to South Carolina to talk with state and federal officials and to seek additional information. Ackerman conferred with Governor Scott and U.S. District Attorney David T. Corbin[47] and informed them of the president's plan to invoke the Ku Klux Act, suspend habeas corpus, and declare martial law. At Yorkville, Ackerman met Merrill, offered him the cooperation of the War and Justice departments, and granted him the authority to make arrests according to the directions of the district attorney.[48]

United States Commissioner Samuel T. Poinier of Spartanburg and United States Deputy Marshal H. C. Moseley of Charleston arrived in Yorkville 10 September 1871 to begin arrests in connection with Ku Klux outrages.[49] About two weeks after their arrival a number of men from the upper part of the county were arrested on warrants issued by the commissioner. Arrested on the night of 25 September 1871, under the Ku Klux Act, were[50]:

O. C. Beamguard	Charles Beamguard	J. Newman Thomas
William C. Thomas	John C. Watson	Thomas H. Lessley
William D. Lessley		John L. Wood

The prisoners were brought into town about daylight of the 26th by a squad of United States soldiers, and placed in the county jail to await a preliminary examination before the United States Commissioner. These men were accused of whipping Phoebe Smith, a black woman who lived in the same area. The outrage took place on 12 May. Also accused was Robert Faulkner who was not at home the night the others were arrested; upon his return, he heard a warrant had been issued for his arrest and surrendered himself to the marshal. Later in the day Commissioner Poinier examined the witnesses, after which the accused were required to post $2,000 bond, for their appearance before the United States Circuit Court to be held in Columbia in November.[51]

When the Circuit Court convened in Yorkville in September, Judge William M. Thomas instructed the grand jury to summon Colonel Merrill and A. S. Wallace to furnish it with any facts about alleged outrages committed in the county.[52] Upon hearing various reports, an all-white jury was in "laborious session" for nearly two weeks, but it quickly became apparent they were unwilling or unable to deal with the crimes of their peers.[53] The jury, consisting of Klansmen (two of whom had been charged with being an accessory to murder), seems to have spent its time suppressing facts rather than investigating the evidence.

A sampling of the cases studied by the grand jury and their conclusions illustrates its reluctance to render convictions: Merrill's report mentioned a schoolhouse in the Bethel Township that had been pulled down twice by Klansmen. The jury concluded that the destruction had resulted from two rival teachers who desired to occupy the building. In another case, two black men testified that several men in disguises "chunked them," but since they could not identify the men, the case was dropped. Evidence was considered in the murder of Thomas Roundtree, which took place in December 1870, and that of Captain James Williams who had been murdered six months earlier in March. The jury declared that evidence in both cases was insufficient to authorize presentment. Also a raid on the Rose Hotel in which James B. Porter was whipped was studied. Porter testified that he recognized the voices of Pinckney Caldwell and Lawson Armstrong as the men who had participated in the whipping. No other indictments were made for lack of identification. In fact, only indictments for minor incidents were handed down, such as those to R. A. Black, James Sherer and Hugh H. Sherer who had whipped Henry Latham, a black man. Latham testified he had recognized Black because he was left-handed and one of the Sherer men by a missing index finger on his right hand. Sherrod Childers and Mack Sandlin of western York County were arrested for shooting into the house of W. J. Wilson in Bullock's Creek during September 1871.[54] Merrill also reported that six persons had recently been whipped in the southeast portion of the county, but "after a careful examination of the facts, [the jury] ascertained that no such outrage occurred in the county." It was obvious that local persons were little inclined to render convictions,[55] and ultimately, it was the unwillingness of York County's grand jury to demonstrate civil justice that deepened federal intervention.

The jury exhibited more interest in Owens' collaboration with Merrill and began to examine evidence of a possible collusion between the two. One witness claimed Colonel Merrill had been seen giving Owens a pistol and a roll of $20 bills prior to the man's testimony.[56] Hatred and distrust of the Federal commander and his tactics were common throughout the area, and many suspected he was on Scott's payroll to insure convictions in York County. A lack of evidence prevented the grand jury from bringing Merrill to trial.

The difference in viewpoints about actual happenings in York County after April 1871 is intriguing. At about the time President Grant was reviewing reports of violence and unrest in late August, one York County resident T. M. Graham wrote telling of the peace in the county; he went so far as to invite Governor Scott for a visit to ascertain as much for himself. Graham was somewhat skeptical, however, concerning the military presence: "...the country here is perfectly quiet. I think there is better feeling existing among all classes [than] there has been for two years.... I believe if let alone there would be no more trouble ... the military are anxious to see some fuss and if they Succeed Col. Merrill will be to blame for some. I think he is anxious for Martial law. I think he is [a] very bad man. I think if he was removed and all his command there would be perfect quiet.... If you could come up and spend several days with us and have some frank plain talk with the Citizens, both black and white outside of the political Gentlemen I have no doubt you would be ... better Satisfied."[57] Also sometime during the summer of '71, Doctor L. A. Hill made similar remarks to the Governor concerning the peace that prevailed in the county, but rescinded his view on October 28. He had discovered that "a large majority of ... [his] neighbors & supposed friends were Ku Klux." Fearing his credibility with Governor Scott and the Republican party might be damaged, he wrote to the executive hoping to "be set right in the eyes of our government." Hill related that "recent developments" revealed his former statement on the "state of perfect quietude" to be incorrect, and that he had been "ignorant of the true state of affairs."[58]

6

Colonel Merrill Begins Arrests

"I have not slept an hour in too nights nore none of my family... all [may] never meet again."

The worst fears of the Piedmont's white residents were realized on 12 October 1871, when President Grant demanded that all those involved in armed conspiracy disperse and turn in their weapons and disguises to a United States marshall.[1] Publicly relinquishing such materials would have been an admission of guilt; therefore the president's proclamation was ignored. On the 16th, Attorney General Ackerman notified Grant that he should proceed with the suspension of the writ of habeas corpus and declare martial law in nine counties: York, Chester, Lancaster, Edgefield, Spartanburg, Union, Laurens, Newberry and Chesterfield. Several counties in North Carolina also were affected. The president did so the following day.[2]

Mary Davis Brown of the Beersheba Presbyterian Church community helps chronicle events through a diary entry: "...it is reported that martial law is declared and that the yankeyes will commence arresting the men at eney time. Bille & Caty & John, Lawson & Mag is here to night, affraid to lie down to go to sleep. Lawson & John left this morning before day.... I have been down at York to day to see what I could hear, they have made no arests yet but great excitement."[3] Colonel Merrill began making arrests on 19 October 1871,[4] and Brown reveals the uneasiness felt in the community: "Ruff Whitesides was at York to day, came by this evening, he sayes that the yanks has commenced arresting this evening, has put up several. Jackson had his horse saddled to go over to sister Harriets to a shucking to night but when he heard that he did not go, the yankeyes went to sister Harriets that night of the shucking, hunting for Butler. They took Psalm Wood and to of the White boys that night."[5] Not finding Butler Thomasson, the troops returned to the farm of Hiram and Harriet Thomasson on a Saturday evening to search the house.[6]

Federal troops relentlessly canvassed the countryside apprehending those suspected of participating in Klan activities. On the day the cavalry from Yorkville arrived in Blairsville seeking the four Sherer brothers, family tradition has it that John Hicklin Sherer was visiting at the log home of his grandparents, Richard and Jane Sherer. Frightened by the appearance of federal soldiers, young Sherer ran upstairs and hid under the bed while his uncles, James M., Hugh H., William B., and Sylvanus H. Sherer, were taken into custody.[7] Nearby in the tiny community of Hoodtown, brothers John Halsey, George Davis, and William Lafayette Hood were arrested.[8] All four of the Sherer brothers, William Hood, and some others in York County were eventually sentenced to 18 months' imprisonment; most of these men would serve 17 months in the penitentiary in Albany, New York.

During the last week of October, 79 men were confined in the York County jail; most of them had been arrested during the day without resistance. Having been arrested without formal warrants, a preliminary examination of each prisoner before the United States commissioner was held, and if evidence failed to sustain the charge they were released. Attorney General Ackerman and D. T. Corbin were in Yorkville for the examination.[9] Those reported by the *Yorkville Enquirer* as being detained in the county jail were:

A. F. McConnell	Wm. Robinson	J. Henry Wallace	J. Pink Herndon
R. A. Black	Dr. J. B. Hunter	Samuel Wood	E. F. Bell
S. J. Harvey	James White	John White	T. A. Douglas
G. E. M. Steele	J. R. Harper	R. H. Gardner	James Pressley*
S. G. Brown	R. T. Riggins	R. K. Seaborn	J. T. Wilkerson
W. S. Wilkerson	Hugh H. Kell[10]	J. M. Sherer	H. H. Sherer
E. T. Avery	Iredell Jones	W. S. May	R. T. May
J. P. Gage	J. P. Wilson	S. A. Fewell	Henry Toole*
R. D. Gilbraith	James Hampton	W. W. Gaffney	J. W. Dobson[11]
Dr. J. B. Allison	J. W. Mitchell	Scott Owens	John A. Graham
Quintinella McClain	J. C. Chambers	J. L. Wood	J. L. Plexico
J. P. Warlick	John S. Miller	D. H. Carroll†	E. S. Ramsey
S. R. Ramsey	J. H. McDill	W. C. Whitesides	G. D. Hood
J. E. Plexico, Jr.	J. E. Plexico, Sr.	John Rattaree	James Rattaree
Minor Steele*	William Caldwell	Lewis Ramsey	W. G. Gaffney

6. Colonel Merrill Begins Arrests

Sillis Moss	Starnes Wylie	Jacob B. Moore	Adolphus Smith
William Moss	Mack Byers	F. G. Latham	L. M. Hardin
J. M. Hambright, Jr.	J. M. Hambright, Sr.	J. H. Austell	D. M. Stewart
E. J. Downing	J. M. Moss	Berry Moss	A. Kirkpatrick
John Ramsey	Alex. A. Barron	W. E. Camp	W. T. Spencer
	*Black	†Discharged	

The November 2 issue of the *Yorkville Enquirer* reported 21 more men arrested during the previous week; Colonel Merrill claimed to have received confessions of involvement in the Ku Klux organization from over 200 others.[12] The 21 being held in the Yorkville jail were:

S. C. Sadler	W. H. Snyder	Wm. H. White	Riley Moss
D. R. Neely	Reuben McCall	T.B.Whitesides[13]	L. H. Neely
Leander Spencer	H. Z. Porter	W. B. Sherer	S. H. Sherer
Sherrod Childers	R. Hayes Mitchell[14]	J. J. Waters	J. S. Poag
R. W. Wylie	Samuel Stewart	Minor Moore	Cornelius Pride
Frank Fewell[15]			

Others previously arrested, but released before the last of October, were:

Berry Moss	Sillis Moss	W. G. Gaffney	Lewis Ramsey
James Rattaree	Dr. J. B. Allison	W. T. Spencer	

Mary Davis Brown helps detail the two weeks following. "...oure military authorites have seaced aresting so manny of oure men as at first; they have got most of them now ... a good many [have] gone and gave them selves up to the authirities & have been sent home till they call on them and a manny a one rather than be arrested and put in jail [have left] ... they have aresed and put in jail thirteen this week. They arrested one verry ould man, Mr. Thomas Black and put him in jail, but since let him out. Also W. M. Caveny, W. Camp, J. Parker & J. B. Pressly, negro."[16]

Among those arrested at the end of October was Henry Toole, a black Democrat. Tradition holds that he was arrested with his good friend Iredell Jones and was suspected of being a Klan member; Toole spent 41 days in the same Yorkville cell with Captain Jones.[17] That a black man could have been a part of the Ku Klux Klan is difficult to believe. Although the *Yorkville Enquirer* reported a number of blacks in York County had been arrested for Ku Kluxing it should not be concluded that they were members of that organization. Evidently some blacks were robbing businesses and private individuals while impersonating Klansmen. They likely were arrested for violation of the state law passed in March 1871 that forbade "going in disguise," and the publisher of the *Yorkville Enquirer* simply classified the charges against them as "Ku Kluxing."[18] For example, in March 1871, ten or twelve black men disguised themselves and made a raid on the home of a Mrs. Atkinson, seeking to collect any weapons she may have. They told her they were the Ku Klux and to make their plan more believable, several men in nearby woods were shouting and beating a log — they told her they were whipping a black man.[19]

Through the first of November, 103 arrests were made; 88 men were imprisoned in the Yorkville jail, with some quartered in the guardhouse.[20] One elderly black man commented on the large number incarcerated: "They packed a two-story jail so full of men they had orders to turn 'em out. Then they built a high fence 'bout eight foot tall and put 'em in it. They had lights and guards all around it. They kept 'em right out in the hot sun in that pen. That's where the Yankees put the Ku Klux."[21] The *New York Tribune* sent a reporter to Yorkville to cover the activities. In one of his articles published 23 November 1871, he describes the jail and the men it housed.

> The county jail is an ugly, three story brick building, standing on the western outskirts of the town. The ground floor is occupied as a residence of the jailer's family. The two upper stories are divided into cells and corridors, and now contains more than 100 Ku Klux.... Every day or two a scouting party of cavalry picks up a few ... fellows who have ventured back to their houses after hiding in the woods for a fortnight, and whose whereabouts have been betrayed by the Negroes in the vicinity. The blacks all over the county keep a vigilant watch for the raiders who are especially wanted at headquarters, and will frequently walk 20 miles by night to announce the discovery of the hiding place of some chief of a Klan, and to pilot a squad of Cavalry back to capture him.
>
> The prison is guarded by sentries and is under the charge of Captain Ogden of the 18th Infantry. From the lower floor of the jail a flight of stairs leads to vestibules in each of the two other floors, lighted by large windows fronting on the street. In front of each of these vestibules stands a soldier with his musket, in front of a very large grated double door which opens into a corridor running the length of the building, with the doors of the cells open. On the second floor the cells have ordinary wooden doors, and the windows, which are quite large, are in the outer walls. The cells in the upper floor have massive iron doors and windows opening on a narrow corridor, which runs around three sides of the building. The prisoners are not confined in the cells, but have the limited range of the corridors. They are so closely crowded that there is not much more than room enough on the floor of the cells and corridors for all to lie down at night. Their friends furnish them with bedding and with much of their food. Everyday from 10 to 12 of their friends are permitted to visit them, and during those hours, rows of saddle-horses, and teams, attached to a variety of country vehicles, stand hitched to the fences along the roadside near the jail, and crowds of

6. Colonel Merrill Begins Arrests

people, chiefly women, flock down from the village.[22] The prisoner's lawyers have access to them all the time.

Nine-tenths stoutly deny their guilt. One prisoner said that $200,000 had been sent from Washington to [secure] witnesses [and] that 50 cents would buy a testimony. One prisoner burst out, "The Yankee soldiers are the only Ku Klux here, and President Grant is the greatest Ku Klux in the country." One cell [was] occupied by men who were all farmers and landowners expressing [that] their cotton and corn would perish in the fields as it has not been gathered. Some complained of their treatment while others said Captain Ogden had shown great kindness.

Weather permitting, the prisoners are taken out and marched to a nearby field where they can enjoy 2 to 3 hours of fresh air and exercise. A few infantry soldiers guard them as well as three cavalrymen. The prisoners ran about, wrestled, danced to music of a fiddle and exercised various ways. Most remained cheerful and hopeful. One man who confessed he helped murder a Negro had grown nearly insane and spent hours crying and repeating, "I shall be hung! I shall be hung!"[23]

Arrests for Klan Associated Violence
1871–April 1872

Spartanburg	230 arrests
York	183 arrests
Chester	43 arrests
Laurens[24]	40 arrests
Union	36 arrests
Newberry	1 arrest
TOTAL	533 Arrests[25]

When word was received that the arresting activities of the federal troops were about to begin, men fled. An estimated 200 white men from York County departed the state as a result,[26] and flight to avoid capture sporadically continued into 1872.[27] Brown wrote: "Theire is a good manny of the men left York; John Hunter, Wille Colcox & Cal Parrish is all gone.... Martin Hall was here this evening and took supper with us & is now gone fore parts unknown, whether we shall ever see him again God only knows.... John Brown has come back to day and got his close & him & Ruff Allison is gone.... Oure children & grandchildren is all under oure roof to night but it has the apperance that ... all [may] never meet again."[28] She continued the following day: "...[this] has been a night to be remembered. I have not slept an hour in too nights, nore none of the family.... Lawson, Eb & Wille Jonson, Harve Gunings, Gim Love, left this morning at thre o clock fore parts unknown ... it was hard to see them leave, we don't know whether ever to return.... Hiram & Lawson put on their hats this evening and steped off. Butler & Wille left last week. I left Sister with her three little girls.... I dont know how they will git allong...."

James L. Strain, who resided in the post office community of Etta Jane in the 1870s, recorded that Emsley Osment moved his family to Greene County, Tennessee, to avoid the arrest of his sons. Strain wrote with his usual flare: "Mr. and Mrs. Osment raised a family of sons who were ripe for the work when the unfortunate Ku Klux broke out, and for whose safety, more than any other cause, they went to Tennessee, just before the Federal government laid its iron grasp upon their sons for alleged complicity in the deeds of the mystic order." Doctor J. Rufus Bratton's flight from York County, and the search for and arrest of him (discussed in Appendix 3),

Dr. Rufus Bratton.

6. Colonel Merrill Begins Arrests

became one of the most publicized incidents during the Ku Klux era. Every road from the county was used as men and sometimes families relocated to North Carolina, Tennessee, Alabama and Georgia. Some went to the homes of family members living in those states. John Plexico "Squire" Hood and his brother, J. Simpson Hood, the head of the local Klan, along with their cousin Edward Good, took flight to Cedartown, Georgia.

In 1927, Thomas J. Robbins wrote an article discussing those who escaped arrest in western Chester County:

> In the Ku Klux time he [William J. Robbins] was a member of that Klan, and was never molested by the Yankees while they were here, though they camped near his home for a long time. No Negro ever reported him and he was never suspected of being a member.... William Carter, M. P. Faris, Garland Smith and Walker Smith out-witted the Negroes and Yankee troops for nearly a year. They would lie out at night and in the daytime they would get up on the hills of west Chester County and watch the Yankee troops search around in the valley below them. They all four had Winchester rifles.
>
> At the time, it was all the other three men could do to keep Garland Smith from shooting up the Yankee troops. They would stay in Chester County, awhile in Union and York Counties. They were royally entertained by friends, and went to rest on a good feather bed, a great improvement from a quilt in a pine thicket. William Carter had a narrow escape from being caught by the Yankee troops. He was at home when the dogs warned him, and when he went to the door the troops were within fifty yards of his house, on horses, coming in a run. There happened to be two rail fences, one about 30 yards, and the other about 100 yards from the house. Carter ran and jumped the first fence, and was over the second fence by the time the troops got their horses over the first one. That was the last they saw of Carter, as he went on over the hill, waded Turkey Creek, got some dry clothes at the home of J. Craig Kirkpatrick and kept on going.
>
> M. P. Faris also had a narrow escape from being arrested by the Yankee troops. He went to bed with E. L. Gaston, in the home of a man by the name of Reynolds. This house had a potato cellar, which was entered by raising some planks from the floor. When the Yankees surrounded the house, Faris, being a small man, got into the cellar, while Gaston, being a large man, could not get in. When the troops entered the house, they could see that there had been two men in bed, but could only fine one, Mr. Gaston, who was arrested and carried to jail. They didn't find Faris, who stayed in the cellar until they had gone.

T. J. Wright of Hickory Grove, in 1932, provided a list of names of men he knew who left York County for Sanatobia in Tate County, Mississippi, to escape arrest:

John DeVinney	Greyson DeVinney	Bill Lamaster
Joe Brown	Calhoun Alexander	Jim Smith
Ed Smith	Tom Montgomery	John Chambers

Lenn Cook	Jeff McKnight	Ross McKnight
Jess Mabrey	Andrew Kirby	Bob Caldwell
Sam Wright	Henry Wright	John Knox

Wright mentioned that two "Blue Coats" by the name of John Taylor and John Sigmon were among the group that fled to Mississippi. These men were military deserters from a camp "near the old depot in Yorkville."[29]

With the head of the household hiding in "parts unknown," strained financial conditions became a day-to-day experience for many families in York County. Since many men returned to their farms only after the crisis passed, the lives of their wives and families obviously were disrupted. Sometimes, in the absence of their husbands, the younger women would move themselves and their children back into the homes of their fathers. In certain cases, an abandoned farm might require a relative to occupy the house until the self-exiled kinsman returned. The *Yorkville Enquirer* reported in late October 1871, "Crops remain in the fields unharvested ... a large number of persons have left the county, rather than incur the unpleasant and uncertain consequence of arrest." Paid laborers or sharecroppers had to be relied upon to work farms already in dire straits. When a farmer's debts became outstanding, the family could expect a visit from Sheriff Glenn warning them that the farm could go on the auction block to settle a judgment. It was the fortunate farmer who had relatives with a sufficient financial base to support them or extend them a loan during a crisis. In February 1872 while his son Lawson was in hiding, Robert Jackson Brown was approached by Sheriff Glenn regarding his son's debts. Brown went to "Cousin Daubson [Dobson]" in York seeking a loan.

7

The Klan Trials

"Oh! When will this trouble end?"

Before the trials began for men arrested for Ku Kluxing, Chief Prosecutor David T. Corbin[1] had expressed doubts to Attorney General Ackerman about his ability to obtain an overwhelming number of convictions.[2] Many of the outrages had been committed prior to the passage of the third Enforcement Ku Klux Klan Act of 20 April 1871 and thus could not be prosecuted under federal law.[3] Ackerman, too, had concerns and doubted if the United States Court system could bring all the perpetrators to justice because his department lacked the necessary money and personnel to handle the workload. He therefore adopted a policy of "selective prosecutions," ordering Corbin to prepare cases only against those suspected of being Klan leaders or those who were involved in "deep criminality." All prisoners subsequently were reclassified, and all who did not meet Ackerman's prerequisites were released. Of those being held for trial, hundreds were allowed to return to their homes, farms and businesses after pledging to appear at court if ordered.[4]

South Carolina in the 1870s contained two Federal Circuit Court districts. The Western District consisted of Lancaster, Chester, York, Union, Spartanburg, Greenville, Pickens, Oconee, Anderson, Abbeville, Edgefield, Newberry, Laurens and Fairfield counties; the remainder of the state was within the Eastern District. Trials of those suspected of Klan activities in the Western District began in Columbia on 27 November 1871.[5] Seated at this session of the United States Circuit Court was the Honorable Hugh L. Bond of Baltimore, circuit judge, and the Honorable George S. Bryan of Charleston, district judge.[6] Judge Bond had not wanted Bryan to share the bench because he had previously hampered convictions in Greenville during August and September 1871. A Democrat, former slaveholder, and viewed by the Radicals as too sectional in his thinking, Bryan took his seat with Bond at Wade Hampton's urging in order to promote justice and to keep the Radicals from having free rein over the court system.[7]

The first matter argued before the court were the charges against Allen B. Crosby of the Blairsville community. He, among others,[8] was accused of violating the first section of the Ku Klux Klan Act[9] and injuring Amzi Rainey, a mulatto who supported Republican Alexander S. Wallace for Congress. On the night of the raid, a large body of Klansmen burst into Rainey's home, fired on the family and wounded one daughter. They raped another daughter, and beat Rainey's wife until she was senseless and Rainey until he promised never to vote the Republican ticket again. Crosby pleaded guilty and received a fine of $100 and 18 months in a federal prison.

The second case argued was *U.S. v. James W. Avery* in which he was accused of planning and executing the murder of Captain James Williams. Avery, who had helped organize the Klan in York County and held the position of county chief, was self-exiled in London, Ontario, with Dr. Rufus Bratton when his case was argued.[10] Because Avery's case involved murder it was certified to the Supreme Court for clarification on two constitutional points: the Second Amendment which guarantees the right to bear arms, and secondly whether the federal courts had the authority to use capital punishment in civil rights cases. Corbin prepared an indictment for conspiracy under the first and sixth sections of the First Enforcement Act and attached a murder charge to test the seventh section, and certified his case to the Supreme Court.[11]

Most federal lawyers across the South doubted the Fourteenth Amendment was meant to secure the right to bear arms to the freedmen, as that would entail a radical change in the federal system and warrant a "Second American Constitution."[12] Meanwhile hundreds of Klansman waiting trial, both the defense and the prosecution, were eager to hear the court's rendering.[13]

Attorney General Williams refused to provide the Supreme Court with a broad nationalistic interpretation of the Fourteenth Amendment, but continued the conservative interpretation that ensured a states' rights view. When the defense sensed the federal government was tiring of the responsibility of enforcing civil rights and was seeking a way out of the morass, they mounted a campaign that insured a ruling compatible with conservative views.[14]

As predicted by many, the Supreme Court denied that security and protection of civil rights were not transferred from the states to the federal government. The constitutionality of the First Enforcement Act was upheld.

On December 11, the first case presented was two counts against Robert Hayes Mitchell, charged with preventing a Negro from voting in the election of October 1870 and threatening Captain Jim Williams on 19 October 1870 while he was voting.[15] Mitchell confessed and received a sentence of 18 months in prison and a $100 fine.[16] Under Section 7 of the First Enforcement Act of 31 May 1870, crimes normally under the province of a state, such as burglary or murder, could fall within the jurisdiction of the federal court if the crime was committed "in the process of violating other sections of the law." In addition, the state penalty for the crime could determine the punishment.[17] Those involved in the death of Captain Williams were charged only with the federal offense of "conspiracy to deprive a citizen of his right to vote on account of race and color."[18]

Captain John W. Mitchell and Dr. Thomas B. Whitesides in the second case tried were accused of whipping a black man, Charles Leech.[19] Whitesides denied being a Klan member. Informant Kirkland L. Gunn[20] testified that while attempting to give Doctor Whitesides the secret grip[21] he did not respond accordingly; Gunn further testified that Whitesides had remarked on one occasion that the Klan was "the most damnable affair in the country."[22] Nevertheless, Judge Bond sentenced Doctor Whitesides to a year in prison and $100 fine. Bond lectured the western York County physician, telling him that the situation might not have continued "…if gentlemen in your position in York County, having found out what was going on, had united to put it down."[23]

The cases of John S. Miller and Dr. Edward T. Avery were next. Miller was convicted on one count of conspiracy because he allegedly prevented a freedman from voting, but he was given a light sentence when it was proven that he never rode with the Klan. The fourth and final trial of the 1871 Fall court term began on December 31. Doctor Avery was charged with crimes against Samuel Sturgis, a Republican. Led by Avery, the nightriders placed a rope around Sturgis's neck and dragged him about, and in a mock hanging, they lifted him off the floor by the rope. Leaving Sturgis's home, the Klan visited Isaac Postle, a black minister known as "Isaac the Apostle." When Postle's wife refused to reveal his hiding place, Doctor Avery knocked the pregnant woman to the floor and pinned the baby she was holding with his foot, while another Klansman stepped on her. In an effort to get information about Postle's hiding place, Klansmen beat her head against the side of the wall and Avery placed a rope around Mrs. Postle's neck and proceeded to "hang" her in the same manner as

Sturgis. When Postle was discovered, he was taken outside to a tree and "hanged" repeatedly. Tiring of their cruelty, they eventually released the man with a warning.[24]

Avery, who had been recognized at both houses, was arrested and placed in the Yorkville jail.[25] Mrs. Mary Avery sought the help of Reverend Robert E. Cooper[26] and two of her house servants in an effort to get the doctor freed. Cooper and Mrs. Avery visited Postle and insisted that he sign an affidavit claiming false charges. He was assured that both Mrs. Avery and the two house servants would swear that Avery was home that night. When Postle refused to sign the paper, they threatened to have him charged with perjury and sent to a penitentiary. Eventually they wore the preacher down, and Postle affixed his name to the affidavit. In court he testified that Mrs. Avery and Reverend Cooper had forced him to sign the paper under duress. Charges of conspiracy by force and intimidation were brought against Mrs. Avery, Reverend Cooper and the two female servants, Louisa Chambers and Kizzy Avery. Although the grand jury found a true bill, they were never tried.[27]

As his trial proceeded, Avery realized he would be convicted. With the knowledge of his attorney, F. W. McMaster of Columbia, he forfeited his $3,000 bond and fled to Canada. Discovering that Avery was absent from the court during the closing remarks, Prosecutor Corbin demanded the whereabouts of the defendant. McMaster was uncooperative and Judge Bond became furious. Bond ordered the trial to continue, and the jury brought in a guilty verdict after 15 minutes of deliberation.[28] Mrs. Avery subsequently obtained an affidavit from a man who claimed he was on the Postle raid which stated that Avery was not along with them.[29] She presented this to Attorney General George H. Williams, who ordered Corbin to allow Avery to return home to his family. Judge Bond, however, was not as agreeable. In signing the closing orders of the court session in April 1873, he struck through the part that would have exempted Avery from arrest. Avery remained in exile until his case was discontinued in April 1874 along with hundreds of others.

The expectations of District Attorney David T. Corbin proved true. Though hundreds of men awaited trial, the November 1871 term of the Circuit Court closed in the early part of 1872 with only 54 men being sentenced. Only five were convicted by trial; the remaining 49 had pled guilty. The April 1872 term of the Circuit Court faced a carry-over of 278 cases involving more than 400 men.

While the trials were in progress, friends and families awaited the outcome and countywide arrests continued. Mary Davis Brown lamented in early December: "They are still arresting some yet. They have arrested six in the last week, have let out about fifty out of jail & have sent twenty too

7. The Klan Trials 101

Looking down Congress Street in Yorkville, S.C.

to Collumbia to the United States court. It convened on last Monday. Mr. Stanberry, Reverdy Jonson & Judge Barnet of newberry is all there to see that the Ku Klux prisiners get their justice done them. Theire is still fifty one in jail yet."

Prior to the April 1872 term of the Federal Court, which was to be held in Charleston, 49 of the men sentenced for conspiracy during the fall 1871 term boarded a train in Columbia in early January under a military guard of 13 privates from the 18th Infantry. On 8 January 1872 they arrived in Charleston. Those prisoners sentenced to a $100 fine and 18 months' imprisonment at Albany, New York, were marched between a bayonet-bearing detachment of the Third Artillery from the depot, down Meeting Street and Broad Street, to the docks. They were a sad, forlorn lot, causing one reporter to describe their condition: "Many were imperfectly clothed, some had gaping shoes, and their persons and clothing seemed to have declared eternal war with such domestic appliances as soap and water." At the docks the following prisoners boarded the steamship *Charleston*:

Sherrod Childers	Hezekiah Z. Porter	William Montgomery
Evans Murphy	Robert H. Mitchell	William B. Sherer
Sylvanus Sherer	Hugh H. Sherer	James B. Sherer
Henry Warlick	Milus Carroll	Eli Ross Stewart

Josiah Martin	Thomas B. Whitesides	John L. Moore
Charles Tate	Tibion Cantrell[30]	Junius B. Tindall[31]
Aaron Ezell [32]	Alexander Bridges[33]	Jonas Vassey[34]
Stephen D. Splawn[35]	John W. Mitchell[36]	Samuel G. Brown[37]

The other men who were to serve their sentences in Charleston were escorted down King Street before turning at Clifford Street to reach the jail. Most in this group appear to have been from Union County and part of what now is Cherokee County.

Sentenced to Six Months' Imprisonment

William Jolly	W. Shefflin Blackwell	Thomas J. Price
Taylor Vassey	Christenbury Tate	Frederick Parrish
William P. Burnett	John F. Burnett	Chesterfield Scruggs
Martin Hammett	Columbus Blackwood	Monroe Scruggs[38]

Sentenced to Three Months' Imprisonment

King Edwards	William F. Ramsey	Marion Gardner
John Cantrell	Louis Henderson	William D. Self
Andrew Cudd	James Wall	John C. Wall
D. C. McClure	Calvin Cook	Dillard N. Cantrell
John S. Miller[39]	Melvin C. Blackwood[40]	Henry Surratt[41]

On the same day that the convicted Klansmen arrived in Charleston, Agnes McDill of New Centre (Bethel Township, York County) wrote to William D. Knox at Davidson College. A portion of her letter, composed after a visit to Chester, relates that:

> Everything quiet in the county. The Marshals are making no arrests & hope they will not but no one knows how soon they may begin. Brother Nixon came to Yorkville to see me. He & I went to the jail to visit some of our friends who are imprisoned there charged with being KK. They are looking well say they get plenty to eat & nothing to do. Oh! I am sorry for them but cannot do any thing for them except to visit them. I baked them some cake & took with me. The lawyer who is working in their behalf told me he was hopeful he would get bail for them in a few days. Oh! when will this trouble end?[42]

The quiet of the countryside reported by Miss McDill was short-lived. On 26 March 1872, 30 men of Company K of the Seventh Cavalry, under the command of Lieutenant Edward Settle Godfrey, were transferred to Chesterville in preparation for making arrests.[43] A few days later, armed with warrants issued in December, this squad made a night assault on the Turkey Creek area.[44] Arrested were J. D. Smarr, S. Howell, M. Good, John Jones, John McCarley, J. T. Love, Lee Gaston and a black man, Amos Scaife.[45] Also in the Turkey Creek area, a detachment from Yorkville seized brothers J. M. and John B. Kirkpatrick. That same night a raid was conducted in the western part of York County. F. T. Castles, Richard Woods, William McCallum, Martin Wade, Thomas A. Anderson, William Leckie, James Darby and Joseph Sims were arrested as well as T. M. Sanders, who was hiding at the home of his father-in-law, A. T. Walker. Later it was discovered that Sims had been apprehended by mistake, and he was released. Apparently believing that the constitutional rights of the men arrested were violated, publisher L. M. Grist reported, "Arrests were made by the military authorities without any pretense of acting as an auxiliary to the United States Marshal ... [since] neither [a] Commissioner nor Marshal [is] here."[46]

Transfers and arrests created a great deal of activity in and around the Yorkville jail; William L. Spencer, Pinckney Caldwell, William H. White and George Wright were transferred to Charleston on April 11 in preparation for the April term of federal court.[47] Two days later, John W. Gaffney of Spartanburg County, Marion Harris of Union County, Jerome P. Moss, Daniel Dover, J. B. Fulton, all of York County, as well as Ed A. Turner and P. W. Randall of Cleveland County, North Carolina, were incarcerated.[48] At the time, there were 12 men in the York County jail charged with Ku Kluxing.[49]

Meanwhile in Charleston, the federal court commenced on April 17, and Judge Bryan, seated with Judge Bond, charged the jury with its duty. The jury worked into the night preparing for the trials that began the following day.[50] This term produced a few more convictions (18). Included in this number were those for Elijah Ross Sepaugh for conspiracy and the murder of Thomas Roundtree, and Robert Riggins for conspiracy. The case against Wesley Smith and Leander Spencer ended in a mistrial. The prosecution allowed Spencer to plead guilty to conspiracy and dropped a murder charge rather than retry him. He was sentenced to ten years' imprisonment and a $1000 fine. Smith also pled guilty to conspiracy. An additional 18 persons pled guilty,[51] bringing the total number to be sentenced to 36. Nonetheless, a backlog of hundreds of cases remained on the docket.[52]

Judge T. J. Mackey[53] came to Yorkville a month after the April term of federal court convened. In a May speech before Republicans and other interested citizens of the area, he informed the audience that he had spoken to Grant, and that the president had heard with "extreme sorrow that the Ku Klux organization was composed of men who had fought valiantly under the Confederate flag...." Mackey, evidently under an extremely false perception, claimed that he reassured the president that out of all the Ku Klux who made confessions in the state "no more than two ... were honorable fighting soldiers in the Confederate Army." Mackey also made several remarks for the audience about Scott's "mal-administration," and the direction in which the Radicals had carried the state. He admitted that an army of blacks in exclusion of whites was wrong and a "blunder for who [sic] Governor Scott was responsible." While he agreed that "vast amounts of public funds had been misapplied or misappropriated," he circumvented placing the blame on the Republican Party by saying that the bad men who had been elected to office, rather than the party, were responsible for the condition of the state.[54] Judge Mackey's remarks, if taken at face value, may have signaled a change in the way Republicans were viewing their policies.

Most York residents probably had little interest in anything Mackey had to say because of continuing concerns about themselves, relatives and friends. By midsummer the Yorkville jail was quiet and nearly empty. P. S. Williams of Union County had been released on July 12; he was the last alleged Ku Kluxer, excepting Eli Ross Sepaugh, under confinement there. Sepaugh soon had some company; A. J. Martin and R. T. Riggins, both sentenced in early July in Charleston, were transferred to the Yorkville lockup to convalesce from sickness. Despite the momentary quiet at the jail, some arrests, transfers and releases on bail continued in York County and the surrounding counties throughout the remainder of 1872.

John Benfield was taken into custody in November 1872 and incarcerated in Yorkville on a warrant issued more than a year earlier. The warrant, which was reported to have been in "State and Federal hands," charged Benfield with robbery and Ku Kluxing.[55] He and an accomplice were charged with robberies and outrages taking place on 1 September 1871. The first incident took place when two disguised men broke into the home of Andrew Cathcart, planning to rob him of money he had received by selling several cattle. When Cathcart's wife refused to tell them where the money was, they abused the family and left. On the same night the men visited the residence of a black man by the name of Miles Watson who lived on the farm of the deceased Joseph Miller. After stealing a shotgun, the men attempted to rape Mrs. Watson, and in defending herself she cut Benfield on the arm with an axe, after which they fled. The following day John Benfield and Romulus Hopper were charged with the outrage. Warrants were issued and the sheriff was successful in arresting Hopper, but Benfield escaped. Upon examination of Hopper, it was ascertained that he was not involved; but he was able to give evidence that implicated Benfield and James Bennett. Both men eluded the sheriff until Benfield was apprehended in November 1872.[56]

Also during November, the grand jury in Yorkville was busy considering a number of indictments against those charged with violations

7. The Klan Trials

York County Court House as it appeared prior to the turn of the 20th century.

falling under state law. The names of men indicted as gleaned from the *Yorkville Enquirer* include[57]:

For riot and assault on William J. Wilson[58]

Julius Howe	Joseph Mitchell	Edward Leech
George C. Leech	C. Chesterfield McKinney	John Morrow
Sherrod Childers	Thomas Wilkerson	Jefferson Smith
Marion McAfee	Alonzo Brown	Harvey Gunning
Chambers Brown	Robert Caldwell	John Ramsey
Hugh Kell	Joseph W. Leech	William Johnson

For riot and tumult on John R. Faris

Edward Leech	Joseph Mitchell	Banks Childers
Dudley Jones, Jr.[59]	Allen B. Crosby	Rufus Garvin
Sylvanus Sherer	Peter Brown	Banks Kell
John A. Brown	William Johnson	Frank Smith
Harvey Gunning	Robert Caldwell	Daniel Smith[60]
Joseph W. Leech	Rufus Dobson	Butler Dobson

For the murder of Anderson Brown

John Gardner	Levi Gardner	Green Culp
Robert J. Caldwell	James M. Caldwell	O. J. Gwinn

For the murder of James "Jim" Williams[61]

James Rufus Bratton	Chambers Brown[62]	Sylvanus Sherer
Elias Ramsey	Robert Riggins	Hugh Kell
Henry Warlick	Robert Hayes Mitchell	Napoleon Miller[63]
Andrew Kirkpatrick	Alonzo Brown	William Johnson
James Neel	Addison Carroll	Miles Carroll
Harvey Gunning	Pinckney Caldwell	Robert Caldwell
Rufus B. McClain	Eli Ross Stewart	Holbrook Good
John Caldwell	Samuel Ferguson	Josiah Martin
	Robert Dickson Bigham	

Since testimony revealed at least 30 to 40 men who went on the infamous raid that concluded in the hanging of Jim Williams, there were additional indictments:

Layfette Hood	Pinckney Carroll	Robert Sherer
W. H. Montgomery	Evans Murphy	Hezekiah Porter
Hugh H. Sherer	William B. Sherer	James M. Sherer

The indictments caused considerable anxiety and anger among members of the York County white community. One man, writing to Samuel G. Brown after he was incarcerated in the Albany Penitentiary, probably expressed the feelings of many:

And it has come to this at last that our boasted model Republic no longer affords protection to her best citizens, but has become an engine of persecution to her children (through her courts, too) as furiously insane as were ever the Inquisitions of Portugal or Spain! As yet (thank God!) I have my personal liberty, but I feel that I have no country, no protector, of my purse, property, or reputation, when I hear every day the military bugle, drum, and clank of arms, and see every hour before my eyes the attired soldiers, cavalry, infantry, and artillery crowding our streets, and hunting down my neighbors and the best citizens we have; and find our jails packed with men charged with offenses of grave sort which they did not commit, and tried by juries packed for the purpose of a sure conviction and witnesses paid in money or otherwise to swear to suit the tastes of the prosecutors; and a prejudiced judge to impose a fine and pass sentence which is equivalent to confiscation of a whole estate and confinement for the remainder of the term of life! When I see all this, and worse, daily occurring I am appalled at the sad and sickening spectacle! For we all well know that this is done, not for the public good but for the support of a political party. I venture to affirm that there has not been, nor is now, a single man from this state sent to Albany prison who ever was or is now, a member of any organization, or single handed, who has opposed the Federal laws; and it is only by a forced and far fetched construction that even the most violent act of Ku Kluxism can be so regarded by a Court, etc., etc.[64]

Concerns eased slightly beginning in January of 1873 when President Grant issued pardons to several men from York County who had violated federal law; approximately 12 were released because they had been partially forced into joining the Klan rather than associating of their own volition. On the heels of these pardons, the president announced his decision to remove occupying forces. While the president's action may have been taken with the hope of restoring peace and good will between the North and South, these troops in fact were desperately needed in other parts of the country. The Northern Pacific Railroad surveyors had met with a "persistent hostility" from Indians and asked the government for military protection.[65] Shortly after the president's decision, the post at Chester was discontinued and a detachment of men of Company K of the Seventh United States Cavalry stationed there went to Yorkville. Two companies then were in Yorkville: Company C of the 18th Infantry under Captain John Christopher, and Company K of the Seventh Cavalry under Captain Owen Hale.[66] On 12 March 1873, Company K of the Seventh Cavalry left under Hale's command. Boarding the Kings Mountain Rail Road they were under order to proceed to the Dakota Territory.[67] Also in March, Colonel Merrill, who had been commander of the post at Yorkville for about two years, was relieved of his command and ordered to report to Attorney General Williams for service in connection with the trials. Captain John Christopher of the 18th United States Infantry once again became commander of the Yorkville post.[68] Southern Republicans had strong reservations concerning the president's order for the troops to vacate the region and made loud protests following the announcement. They contended that the removal of the military force would cause a rise in violence as perpetrated by the Klan. However Southern Democrats saw Grant's action as a further demonstration of the president's "confidence in the peaceful disposition of the South."[69]

8

Peace Returns to York County

"The K.K.K. have all gone home."

The Klan, rarely remiss in its duty or attention to its goal, had accomplished much on its political agenda by spring and summer of 1871. So effective was the Klan that the black militia companies in Spartanburg, Union, Chester and York counties were disbanded. Additionally, it brought attention to the negligence and dishonesty of many men holding office under the Radical government. In some cases, honest and frugal men replaced these officials.[1] Its successes, however, came at a price. As was told at the Klan trials, "Persons have lost a great deal on [York County] farms by running off the colored people, not being able to work them." The *Yorkville Enquirer* confirmed the problems faced by many county white residents. It reported in the fall of 1871 and in early 1872, "Crops remain in the fields unharvested ... a large number of persons have left the county, rather than incur the unpleasant and uncertain consequence of arrest," and "[that] the prosperity of the county is injured by the late difficulties cannot be truthfully denied. A feeling of uncertainty is connected with everything."[2]

During the first half of 1871 the *Yorkville Enquirer* frequently carried reports about the Klan. No further articles about its activities appear in the newspapers after June,[3] and the *Charleston Courier* reported York "county is in a state of profound peace and quiet." Some researchers in the recent past have debated whether the presence of the United

States military and the increased activities of the federal government brought peace to the area. Most writers agree, however, that a truce was already in effect before the government became so deeply involved: the federal powers could not lay claim to stopping the violence in the upper counties of the Piedmont. A study of the outrages listed in the Klan trials reveals a peak in activity in May 1871, followed by a drastic decline only a month later. Richard Zuczek in reappraising the Klan in South Carolina relates:

> Soldiers on the scene also noticed a decline in Klan activity before the federal crackdown. Sergeant Winfield S. Harvey, a Seventh Cavalry farrier, arrived in Yorkville on March 26, 1871, and recorded in his diary that "plenty of Ku Klux" was in the area. He continued to record Klan activity until about mid–June, when his entries started sounding like the one for June 15: "no further news of the KKs, all have settled down and gone home to stay." By July 28 the comments were the same, that "the K.K.K. have all gone home and no more heard of them." Major Marcus A. Reno[4] of the Seventh Cavalry had established a post at Spartanburg in July — Klan activity had been intense there — but reported in September that not a single outrage had occurred since his arrival. Reno attributed the calm to "the active part taken by some of the men of property, to show the folly of such deeds & the harm it might bring the county...." Even Major Merrill noted a "lull of acts of outrages" in his region before the October suspension [of the writ of habeas corpus and the declaration of martial law in mid October].[5]

The congressional investigating committee visiting York in June 1871 likewise reported that Klan activities had subsided; U.S. District Attorney David T. Corbin would only echo their opinion as he made plans for the Klan trials that began in November 1871. Although the "reign of terror" had ended, the government ignored the altered situation and launched an out-and-out assault on the Klan anyway.

The federal attack on the Klan was short-lived since interest in reconstruction and enforcing civil rights began flagging in 1872. Even so, the state remained under military occupation. Later in 1872, Colonel Merrill and U.S. District Attorney David T. Corbin shifted their focus from York, Spartanburg and Union to Newberry and Laurens. Their efforts there produced no better results; large numbers were arrested, few were convicted, and many fled to safety. Officials simultaneously pushed for extradition of refugees, and Corbin sent marshals as far as Arkansas to apprehend high-ranking Klansmen.[6] The most famous case, the capture of Doctor J. Rufus Bratton of Yorkville, illustrates the inept way in which this procedure was handled. (See Appendix 3.) As Colonel Merrill became apprehensive about declining federal interest in convicting Klansmen, his optimism turned to pessimism and he openly criticized his superiors.

8. Peace Returns to York County

District Attorney Corbin had requested an extra court term, but Attorney General George Williams denied his request.

The year 1872 also marked the beginnings of severe divisions within the Republican Party, as well as a congressional shift from vindictiveness to a more conciliatory mood. Weary of Reconstruction, Congress increasingly was ready to disengage itself from South Carolina and the enforcement of civil rights. In the spring, an amnesty bill easily passed while rabid Radical Charles Sumner's civil rights bill was defeated, and Congress refused to extend the suspension of habeas corpus in South Carolina once it expired in June. All of this was done prior to an increase in violence that began to be re-experienced throughout the Piedmont in the early fall after a lengthy intermission. During September, Chief Constable Hubbard informed Governor Scott that the Klan had not been disbanded but was in reality preparing itself for continued warfare. He wrote:

> I am satisfied that a complete organization exists from the Savannah River to Chester County a distance in length of nearly 200 miles ... that its object is to intimidate Republican voters on election day and if necessary murder leading republicans, and that large numbers of the citizens of Georgia and North Carolina are employed to come into the state just before the election for the purpose of voting and ordering their organization. I have also learned that five thousand Winchester Rifles have been shipped to the uper [sic] country within the last month.[7]

While only limited information can be obtained from local newspapers, arrests of men suspected of Ku Klux activities continued sporadically through late 1872 and into 1873.[8] Martin Hall of the Beersheba community eluded capture by the federal troops during the early months of 1873. Mary Davis Brown relates how events connected with this man disrupted the lives of her family. Hall and Margaret Brown, the daughter of Mary D. Brown, were to be married 13 March 1873.[9] He received word on March 8, however, that a warrant for his arrest had been issued. His future mother-in-law observed he was "in a fret." The day before the wedding, Hall told his fiancée that "the yankies sayes they will have him dead or alive," and that they would be unable to marry because he was about to go into hiding. With the wedding cake baked and "Mag's" wedding dress prepared, Hall obviously was "not in a good humour" when he secreted himself nearby. The next day Mary tried to console Mag by talking with her about people "bearing crosses," and telling her that "it will all be right in time." Certainly Mag's "cross" was made even heavier when her cousin, Davis Brown, and Ann Scoggins were married a week later. Overcome with love and loneliness, Hall slipped into the Brown home on March 23 under the cover of darkness, visited with Mag and her mother, and spent the night with the Brown family. He declined to attend church the next day, however, for fear of being seen. Hall left Sunday evening without being able to tell Mag when he would return. "Not till the United States court is over and our civil court [is back in force, and] that will be the first of next month" surmised Mary Brown.[10]

Mary Brown's "trials" increased. On Monday, Sheriff Glenn "sent out after" her son Lawson.[11] Some days later, on April 5, Lawson surrendered to the sheriff and was released on bail. (A cousin, Samuel Brown of Sharon, was confined in the Yorkville jail at the time, but the family "...was in great hopes that cousin Psalm [Samuel] will be pardened & git home soon."[12]) Lawson appeared in court on April 9 but was released for lack of evidence.[13] Whether Lawson was arrested as a result of Klan activities is unknown, but his release roughly coincided with actions Attorney General Williams took in April 1873 that decreased the Justice Department's activity in the state by "discontinuing or postponing" all cases already carrying indictments.[14] In July Williams allowed all refugees to return to their homes without fear of prosecution. Also during the summer a committee consisting of the Honorable W. D. Porter, J. B. Kershaw of Camden and the Honorable W. E. M. Sims met with the president for the purpose of interceding on behalf of the men under indictment or sentenced. After meeting, they reported to Williams that he had "expressed views of clemency"[15] and Grant soon announced such a policy "for those Klansmen who had not yet been tried and pardon for [most of] those who had."[16] In a letter to the committee, Williams stated the president had communicated to him "that the persons accused and convicted of offenses under said [Enforcement] Acts should be treated with as much leniency as possible."[17]

Before Attorney General Williams determined to "discontinue or postpone" those cases carrying indictments, the trials had continued in Charleston. George C. Leech along with two other men (Moore and Wallace) from York County were convicted in April by the United States Circuit Court for violation of the Enforcement Act[18] as would be others in South Carolina in years to come. This conviction however seems not to be part of the Klan trials which appear to have ended during the November 1872 term of the Circuit Court held in Columbia.

During late spring of 1873 it was learned that "steps [were] being taken in various sections to organize colored militia companies" across the Piedmont, and that an effort was being made to form a company in Yorkville.[19] This may have been in reaction to the increased violence that began near the end of the previous year. In August of 1872 Corbin told Williams that the Klans in the Piedmont "are becoming very much emboldened" and that there was a "general feeling of alarm among the

8. Peace Returns to York County

colored people" who had testified against the whites. Merrill also reported, "Affairs are getting into a very bad condition by reason of hopes excited by refusal of Congress to extend suspension of Habeas Corpus."[20] Returning to the formation of militia units in 1873, some surmised certain "scheming politicians" were hoping to promote Republicans to some position of importance. The *Yorkville Enquirer* hoped the "colored citizens will reflect before taking a step which cannot confer the least possible benefit ... that it may possibly involve them in trouble ... and cause a repetition of the trouble of only two years ago, from which the immediate area has not yet recovered." As a final warning he wrote, "We want the colored men to beware of the dangerous trap to which it will surely lead them."[21]

When the South Carolina Circuit Court convened at Yorkville in July, Judge T. J. Mackey announced before the grand and petit juries that a black militia company had been organized in York County, and that it had been, or was about to be, armed. Admonishing the juries, he claimed there were two classes of people in the county: one, composed of "quiet, law-abiding, good citizens" who feared the situation might lead to violence and disorder; the second class, he said, would "take the offensive and dissolve the organization by force."[22] Mackey reminded the juries that the "militia is part of the governmental organization," and that law prescribed all able-bodied men between 18 and 45 to be liable for service and subject to fine for failure to serve, but he continued, "having observed the repugnance of the whites to enroll themselves in the militia, the authorities have not attempted to enforce the law with rigor." Possibly hoping to quiet fears, Mackey told the juries that Charleston County had ten volunteer companies of whites and 15 companies of blacks, and that the two groups had never suffered a collision.

Mackey's address before the York County juries reveals a dramatic change in the mood of the state government leaders from two years prior. He assured the panel that should violence occur, no assistance would be solicited from the federal government, and claimed that the state was "able and determined to protect the militia organizations." They also were told that "any white company, composed of law abiding citizens, if organized under the requirements of the law, will be accepted." Evidently the mood of white conservatives had also changed. Speaking about the controversy, the editor of the *Yorkville Enquirer* reported that whites did not want to organize a militia since they saw no necessity for one "of either race."[23]

Although the federal government was growing tired of the situation in the South and was exercising leniency toward the offenders of the Ku Klux Klan Act, arrests continued.[24] A number of these arrests ended in nolle prosequi (unwilling to prosecute) since they fell under the president's exception whereby crimes committed prior to the signing of the Ku Klux

Klan Act on 20 April 1871 were exempt from prosecution. In February 1874, Deputy Marshal Hubbard arrested J. Blackburn Wilson and Robert M. Steele for violations of the Enforcement Act and for crimes committed in 1871.[25]

As the Ku Klux era was drawing to a close, a number of men who had played important roles in the enforcement of federal and state laws turned their attention to more pressing matters. Captain J. B. Hubbard had been chief of the constabulary in Columbia, but during 1874 he became a federal government employee serving as an internal revenue agent.

Although Judge Mackey's comments to the grand jury in July had been conciliatory, other Radicals continued to inflame emotions with their rhetoric, sometimes lacing their speeches with suggestions of violence. In August 1874, Congressman Wallace spoke to an assembly of Republican blacks at Gowdysville in Union County. Some claimed he said, "If you don't get them [civil rights] at the ballot box, you must resort to the cartridge box." Although Wallace denied the accusation, 12 white men of the area publicly swore they had heard him. Wade Fowler disagreed slightly with these men and provided a more exact quote: "Your rights are imperilled, you must *rally* to the ballot box — if need be to the cartridge box."[26]

Grave of U.S. Senator Alexander S. Wallace. Rose Hill Cemetery, York, SC. "A self-made man. He became a member of the S.C. Legislature, Collector of Internal Revenue and member of U.S. House of Representatives. He filled these positions with marked ability and left to his family the proud heritage of an unsullied name. A good citizen, a consistent Christian, a friend of the poor. His deeds will not be forgotten."

As the fall elections neared, Democrats believed they had another opportunity to restore the state to its rightful owners — the landed, educated and taxpaying whites. Believing the blacks were the root of all their troubles, outrages increased and Republicans called for armed units to keep the peace. The state responded to their appeal and the 3 November 1874 election passed

8. Peace Returns to York County

Grave of Captain George D. Wallace, son of Senator A. S. Wallace. He was a memner of the Seventh U.S. Cavalry and was killed at Wounded Knee, South Dakota.

with little trouble.[27] The results were not as Democrats had hoped; Mary Davis Brown lamented, "…the radicals has beet us badly."[28] She was correct, for all the Republican nominees for the Legislature and county offices were elected.[29] The Democrats' disappointment was lessened slightly (although only temporarily) a little more than a week later, when a number of soldiers were mustered out of the ranks of the Yorkville post, giving rise to a rumor that the remaining troops were being withdrawn. When questioned by the *Yorkville Enquirer*, however, Captain Hyer reported that the mustering out was due to the fact that Congress had made appropriations for only 25,000 and the rolls exceeded that number.[30] Three months later in February 1875, the military post headquartered at Yorkville numbered 48, including officers. That group included 21 recruits who had arrived in Yorkville from Governors Island, New York.[31] Evidently there was a yearly rotation of troops as approximately the same number of recruits had arrived in February the year before.[32] Since the troops were being utilized to make state civil arrests, it would appear that their work involving Klan activities was minimal.[33]

Crimes connected with earlier Ku Klux Klan action were being prosecuted as late as 1875. In April, J. E. Leech, A. B. Crosby, Rufus Dobson, J. D. Jones, Butler Dobson and Joseph W. Leech were being tried in Yorkville for assault and battery, riot and tumult. This case was called a "Ku Klux trial" because the acts of violence took place in the early part of 1870, but the charges appear to be related to violations of state rather than federal statutes.[34] Prosecutors of the case were John Fair, Wilson Wilson and W. J. Wilson. Rufus Dobson, tried separately and charged with a raid on the home of John Faris on 10 February 1870, was found guilty, but was allowed a new trial with the others. All the charges were settled through an agreement that compensated the victims with a $500 payment.

In what the local newspaper in July labeled as "the latest Ku Klux case," James Finely, S. W. Robinson and Isaac Griffin were arrested and charged with "intimidation with intent to bury." Reuben Goins, alias Shedd, resided on Robinson's farm and had been living in bodily fear for some time prior to the arrests. Robinson had made several threats on Goins, and, to intimidate him further, Finely and Griffin told Goins that Robinson had dug a grave on Griffin's land where his body was to be "quietly and forever hid from mortal view." Goins testified that Griffin and Finely related to him Robinson's plan to lasso and drag him into the pit and then give him the choice of either leaving the state, or being killed and buried in the hole. After a lengthy argument by both the defense and the prosecution, the judge charged each of Goins' intimidators $300 apiece.[35] This case apparently was the last in York County to be called a Ku Klux trial, even though the description may be incorrect.

Though the Ku Klux Klan of the Reconstruction period was little discussed by 1876, it must be recognized as one of the most powerful and effective grass-roots movements that the state ever witnessed. This clandestine organization did what four years of a Civil War failed to accomplish — it brought the powerful federal government to its knees and revealed its ineffectiveness. Although District Attorney Corbin believed the prosecution of some of the Klansmen had a demoralizing effect on the group, the record of convictions speaks strongly to the ineptness of the government. According to Corbin's tally, out of 1355 indictments, the government was able to convict only 27; another 75 pled guilty, five were acquitted, and 54 fell nolle prosequi (unwilling to prosecute). Nearly 1200 of these cases were still pending at the end of 1872. Also, the federal government's efforts to destroy the Klan, restore peace to the area, and send a message to the Conservatives utterly failed.[36] On the other hand, the Ku Klux Klan affected their aim and helped to bring Reconstruction in South Carolina to an earlier conclusion.[37]

Before the end of 1876, President Grant pardoned all convicted Klansmen. When these men returned home, the Ku Klux Klan in name was consigned to history, for a few decades thereafter at least.[38] On the horizon, however, was another movement which would exhibit a number of similarities to the Klan, which would sweep many of the same men into a political action that ultimately dismantled Republican rule in South Carolina, and which would subjugate the blacks. After a short interval, hoods and robes would be exchanged for red shirts. In the wings of the political arena, ready to portray the conquering hero, was Wade Hampton.

Appendix 1

Oath, Constitution and Bylaws of the Ku Klux Klan

Each Klan member was required to supply his own robe and pistol, as well as a whistle to be used for signaling. Induction into a local Klan usually involved a simple, but secret, ceremony with the inductee kneeling before the chief and swearing to the following oath or obligation[1]:

I, (name) before the Immaculate Judge of Heaven and Earth, and upon the holy Evangelists of Almighty God, do, of my own free will and accord, subscribe to the following sacredly binding obligations:

1. We are on the side of justice, humanity and constitutional liberty, as bequeathed to me in its purity by our forefathers.
2. We oppose and reject the principles of the Radical Party.
3. We pledge mutual aid to each other in sickness, distress and pecuniary embarrassment.
4. Female friends, widows and their households, shall ever be special objects of our regard and protection.

Any member divulging, or causing to be divulged, any of the foregoing obligations, shall meet the fearful penalty and traitor's doom, which is Death! Death! Death!

CONSTITUTION

Article 1. This organization shall be known as the _____ Order, No. ___ of the Ku Klux Klan, of the State of South Carolina.

Article 2. The officers shall consist of a Cyclops[2] and Scribe, both of whom shall be elected by a majority vote of the Order, and hold their office during good behavior.

Article 3. It shall be the duty of the C[yclops] to preside in the order, enforce a due observance of the constitution and by-laws, and an exact compliance to the rules and tisages [sic] of the Order; to see that all the members perform their respective duties; appoint all committees before the order; inspect the arms and dress of each member on special occasions; to call meetings, when necessary; and to draw upon members for all sums needed to carry on the order. The S[cribe] shall keep a record of the proceeding of the order; write communications; notify other Klans, when their assistance is needed; give notice, when any member has to suffer the penalty for violating his oath; see that all books, papers, or other property belonging to his office, are placed beyond the reach of any one but members of the Order. He shall perform such other duties as may be required of him by the C[yclops].

Article 4. Section 1. No person shall be initiated into this order under eighteen years of age.

Section 2. No person of color shall be admitted into this order.

Section 3. No person shall be admitted into the Order who does not sustain a good moral character, or who is in any way incapacitated to discharge the duties of a Ku Klux.

Section 4. The name of a person offered for membership must be proposed by the committee appointed by the chief, verbally stating age, residence and occupation. State if he was a soldier in the late war; his rank, whether he was in the Federal or Confederate services, and his command.

Article 5. Section 1. Any member who shall offend against these articles, or the by-laws, shall be subject to be fined and reprimanded by the C[yclops], as two-thirds of the members present, at any regular meeting, may determine.

Section 2. Every member shall be entitled to a fair trial for any offense in violating [involving] reprimand, or criminal punishment.

BY-LAWS

Article 1, Section 1. This Order shall meet at _____.

Section 2. Five members shall constitute a quorum, provided the C[yclops] or S[cribe] be present.

Section 3. The C. shall have power to appoint such members of the order to attend to the sick, the needy, the distressed, and those suffering from Radical misrule, as the case may require.

Section 4. No person shall be appointed on a committee, unless the person is present at the time of appointment. Members of committees neglecting to report, shall be fined thirty cents.

Article 2, Section 1. Every member on being admitted, shall sign the constitution and by-laws, and pay the initiation fee.

Section 2. A brother of the Klan wishing to become a member of this order shall present his application, with the proper papers of transfer, from the Order of which he was a member formerly, and shall be admitted to the Order only by a unanimous vote of the members present.

Article 3, Section 1. The initiation fee shall be _____.

Article 4, Section 1. Every member who shall refuse or neglect to pay his fines or dues shall be dealt with as the Chief thinks proper.

Section 2. Any member refusing to serve, or neglecting his duties, when appointed on a committee, shall be dealt with as the Chief thinks proper.

Section 3. Sickness, or absence from the country, or being engaged in any important business, shall be a valid excuse for any neglect of duty.

Article 5, Section 1. Each member shall provide himself with a pistol, the Ku Klux gown and signal instrument.

Section 2. When charges have been preferred against a member in proper manner, or any matters of grievance between brother Ku Klux are brought before the Order, they shall be referred to a special committee of three or more members, who shall examine the parties, and determine the matters in question, reporting their decision to the Order. If the parties interested desire, two-thirds of the members present voting in favor of the report, it shall be carried.

Article 6. Section 1. It is the duty of every member who has evidence that another has violated Article 2, to prefer the charges and specify the offense to the Order.

Section 2. The charge for violating Article 2 shall be referred to a committee of five or more members, who shall as soon as practicable summon the parties, and investigate the matters.

Section 3. If the committee agree that the charges are sustained — that the member on trial has intentionally violated his oath (Article 2) they shall report the fact to the Order.

Section 4. If the committee agree that the charges are not sustained — that the member is not guilty of violating his oath, (Article 2) they shall report to that effect to the Order, and the charges shall be dismissed.

Section 5. When the committee reports that the charges are sustained, and the unanimous vote of the members is given thereof, the offending person shall be sentenced to death by the Chief.

Section 6. The person, through the Cyclops of the Order of which he is a member, can make appointment for pardon to the Great Grand Cyclops of Nashville, Tennessee, in which case execution of the sentence can be stayed until the pardoning power is heard from.

Article 7. Section 1. Any member who shall betray or divulge any of the matters of the Order shall suffer death.

Article 8. Section 1. The following shall be the Rules of Order, to any matter herein not provided for, which shall be managed in strict accordance with Ku Klux rules.

Section 2. When the Chief takes his position on the right of the Scribe, with the members forming a half circle around them, at the sound of the signal instrument, there shall be profound silence.

Section 3. Before proceeding to business, the S[cribe] shall call the roll and note the absentees.

Section 4. Business shall be taken up in the following order:

1. Reading the Minutes.
2. Excuse of members at preceding meeting.
3. Report of committee on candidates for membership.
4. Collection of dues.
5. Are any of the Order sick or suffering?
6. Report of Committees.
7. New Business.

Appendix 2

Captain James Williams

One of the more infamous crimes committed by the Ku Klux Klan was the murder of militia Captain James Williams.[1] The captain became extremely unpopular among whites when it was rumored he planned to form a Ku Klux to war against them, intending to "kill from the cradle to the grave."[2] Specifics of Williams' death are revealed through the journal of M. S. Carroll, one of those convicted of the murder.

> Jim Williams was a slave and belonged to the late Samuel Rainey[3] who lived just below Brattonsville on the York to Chester road, 20 miles from Yorkville. Sometime during the Civil War he ran away and went over to the Yankee army where he remained until the close of the war, when he returned to his old home and changed his name from Rainey to Williams.
> Sometime thereafter he was commissioned as Captain and organized a company of militia[,] and the Carpet Bagger Scott, then acting governor, supplied the company with improved army rifles and ammunition. He and his company became a nuisance to the surrounding country.
> But what brought about his downfall was a speech he made in Yorkville on a certain day. I do not remember the date. Anyway it was a public day, sales day perhaps, and there was a large crowd in town. Late in the afternoon he mounted his mule and rode down to Rose's Hotel, which was headquarters for the radical party, and delivered his speech in which he boasted that if ever the KKK came into his country very few, if any, of them would return to their homes.
> In less than two hours thereafter, plans were perfected to raid his place that night and were carried out as follows. The York Klan under leadership of Dr. J. R. Bratton, the Rattlesnake Klan, Will Johnson, Chief and the Broad River Klan, [and] Chambers (Pete) Brown were to meet and did meet at a place five miles west of Yorkville, on Howell's Ferry Road, known as Briar

Patch Muster ground near where R. B. Hartness now resides. It was agreed that Dr. Bratton take charge of the raid.

From there we went across country to McConnellsville and then across to near the Rainey Place. Dr. Bratton and myself were the only ones who knew just where Jim Williams lived. We followed a blind sort of road leading in back of where he lived. When we got in 3 or 4 hundred yards of his house, we halted and here we selected ten or twelve men to go to the house and left the rest of the men with the horses. We proceeded on foot to the house and knocked on the door. The door was opened by Rose, Jim's wife, and we went in. The only occupants of the house were Jim's wife and one negro man. When asked were Jim was, his wife said she did not know. He had gone off somewhere, she said. We made a thorough search of the house but did not find him. After a moment's reflection Dr. Bratton told someone to pull up some of the plank flooring. "He might be under there," he said. And sure enough, there was Jim crouched down under the floor. We hauled him out and placed a rope around his neck and started back toward our horses. We had got back about half way to the horses when someone spied a large tree with a limb running out 10 or 12 feet from the ground and suggested that that was the place to finish the job. And we left Captain Williams dangling from that limb.

We then began a search for the guns of the company. We succeeded in getting 23 of the guns but never found a member of the company. They all had business away from home that night. I remember going to the house of Henry Haynes, whom I knew was a member, and when I knocked on the door his wife opened the door and thrust the rifle out and said, "Here take it for Gawd's sake."

Sometime between midnight and morning we reassembled in the road opposite to the gin house of John S. Bratton and some kind and thoughtful, well-wisher served us with a bountiful lunch and then for home.[4]

At the end of Carroll's account of the incident, a notation apparently added by some member of the family at a later date gives a few more details concerning the hanging:

In conversations with M. S. Carroll's grandchildren, he told some of the details of the Jim Williams raid — the conversations, the terror of Rose and the negro man, how Jim pleaded and prayed, how the Klansmen appeared in uniforms, how Bob (R. L.) Caldwell climbed up and pushed Jim from the limb when he refused to leap from the limb. (He, Jim, climbed up himself.) He said that Jim grasped the limb and held on until B. Caldwell hacked his fingers with a knife forcing him to drop. He died cursing, pleading and praying all in one breath.

Prior to his death in 1919, ex–Klansman John D. McConnell of McConnellsville recalled the night that Jim Williams was hanged:

The Klan determined to hang Capt. Jim and orderly Sergt. "Yaller Joe McConnell" in [the] spring of '73. So one night our house was suddenly surrounded by a company of Ku Klux in their disguises. I was called to the door. This scared Sally terribly as she thought they might take me out and whip me because I had pulled out at the re-organization. I did not fear that, but was afraid some drunk would shoot me accidentally. As I found out later the raid on our home was a mistake. They always had a Klan from a distance to do "discipline" and they mistook our place for Uncle Jno. B. McConnells where Sergt Yaller Joe lived.

Our kitchen was a double log house, the cook living in the west end. Bert Latta was her husband. The two KKs on each side of me with drawn pistols told me to call out my Negro. I protested that Bert was a harmless Negro. He was in the room and called out, "I will come out Mass Johnnie if you will protect me." I told him, "They won't promise me anything and I can't promise you anything." Bert's wife, Mary, was slow fumbling at the bar across the door. They had a man stationed at each corner of the house, but no doubt they were watching the commotion at that door so Bert raised a loose plank and on his all fours escaped. The K.K.K. took his gun and uniform and went on about three miles to Jim Williams and hanged him, thereby causing a great deal of trouble....

Appendix 3

James Rufus Bratton, M.D.

Various accounts, as well as family tradition, say that James Rufus Bratton of Yorkville was a leader in the Ku Klux Klan and fled to Canada to escape arrest by federal officials. Though holding a leadership role in the clandestine organization, he superficially gave the impression of abhorring violence and frowning on the activities of the Klan.[1]

Bratton was born 12 November 1821 at his ancestral home in Brattonsville, York County, South Carolina, at the site where his grandfather, Colonel William Bratton, defeated Captain Huck of the British army during the Revolutionary War. Bratton attended Mt. Zion Academy in Winnsboro and graduated from the College of South Carolina in 1843. After completing his medical training in 1845, he took a full course in the hospital of the University of Pennsylvania.

Returning to Yorkville, he set up his practice in partnership with William Moore, but after about a year he determined it would be financially more beneficial to practice alone. Doctor Bratton, in his short memoirs, intimates that his older partner was not as well trained as he and was not working to enhance the partnership. Bratton next established a practice in Yorkville in 1847 that grew beyond his own expectations, and he soon took on a young, well-trained partner.

In 1850 Bratton married Rebecca Massey of Lancaster County, and they subsequently had five sons and two daughters. When the Civil War broke out, he volunteered his service as assistant surgeon on 13 April 1861 to Colonel Jenkins of the Fifth Regiment, South Carolina Infantry Volunteers. Bratton was in charge of the Fourth Division of the Winder

Hospital in Richmond, Virginia, where he served for three years and was promoted to the rank of surgeon. Failing in health, he requested lighter duty and was ordered to the 20th Regiment of Virginia surgeons under General Bragg at Milledgeville, Georgia. In the wake of Sherman's march, the hospitals were dismantled and Bratton went home on furlough. Doctor Bratton was in Yorkville on 28 and 29 April 1865 when President Davis and his cabinet arrived on their flight South; the president and two of his aides were invited by Bratton to spend the night at his home.

Following the close of the war and emancipation, labor became an acute problem. In order to meet obligations for the coming year (1866), Bratton found himself working daily in his fields with the few freedmen who remained on his plantation. That year's cotton crop yielded no more than four bales, and he killed the last of his hogs on the day before Christmas. At that time, he told the Negroes to "go their way with their freedom either in peace or misery." A few apparently remained and worked for wages, but these left the plantation in June, to be followed by "Lancaster, Allston, Fred and his wife" in August, and "Bill left me in Sept." In October, a fire destroyed Bratton's gin and 100 bales of cotton at a loss of $12,000.[2]

Although spending much of his time at his plantation, Bratton attempted in January 1866 to resume his medical practice in Yorkville. "The crops made by the negroes on the farm for 1866 & 1867 were not sufficient to pay fully for the meat bread and etc. advanced to them...." Early in 1868, he sent "the man Bob & his family" away from his farm "on account of his radical politics — and worked the farm with white & black hired labor." "Crops [for 1868 and 1869] were rather deficient both in cotton & corn. The price of both was high & yet the negro laborers were not able to pay for the advances made to enable them to make a crop." After a few years of freedom, Hannah and Heyward came back to the Bratton farm in 1869 and there remained.

As a result of his involvement in the Ku Klux Klan[3] and a pending warrant for his arrest, Doctor Bratton fled York County in 1871 for the home of his sister, Mrs. Sophia O'Bannon, in Barnwell, South Carolina. Some family members say he went from Barnwell to Selma, Alabama, where he remained with some friends from South Carolina for one year. There he lived under the name of "Simpson." Thinking himself out of reach of the federal agents seeking him, Bratton became interested in coal mines. As he was preparing to buy a vast tract,[4] he discovered that federal agents had located him. He fled to Memphis where he met his fugitive brother John, who ironically was also living under the name of "Simpson."

Around 22 May 1872, Doctor Bratton under the assumed name of

"John Simpson" arrived at the home of expatriate G. Manigault in London, Ontario, Canada. Bratton asked his friend to seek lodging for him, and quarters were found at the Revere House on Wellington Street.[5] A large number of southern men, including a few of the Mazycks and Manigaults of Charleston and James W. Avery of Yorkville, reportedly had sought sanctuary in that city.[6] Close behind Bratton was Isaac Bell Cornwell, a hireling of Governor Scott's. Arriving at the Canadian border and knowing that the warrant from Scott had no authority, Cornwell applied to the United States Secret Service Department for assistance. He received a warrant ordered by President Grant, and a man named Joseph G. Hester was placed at Cornwell's disposal. They then proceeded to Canada seeking their fugitive. A London, Canada, newspaper reported "they dogged him [Bratton] around the city for some days before they got an opportunity of carrying out their nefarious project."[7]

On Tuesday, June 4, at about 4 P.M., Doctor Bratton was on a walk along Waterloo Street in the northern part of London when he noticed three men in the distance; two were standing in the road and another was seated in the cab. As the two men on the road approached him, Bratton recognized one as Cornwell. Cornwell lunged at Bratton seizing him "in a rude and violent manner by the arm and shoulder telling him he arrested him under a warrant." Bratton demanded the warrant be read, but Cornwell said he would take care of that at a later time. A struggle ensued and Bratton was wrestled to the ground. Trying to place handcuffs on Bratton, Cornwell called out to the cab driver for his assistance. The doctor also tried to get the cabbie to come to his rescue, yelling that his captor did not know who he was arresting. Bratton's call went unheeded and the driver helped Cornwell. A little girl who witnessed the capture gave sufficient evidence to suggest that chloroform was used to subdue Bratton.[8]

On Bratton's way to the train depot, after not being allowed to go by his boarding house for clothing, he again demanded the warrant be read. Cornwell acquiesced but the warrant did not contain Bratton's name. Charles Hutchison, a clerk and employee of Cornwell, later testified that Cornwell's warrant was not for Bratton, but for James William Avery.[9] Both Bratton and Avery were on the most-wanted list of the federal government for the murder of Jim Williams because one had ordered the raid and the other had commanded the ride. At 5:30 in the afternoon when Bratton and his captors boarded the train to Detroit, an inn-keeper remarked to a companion about Bratton's "stupid, vacant look," likely the result of chloroform sedation.

Upon their arrival in Detroit, Bratton was placed into the hands of Joseph Hester[10] who formally arrested him under a warrant signed by

President Grant. Bratton protested, "I am under Canadian law ... and I, under protest, refuse to obey you; neither your government, or you, sir, have a right to detain me here, and if you do, you will pay for it."[11] When Hester showed Bratton the warrant, his name was not on it. He was taken to a local police station at Leavittsburg, Ohio, where he was jailed for about two hours before being allowed to send a telegram to his friends informing them of his abduction and illegal transport to Detroit under the influence of chloroform.[12] Bratton, Hester and Cornwell took a room in a hotel and prepared to spend the night, but Cornwell departed before morning. He left Bratton in custody of Hester and ordered him to deliver the doctor to authorities in Yorkville.[13]

One written account of Doctor Bratton mentions that he escaped while passing through Virginia and temporarily hid out in the nearby woods. The next morning Bratton accidentally met Hester at the train depot; after a short, pleasant exchange, Bratton submitted quietly to him and they continued on their way.[14]

Bratton and his captor arrived in Yorkville on the Monday, June 10.[15] On the orders of Judge Bryan, Bratton was released by Wednesday on a $12,000 bond.[16] He evidently returned to Canada immediately upon his release, as Bratton was in London, Ontario, by July 16 when he appeared as a witness at the trial of Cornwell, accused of kidnapping a Canadian resident.

Some stories relate that an international incident occurred when Hester and Cornwell crossed the Canadian border and apprehended Bratton. This seems highly unlikely, though since the warrant used in his arrest was signed by President Grant and specifically mentioned "...respecting the Treaty between Her Majesty and the United States of America...."[17] According to one newspaper report, Cornwell failed to have the proper papers issued by a Canadian commissioner under the extradition treaty. In fact, the only papers he had obtained were for Avery and not for Bratton. The Canadian government, having been notified of the abduction, laid a memorial before the Commonwealth praying for their action in this unlawful violation of sovereignty. The British Minister demanded Bratton's return to Canada, stating that "under the Extradition Treaty regular legal proceedings could then be instituted against him."[18] Apparently, no effort was made to rearrest Bratton after he arrived back in Canada.

Remaining in Canada, Bratton set up his medical practice in the city of London,[19] and acquired the reputation of a good and compassionate physician, well loved by local Canadians. His wife and several of their children left Yorkville in July 1872 to join him. The Brattons remained in London until a blanket amnesty was offered to the members of the Klan in 1876.

Doctor Bratton's Klan activities were purportedly the subject of Thomas Dixon, Jr.'s novel *The Clansman*, which served as the basis for the movie, *The Birth of a Nation*.[20] The author was reared in North Carolina. Dixon had relatives in York, whom he frequently visited, and probably heard family stories about the Klan.

Appendix 4

John Hannibal White[1]

[From a sketch originally appearing in the Columbia, SC, *Union Herald*]

During the war, in the town of Yorkville, in this State, the colored people were in the habit of meeting together at night[2] to hear and discuss the tiding that came from that conflict, in which they had so wondrous an interest. As the tide surged, and as victory in grim dalliance flitted in changeful course amid the smoke and roar, the hearts of these watchers of the drama, keeping vigils in the nights, alternately beat with the quick pulsation of hope, or slackened to the slow and anxious throb of doubt. At these gatherings, John Hannibal White, one of the watching group, being able to read, was in the habit of gleaning from the papers all the news of the war, and used to impart the intelligence to his comrades. This circumstance invested him with the attributes of a leader and counselor among them. This leadership he maintained, being ever on the alert to know all that interested his people, and occupying as it were a superiority of advantage, was able to foretell and to counsel as to their best course.

It is not surprising then, that when the military order was promulgating, bidding the people of the various counties to meet and choose delegates to a convention to re-establish the overthrown structure of government, that John Hannibal White should be selected by the new voters of York, to be their delegate to the constitutional convention. Nor is it strange that his consistent course as their representative, should have induced that people to continue to select him for two terms in the House, and now in the Senate of the State.

Senator White was born in Yorkville, December 26, 1828. He grew up in his native town, and was one of the fortunate ones of his race who had some advantages of acquiring the first principles of education, at the hands of those who held a title of property in his person. He first learned to read and write under the instruction of his young mistress, and afterwards continued his course of study by his own efforts at night.

At the age of nineteen, he went to the trade of blacksmith, at which he continued up to, and during and after the war, until the year 1868, when he was elected a delegate to the constitutional convention. He applied himself diligently to his trade, and excelled in its work. From his apprenticeship, up to the date of his emancipation, he earned upwards of four thousand dollars, a little fortune, which went to enrich his owner.

In 1868, at the first organization of his people into a political party, he became their chief in all their councils and deliberations. At the first general election, when the constitution was submitted to the people for ratification, and the first officers were elected under its provisions, White was chosen by his people as their representative in the House of Representatives, in the first General Assembly of the reconstructed State. During his first term he felt that it became him better to overcome than to exhibit his want of a proper acquaintance with the new duties of his position as a legislator. He, therefore, declined taking any active part in debate, but devoted all his time and energy to a close study of the interests of his people, of the principles of government, and of the routine of legislation. He was a member of [a] committee on contingent accounts and other committees, and was prompt and careful in the discharge of his business.

At the second general election in 1870, Mr. White was reelected to the House. He had now made wonderful progress in understanding his duties, and was, if not the most erudite or eloquent member on the floor, still a competent and trusty steward of the interests of the people who reposed in him their fullest confidence.

It was during this, his second term, that the question arose as to the governor's duty to call out the militia of the State, to protect the victims of lawless violence that reigned in the up-country. Mr. White took the ground that this measure was impolitic and unwise. His maintenance of his position was most manly, vigorous and distinguished. His speech on the subject in the House, attracted a great deal of attention in that body and over the State. His argument was published at the time in the papers, and remains upon the record, as at once an instance of brave words, earnestly uttered in the maintenance of a good cause, and full vindication of the ability of Mr. White, as a representative of his race, to foresee and to point out the course of wisdom and right. Representative White, by his effort, prominently came out before the attention of the Legislature, and advanced another degree in the golden opinions entertained for him by his people at home. He was the author of the bill to pension the widows and orphans of persons killed because of their political opinions, which became a law. During this term he was on the same committees, and by his devotion and constant attention to his legislative duties, took a prominent position in the deliberations of his house.

At the third general election since reconstruction in 1872, he was elected to the Senate, victoriously triumphing over two strong opponents. In the Senate he is a member of several important committees and is faithful in the performance of his functions.

Senator White's record evinces an invincible determination to acquire education, an absorbing interest in the elevation of his race to a full appreciation and use of their freedom, and its concomitant blessings in the pursuit of comfort, peace and happiness, and in the attainment of wealth and honor. Of his devotion to this good cause, it may be justly written, "he knows their rights, and knowing dares maintain them."

White received an appointment in Washington, DC, in June 1877. He died in the Freedmen's Hospital in Washington 26 July 1878, and was buried in the Young Men's Burial Grounds in Washington.[3]

Appendix 5

Elijah Ross Sepaugh

Elijah Ross Sepaugh (also spelled "Sapoch") was brought before Judge Miles Johnson in the last week of April 1870 on an affidavit of William Wright, a black man, and charged with whipping Wright during a Ku Klux Klan raid.[1]

According to Wright, the assault took place in January of 1870 when the first reported violent raid perpetrated by the Ku Klux Klan in York County occurred. The *Yorkville Enquirer* says that Wright was living in a tenant house with a white woman on the farm of Henry J. Hullender. This relationship caused indignation among local farmers. When Wright's house was burned, he was said to have escaped capture by the Klan.[2]

Wright told the grand jury, however, that he was captured and that Sepaugh, assisted by 12 other men, whipped him. Several witnesses testified that on the day of the alleged incident, Sepaugh had driven his wagon to Rock Hill and did not return home until evening. He then nursed a sick daughter for the remainder of the night. The case was argued before a jury of five white men and one black man, and a not-guilty verdict was rendered. Turning the tables on Wright, Sepaugh filed a warrant for his arrest on a charge of perjury.[3]

The case received the attention of newspapers across South Carolina because it offered information about one of the first raids of the Ku Klux Klan.[4] The case was also of particular interest since it was this "outrage" (along with the burning of Hullender's house) that prompted Governor Scott to form a peacekeeping militia.[5] At the time of Sepaugh's trial, the Yorkville correspondent of the Charleston *Republican* hailed it as a "successful attempt of the State constables to arrest a York Ku Klux."[6]

Two years later, Sepaugh was arrested on 8 January 1872 on a six-count indictment charging him with the murder of Thomas Roundtree. Two counts were for murder committed while denying him his political rights, one by shooting and the other by cutting Roundtree's throat. One count charged conspiracy for interfering with Roundtree's Second Amendment right to keep and bear arms.[7]

The murder of Thomas Roundtree was a particularly heinous affair. Approximately 80 night riders raided his home expecting to find guns that were reportedly stored on the property. When they broke into the house, Roundtree shot into the crowd from a loft, injuring Sepaugh. Roundtree then dropped from the loft to the outside, attempting to escape. Someone yelled that Sepaugh had been shot. For daring to defend himself, Roundtree received the full force of Klan fury. A witness related that he had counted some 35 bullet holes in the freedman. In the event that that was not enough to kill him, Henry Sepaugh, brother of the accused, had drawn his knife and slit Roundtree's throat from ear to ear.[8]

Sepaugh was brought before Judge Hugh L. Bond of the United States Circuit Court in Charleston in April 1872. His case, as well as three other cases tried during this session, was designed to test the constitutionality of the seventh section of the Enforcement Act of 1870. The part in question allowed the federal court to consider ordinary crimes committed in conjunction with the denial of civil rights. After the jury of six whites and six blacks were seated, Bond allowed Defense Attorney John F. Ficken "to enter a plea that the circuit court lacked the jurisdiction because murder is a common law offense." During the trial Ficken argued that Sepaugh had been only one in a crowd and there was no evidence that he committed the murder. He also stated that there was no evidence to prove that murder was the result of conspiracy.[9]

As Prosecutor David T. Corbin had argued in previous cases, the law "says that when men commit murder they shall die, and we have no right to complain of it."[10] The defense argued, however, that it had stated throughout the Klan trials that if the state penalties were exercised in cases involving common law, a man might be sentenced to die for violations of political and civil rights.[11]

Evidently swayed by Prosecutor Corbin, who argued that Sepaugh must bear the full responsibility of Roundtree's death, the jury convicted Sepaugh of murder although he had not taken part in the actual killing.[12] The case was certified to the Supreme Court because the Circuit Court was divided on its extent of jurisdiction and uncertain about what punishment it might issue.

Sepaugh was still being held in the Yorkville jail in the spring of 1874, pending his case being heard by the Supreme Court.[13] Even though Reverdy Johnson had been prepared to argue Sepaugh's case before the high court on two separate occasions, a hearing was not granted, and the question of constitutionality was thereby not addressed. Before the end of the year, Attorney General George H. Williams directed Corbin to enter a nolle prosequi on five counts and pass sentence on the remaining charges of intimidation and violation of the Enforcement Act.[14] Entering a nolle prosequi removed Sepaugh's case from the Supreme Court docket and thereby prevented any ruling on the case. Williams believed this was "not for the sake of Sepaugh, but for the sake of the public good."[15] With the murder count dropped, Sepaugh, after being ordered before the Federal Court in Columbia on 11 December 1874, was sentenced to pay $100 and to serve one year in the Albany Penitentiary.[16] On 20 January 1875, Sepaugh was taken to Charleston and about a month later transferred to the New York prison.[17] After serving part of his sentence, he was pardoned, and returned to his home in York County on 14 October 1875. At the time of Sepaugh's release, only three men remained in the Albany Penitentiary: Robert Moore, John Wallace and Pinckney Caldwell.[18]

Appendix 6

York County Men Imprisoned at the Albany Penitentiary[1]

Name	Post Office	Age	Occupation	Sentence	
S. G. Brown	Yorkville	61	Farmer	5 Years	$1000
M. S. Carroll	Yorkville	25	Farmer	18 Mos.	$100
____Stewart	Yorkville	22	Farmer	18 Mos.	$100
Josiah Martin	Yorkville	23	Laborer	18 Mos.	$100
Joseph C. Robinson	Yorkville	25	Laborer	18 Mos.	$100
William Smith	Yorkville		Laborer	10 Mos.	$1000
Pinckney Caldwell	Yorkville	27	Laborer	10 Mos.	$1000
Leander Spencer	Clarks Fork	28	Laborer	10 Mos.	$1000
George S. Wright	Clarks Fork	23	Laborer	10 Mos.	$1000
Robert Riggins	Blairsville	27	Laborer	3 Yrs.	
T. B. Whitesides	Hickory Grove	34	Physician	18 Mos.	$1000
C. W. Whitesides	Hickory Grove	28	Farmer		
Cpt. J. W. Mitchell	Hickory Grove	45		5 Yrs.	$1000
Hezekiah Porter		21	Laborer	18 Mos.	$100
John Montgomery		20	Laborer	18 Mos.	$100
S. Childers		30	Laborer	18 Mos.	$100
Julius Howe		30	Farmer	4 Yrs.	
John Whisonant		24	Farmer		
Jerome Whisonant		22		3 Yrs.	
Robert Moore	Harmony		Laborer		
Walker Moore	Harmony	32	Laborer	3 Yrs.	
Joseph Leekie	Harmony		Laborer	8 Yrs.	$1000
W. B. Sherer	Blairsville	32	Laborer		
J. M. Sherer	Blairsville	28	Laborer	18 Mos.	
H. H. Sherer	Blairsville	26	Laborer	18 Mos.	

Appendix 6

Name	Post Office	Age	Occupation	Sentence	
S. H. Sherer	Blairsville	23	Laborer	18 Mos.	
H. C. Warlick	Blairsville	22	Laborer	18 Mos.	
E. J. Murphy		38	Laborer	18 Mos.	
R. H. Mitchell		42	Laborer	18 Mos.	
E. A. Hays		40	Laborer	18 Mos.	
Walker Dawson	Antioch	23	Farmer	18 Mos.	
Galbreath Hambright	Antioch	42	Laborer	8 Yrs.	$1000
Elijah Hardin	Antioch	42	Laborer	18 Mos.	$100
W. M. Fulton	Antioch		Laborer	4 Yrs.	$100
Felix Dover	Antioch		Laborer		
James A. Donald	Hopewell		Laborer		
W. L. Hood	Bullocks Cr.	29	Clerk		
Miles McCulloch	Hopewell	25	Laborer	8 Yrs.	$1000
H. M. Moore	Blacks Sta.			1 Yr.	
John C. Robinson[2]					

Appendix 7

Prison Life at the Albany Penitentiary

Randolph Shotwell[1] arrived at the Albany Penitentiary on 7 October 1871 amidst rain and dense fog. A great iron door opened in the prison's massive walls, and Shotwell and other men accused of Ku Kluxing walked in. The door "swung shut with a sullen *slam!* that seemed to echo the words—'Gone! Done!'"[2] Upon entry, new prisoners were marched into a large room where they were ordered to stand close to the wall with heads bowed, arms folded and eyes fixed on the floor. One by one the men were called and marched to a desk, where a deputy enrolled them in the prison register.

Once registration was completed, the prisoners were immediately taken to the barber who "was a spiteful, malicious rascal ... [who] made himself truly barbarous to many."[3] Here they were deprived of hair and whiskers. Once a week they returned to experience the craft of the barber — often with excruciating pain. Shotwell wrote:

> He had been a tenth-rate "hacker" in some half-dime barbershop, and being quite as reckless with his razor outside of his shop as within it, came hither on a long-term sentence, and was assigned to repeat his barbarous operation upon the helpless prisoners. It was no light job to shave 600 stubbly faces, and he slashed his way through them with no light hand, or apparent care whether he chopped the nose, eyebrows, and an inch of the chin of his victims, or only a small portion of their ears.... When he appeared in the shop, the overseer thereof sounded his hand-gong, and two of the convicts stepped up to the overseer's desk, by the side of which they ranged

> themselves, and each taking one of the big paint brushes hastened to swab his face all over with white lather from the soft soap stuff in the basins. As soon as one of these was seated in the barber's chair, to be shaved, the overseer tapped his bell for another man to come forward and daub his face.... Here was another ordeal for me, to use the brush and lather just laid down by a filthy negro, or equally revolting white vagabond and after enduring this to undergo the whacking of the mulatto's razors, which if even sharpened at the start were dull as a wedge long before my turn came!... The blood was oozing from various portions of my face for half an hour after the operation.[4]

When fully deprived of hair and whiskers, the newcomers were marched to the bathtub where they were stripped naked. Since some were allowed to skip the dip into cold river water that was piped into a tub, it would appear the bath was more of an excuse for a strip search. The guards were apparently looking for letters and weapons, or money sewed into clothing that might be used to bribe officials.

At induction, an individual's clothing was bundled and tagged and placed in the "clothes vault" until they were freed or pardoned or died. A prison issue of clothing consisted of a shirt that resembled a sack with short sleeves sewed at the sides. It was made of a coarse canvas material having neither "bosom, collar nor cuffs." The short jacket and pants were of linsey-woolsey, gray in color, and several sizes too small. The uniform cap was a pull-on type, knitted and light blue in color. The caps had originally been made for the United States Navy, but subsequently rejected.[5]

Cells were whitewashed rooms measuring three feet wide and 6½ feet long. Doors were a frame of parallel bars a little more than one inch apart. The tiny rooms were equipped with a red, wooden slop-bucket that had a heavy wooden top that might serve as a seat. Every morning as the inmates were led to their work areas, they carried these buckets to a point where they were left to be emptied; prisoners retrieved them on returning to their cells. Iron beds, which hung from the walls by hinges, could be turned against the wall when not in use. Linen consisted of no more than a straw mattress, a straw pillow and three blankets that often went unwashed as the occupants changed. Each cell had a cup for drinking water, a Bible and a small box for salt. Pictures or ornaments of any kind were not allowed.[6]

Personal hygiene was not a major concern at the Albany prison. Convicts were allowed to wash their faces and hands only once a week, but they might rinse them with their drinking water if they were so minded. On Sunday morning prisoners were led to the "wash tank" and given about 16 seconds to "bathe." A common towel of some rough material was shared among 20 filthy prisoners.[7]

Meals were served in greasy, tin pans capable of holding about a half-gallon. The meal might consist of a slice of bread, a piece of dark, gristly meat and several small potatoes. The plate was placed on the pavement outside the cell door. On command, the prisoner was to put their left hand on the bars on the door. When the turnkey unlocked the door, the prisoner swung it open, quickly drew the plate into the cell, and then continued to hold the door until it was locked again.[8] Hugh Hicklin Sherer of the Blairsville community remarked, "the fare was very poor — sour Irish potatoes for dinner and mush and molasses for supper."[9] Sunday breakfast might consist of a mixture of chopped corned beef and bread crusts, a slice of bread, and a cup of weak coffee that might contain a bit of burnt bread, a grain of parched wheat, or occasionally a stray coffee bean.[10] For dinner there was a pan of rice broth, a piece of mutton and a slice of bread. At 5 P.M., a single slice of bread was delivered as supper.[11] For the 1,000 inmates, a Saturday dinner might require 500 pounds of fish, a barrel or two of potatoes and 200 loaves of bread. About 100 gallons of coffee were consumed daily.[12] Thanksgiving Day seemed to be the only holiday observed in the Albany Penitentiary and this was considered a feast. The annual dinner in 1872 consisted of roast beef, ham, cabbage, potatoes, onions, cheese, crackers and apples.[13]

The ringing of a gong preceded all movements of the inmates. When being moved from their cells to another location, prisoners had to line up and march in step with the right hand placed on the shoulder of the man in front. When not at work, arms had to be folded. Men could not speak unless given permission to do so.

The majority of the prisoners were assigned work in the shoe shop that was owned by the Eastern New York Shoe Company located near the penitentiary. This company began in 1861 with capital of $10,000. When those convicted of "Ku Kluxing" were at Albany in 1871, the company was backed by $300,000 in capital.[14] The 1870 census reveals that the shoemaking business was the fourth largest United States industry, producing a product valued at nearly $19,000,000 yearly; this industry was surpassed only by flour milling, iron production and lumber.[15] A quota of 60 pairs of shoes per day was set for each prisoner who had been sentenced to "hard labor." This quota produced 3,000 pairs daily (done by 50 workers), 18,000 a week, and nearly 75,000 a month.[16] The process required 37 operations by one prisoner for every stage.[17] Hugh Sherer and three of his brothers imprisoned at the Albany Penitentiary worked in the shoe shop. Hugh's task "was to cut out heels."[18]

General Amos T. Pilsbury was the superintendent at the time the Ku Kluxers were imprisoned, and he had held the position for approximately 40 years.[19] He believed prisons should be more than just barracks; they should be reformatories where men underwent punishments to teach them that their sufferings were the results of their crimes—yet prison should strive to preserve the inmate's self-respect and manhood. Though he instructed the overseers, guards and watchmen to be stern and firm, his subordinates were often cruel and overbearing and did not always carry out his directives.[20] As part of his approach to rehabilitation, Pilsbury established night classes for the prisoners[21] and sometimes allowed the men to have books in their cells.[22] Out of the five federal penitentiaries, only the Albany prison had a credit balance ($27,000). With this record and the confidence of the trustees, he and his wife sailed to Europe in 1872 to attend an international congress on prison reform.[23] After Pilsbury's death on 15 July 1873, his son, Captain Louis D. Pilsbury, who had been born in the superintendent's living quarters, replaced him.[24] Captain Pilsbury was a man of compassion and understanding. At one time Pilsbury said that he would rather see 50 burglars and murderers sent to prison than one educated and genteelly reared man, who would be crushed under an experience that others there would face no differently than a day's work.[25] He was known for being ever ready to assist any man seeking a pardon or hearing.[26]

Freedom from the Albany Penitentiary was followed by immediate hardships. Hugh Sherer remarked, "After they let us out of prison they drove us to the railway station in a sleigh drawn by four horses. They gave us each $10 to come home on, it was a long trip and tedious one, but we managed to get home at last."[27] Randolph Shotwell, who was released in September 1873, complained that $10 was hardly enough to pay the fare home, much less obtain food, and that $10 would pay railway fare no farther than to Baltimore. On unrolling his clothing that had been stored in the "clothes-vault," he discovered they were covered with white mold from having been put away wet, and filled with vermin. "The moths had helped the mildew, and my coat was literally in shreds, pantaloons like sieves, waistcoat, wasted! As for hat and shoes, they were an insult to any blind beggar! The thought of going out in the world in such attire made me feel almost sorry to be released—so silly is supersensitiveness!"[28]

Leaving the prison and grounds, Shotwell was met by a "large party of city urchins." They immediately recognized him as a convict by his ragged clothes, shorn head and carpetbags. They began to chant. "Here's yere con-wicks. Here's your Tenny-Pentiary fellers! Sa—a—y, fells wot you'ns put in fur? Look's like you went in 'bout time the ark went down Hudson! Bet you them fellers killed somebody!"[29] Shotwell was more fortunate than many. From Albany he telegraphed his brother in Princeton who picked him up, then took him to his home and then on to North Carolina. The other Klansmen released had to return south the best way they could—walking or hitchhiking, doing without food for days, and suffering exposure.

Appendix 8

Presidential Pardons

At the close of 1872, Governor Scott of South Carolina wrote to U.S. Attorney General George Williams regarding the number of appeals for those serving time in the Albany Penitentiary that had been requested by the grand jurors of York and Chester counties. Williams responded on 5 December 1872 from his Washington office, telling Scott that separate applications for pardons had to be made on the behalf of each man "stating substantially the circumstances of the crime and convictions." The governor was also informed that pardons would be considered "as the President's sense of justice will permit."[1]

A number of presidential pardons were extended in 1873 to York County men who had been convicted on Klan charges and who were imprisoned in Albany, New York. These were generally given to those who had been coerced into joining the organization. The first to receive release were D. S. Ramseur, Galbreath Hambright,[2] and George Sylvester Wright,[3] pardoned in January 1873.[4] Eli Ross Stewart, Robert Hayes Mitchell, and William Lowry were freed the following month[5] and arrived at their homes 27 February 1873. Shortly after February 3, someone in the county received a letter from A. S. Wallace saying "the four Sherer boys who were ... alleged[ly] connected with the 'Jim Williams Raid'" would soon be pardoned.[6] They arrived home February 17.[7]

The following month, Miles Carroll, Miles McCullough, and Henry Warlick were granted pardons.[8] Later, James C. Robinson, who had served six months, was released.[9] Sherrod Childers and William Montgomery soon followed.[10] Both Allison Hayes and Andrew J. Martin (being held at the York County jail) were pardoned in April.[11]

Appendix 8

Other parolees in 1873 were: Elijah Hardin, January; __?__ Stewart and E. A. Hayes, 17 February; John Montgomery, 31 March; Walker Dawson, 17 April; James A Donald, 15 August; Felix Dover, 22 August[12]; and Robert Riggins, 16 December 1873.[13]

For 1874: Julius Howe, 1 February[14]; Elijah Hardin, 5 March[15]; and John and Jerome Whitsonant, 17 December.[16]

Appendix 9

Samuel Gordon Brown[1]

Samuel Gordon Brown, charged with conspiracy, was arrested at his home on 19 October 1871[2] by a detachment of federal cavalry. Oral tradition relates that when the troops neared the Brown farm, two of Brown's sons[3] fled to parts unknown just ahead of the squad. Colonel Merrill had the elder Brown arrested in hopes of putting pressure on the sons to surrender in order to save their aged father from prison. Brown was taken to an adjoining plantation and confined in a barnyard while the troops arrested and brought back six other men accused of "Ku Kluxing." He subsequently was confined in the York County jail until December 15, when he was taken to Columbia, South Carolina, and released within the city limits under a $5,000 bond.

Reliable witnesses appearing before Judge Hugh L. Bond confirmed Brown's statement that he did not belong to the Klan; they said, however, that two of his sons were members. Brown had attended one Klan meeting for the sole purpose of using his influence to prevent the severe punishment of a young man who, while intoxicated, had divulged secrets of the order. About the same time, he had been successful in persuading his sons to forsake the Klan because of the laxity[4] that prevailed.

Prior to Brown's arrest, Judge Hugh L. Bond had made it understood that clemency would be granted to all who confessed to the charges. Colonel Merrill assured Brown before his trial that he would be back home in a few weeks if he made a confession, and his lawyer William Blackburn Wilson[5] advised him to plead guilty and throw himself on the clemency of the court. The lawyer argued that Merrill was determined to have a conviction, and he contended that a confession would enable Brown to apply for a pardon later. His advice proved to have ill effects for Brown.

Since the authorities very much wanted to arrest Brown's sons, he likely was classed as highly uncooperative after refusing to reveal their location. Brown was convicted by a jury of 11 black men and "one disreputable white man, a grog shop keeper,"[6] and sentenced to five years hard labor and a $1,000 fine.[7] According to legal historian Lou Falkner Williams, "Bond threw the book at Squire Samuel G. Brown." Brown had served as a magistrate until 1868, and Judge Bond was irate that a man of his position would take part in such an organization as the Klan. Bond considered Brown to have been "appointed to protect the innocent and helpless" and to serve in a position where the "young and ignorant had a right to look ... for direction and advice." Thus he deserved the full force of the law. The sentence Bond handed down was as harsh as that received by any convicted Klansman of York County during the November 1871 session.[8]

Brown's sentence was protested both in the South and the North. Numerous efforts to free the old man were made by various people; one of these was General Amos T. Pilsbury, superintendent of the Albany Penitentiary. Another was Mrs. Maria Jourdan Westmoreland of Atlanta, Georgia. Mrs. Westmoreland wrote on 14 February 1872 to Mrs. John T. Hoffman, the wife of Georgia's governor, pleading:

> ...I appeal to you in the name of humanity — yea, more, I come to beg you, as a Christian woman ... to befriend the friendless and to console the afflicted. There lies in the State Prison at Albany an old man by the name of Samuel G. Brown, who is sixty-five[9] years of age, almost blind and broken in health. He is from Yorkville, York District, South Carolina, and is a victim of Judge Bond, of Ku Klux notoriety, who was sent to Carolina by Grant, for the purpose, it would seem, of prosecuting the innocent and protecting the infamous. This old man was dragged from his home, brought to Columbia, where Bond's Courts sit, and thrown into prison. He was then taken through the mockery of a trial, and notwithstanding [that] he filed an affidavit proving that so far from acting with the so called Ku Klux he had gone at midnight on a recent occasion to prevent the murder of a negro, [he] was sentenced to five years' hard labor in the State Prison of New York, and required to pay a fine of $1,000. As he had no money to satisfy this atrocious demand ... his plantation [is] to be levied upon and sold ... the poor man's family will be turned adrift upon the world homeless, fatherless and in poverty. Knowing your husband to be the champion of constitutional liberty, the embodiment of those qualities which make a true man truly great and noble, and believing that you must imbibe his sentiments, I hope I shall not appeal in vain.[10]

Mrs. Westmoreland received a reply from the governor's wife dated 25 February 1872, and written from Albany:

> The Governor and myself visited Mr. Brown this morning and had a long and interesting conversation with him. He stated the facts of his imprisonment with great exactness, and I am confident with truth.... The Governor is much interested in the case, and has written the President for a pardon.... [I am] hoping to receive news from the President that will gladden the hearts of wife and children, as well as those who have taken such an interest in the old man's troubles.... [11]

Brown suffered the indignities of an abusive deputy superintendent who seemed to have singled out the old man as a target for his meanness. A fellow prisoner, Randall Shotwell, from North Carolina wrote in his journal, "...I can't help feeling worried and humiliated when I see an old man like Brown insulted by a lowborn hound...."[12] Brown, often weak and despondent, was comforted by receiving numerous letters—as many as two to six a week; not all brought good news, however. Through a letter from a relative, he learned that Congressman A. S. Wallace was opposing his release. Wallace publicly stated that "Nothing less than two years will do him any good."[13]

Colonel Whitley, chief of the government's Detective Bureau, inspected the federal penitentiary at Albany on 7 August 1872 to verify the conditions of the Klan prisoners and to determine if there was any necessity to expedite executive clemency.[14] His real purpose was to interrogate the prisoners and tempt the inmates with pardons in exchange for information that might incriminate others who had not been charged.[15] Whitley privately interviewed more than 40 men. While the prisoners were given ample opportunity to speak privately with the detective, there is no evidence that any of them gave the name of any member who had escaped capture or any incriminating information that might lead to another conviction. Whitley thought he received the full cooperation of Superintendent Amos T. Pilsbury, but the prison director did not approve of Whitley's plan to extract information from the prisoners and warned some of the men of the intent.

Whitley's report to Attorney General Williams stated that most of the men (some poor and uneducated) were frank and communicative. A number of them acknowledged belonging to the Ku Klux Klan, but they claimed to have joined without full knowledge of the organization's aims. Some told of being compelled to join to save themselves and their families from nighttime visits of the order, and claimed while talking to Whitley that they supposed the Klan to exist for mutual protection. Only later did they learn that "its real designs were the extermination of the negro race and the driving out of such of the whites as were in favor of the political equality and social elevation of the blacks."[16] They further admitted the oath they had taken was not for mutual protection as they initially had been told; it instead bound them "to oppose the Radical party in all its forms, and committed them to prevent the negroes from voting."

The prisoners, many fully contrite over their membership, stated "the operations of the Ku Klux were widespread, embracing within its fold men of superior intelligence to whom they had been accustomed to look for advice and counsel, and who they did not suppose would lead them into any combinations that contemplated personal violence and even murder...." They all seemed to be of one mind in expressing regret at being drawn into the order, and agreeing "that the government was fully justified in breaking it up."

Whitley evidently believed that a number of those he interviewed exhibited "hearty penitence," and were "absolutely ashamed of this course which they seemed to have unwilling pursued." He also reported that they believed themselves "betrayed by unscrupulous and designing men of more enlightened minds [as well as] their [own] mutual want of intelligence, and their extreme poverty...." Nevertheless, it may have been that the prisoners made a concerted effort not to reveal the names of any other members of the Klan. Feeling honor bound, they probably lied about their knowledge of the purposes of the Klan as well as their involvement in it. While Whitley's reports recommended that 18 of the prisoners from South Carolina be considered for executive clemency, Samuel G. Brown was not among them.

On 8 August, a reporter from the *New York World* visited the penitentiary and interviewed several prisoners, including Samuel G. Brown.[17] The conversation with Brown was reported in the local newspaper:

"Tell me your case, how you came to be here, and what you have to complain of."

"*The greatest hardship of which I complain is being arrested for being a Ku Klux when I never belonged to the Order at all.*[18] *My family are left in a very destitute condition.*"

What family have you?"

"*I have a wife and three daughters* [at home] *and two sons. My wife and daughters have no one to look after them; and there is my stock and farm all left to ruin without attendance.*"

"When were you arrested?"

"*I was arrested on the 19th of October, 1871, and by the advice of my counsel I pleaded guilty, which was a very foolish thing to do, although a gentleman here yesterday — Colonel Whitley — told me that he did not believe me when I said I was innocent; yet such is the fact. It was on the 26th of*

December, 1871, that my counsel pleaded guilty for me, and I am sentenced to five years."

"Did you have no connection with the klan?"

"*I knew of the Order, and I attended one meeting of the klan, and that was the hold they had on me, and that was the reason I plead guilty.*"

"For what purpose did you attend that meeting; did you intend to join the klan?"

"*No, not at all. I had a double purpose in going there. I wanted to save the life of a young man who had in a drunken frolic let out some of the secrets of the Order, and also to induce my son to resign his position as chief of the klan.*"

"Did you succeed?"

"*I did in both objects. My son resigned, and I saved the young man's life.*"

"That was all the connection you had with the klan?"

"*That was all. I never belonged to it; never approved of it. I had two sons, both members of it, but I never was.*"

"Were your sons arrested?"

"*No; they got off, they left the State.*"

"Where are they now?"

"*I don't know where they are now. I think they have left the United States. Since I have been imprisoned my family have written to me that they had heard from them on the 12th of May last, but they did not say where they were.*"

In the latter part of April, 1872, Brown received a letter informing him that the administration had no intention of issuing any additional pardons for the present to those confined on Ku Klux charges. The president, through his cabinet, stated that the prisoners had been "convicted of direct complicity in the deeds of the Klan and while it is the intention of the President sooner or later to pardon all the prisoners convicted under the enforcement act, he does not deem it proper to extend to this class Executive clemency until they have realized by imprisonment that the government is determined to enforce law and order in every section of the land!"[19]

Brown's wife, Mary Margaret Byers Brown, wrote Reverend William Meek McElwee of Frankfort Springs, Pennsylvania:

> Perhaps you will not know me as Mrs. Brown. I was Margaret Byers, daughter of Edward Byers and subsequently married Samuel G. Brown. I feel certain that when you are informed of its contents you will pardon this intrusion upon your time & attention.
>
> Through the press and from other sources of information you have doubtless been informed of the Ku Klux troubles & difficulties in this

section of the Country, & the fact, that numbers of our good citizens have been incarcerated in the Penitentiary at Albany in the State of New York. Among the number of unfortunate, is my husband, who has now been imprisoned there nearly twelve months. He was arrested, & brought to trial as a Ku Klux last winter at Columbia & through the mistaken & bad advice of his Attorney, plead guilty & was sentenced to a term of imprisonment for five years, to pay a fine of one thousand dollars, and now my dear friend, I am not going to approve or condemn Ku Kluxism, the alleged necessity, or lawlessness of it, to attempt to justify, palliate, or censure the many bad deeds said to have been committed by its members, or that the proceedings, & or the trial of my husband were unfair or otherwise. These are now matters & things of the past, & if wrong, can only be rectified in that higher Court, before which Judge, Accuser, & prisoner, must one day appear. One fact I will state however, that my husband has publicly stated that he never was a member of the Ku Klux organization, & I am satisfied that if he ever attended its meetings, it was for the purpose of controlling & influencing its deliberations, so as to prevent violence, & in the interest of peace and good order. Our family at present consists of myself, & three unmarried daughters who reside with me, & I need not assure you that we desire & miss very much, at home, the advice, assistance, support & encouragement of him, to whom, in the course of nature, we should look to, for earthly help and protection. My husband's treatment in the prison, so far as we know, is mild, lenient & humane. We write to him once a week & hear from him once a month, & as far as we can, we contribute from our limited means such things as he desires or that can be conveniently sent to him. But to the point of this letter, I wish you to use your influence, if possible to effect his pardon by the President of the United States. Our neighbors are getting up a petition to send on for that purpose, & I hope, I know that you will contribute your influence towards the same object. Pardon the liberty I thus take in addressing this letter to you, & by attending to the above you will receive as you will merit, the thanks & prayers of myself & daughters. [20]

Reverend McElwee responded by sending an appeal to the president on 2 January 1873. In the meantime, Brown's neighbors and friends continued to work for his release. Andrew A. Kirkpatrick, a member of the Klan that operated in the Sharon area, sent an affidavit stating he had no knowledge of Brown ever being a member of the Klan. Kirkpatrick acknowledged Brown's attendance at one meeting held at the Sharon A.R.P. Church, but denied his being a member. A neighbor, John Caldwell, verified that Brown did not belong to a Klan and knew of no "outrage" Brown had done to anyone. John Ramsey, a tenant living on Brown's farm, sent a sworn statement explaining that while he had been a member of a local unit of the Klan, he had no knowledge of Brown being involved.[21]

Sometime during the summer of 1872, Brown sought aid in his appeal for pardon from the Honorable Gerrit Smith, one of the most infamous

Northern abolitionists and a man who generated much hatred toward the South. Later in the summer, Smith visited the Albany Penitentiary and interviewed both Brown and Shotwell. While Smith's recommendations to president Grant included leniency to be extended to Brown, he did not suggest the same for Shotwell who he found to be defiant, scorning pardon "and engaged in study of law."[22] Smith further recommended that the president postpone Brown's pardon until after the October elections to quell any speculation it was prompted by politics. Evidently the pardon was delayed longer than Smith's recommendation, for in February 1873, Brown wrote him once again:

> The kind interest which you were pleased to manifest in my case some six months ago, encourages me to venture a line to you soliciting your influence to obtain a renewal of the pardon which was then granted by the President (as I am informed) upon your recommendation but afterward rescinded for some reason to me.
>
> I think I informed you at that time how unhappily I was circumstanced with respect to my family (wife & four daughters) without a protection and without the means of making a subsistence so that I need add no more than that my advancing years (sixty-one next Friday), and infirmities agravated [sic] by sixteen months confinement cause me to feel the most extreme solicitude to be restored to liberty and my helpless ones before I shall lose all ability to aid them.
>
> A Petition praying for pardon has been forwarded to the Attorney General signed by my neighbors in York County, S.C., irrespective of Party or Color and our Representative in Congress, Hon. A. S. Wallace has signified to my family his intention to urge its passage but I learn Major Merrill the Commandant of that post did not sign my petition and as he seems to have some enmity against me I fear his influence may be thrown against it. At any rate it is likely the application will make very little progress unless brought to the particular attention of the President by some one in whom he has confidence.
>
> I therefore throw myself on your known generosity and benevolent spirit and venture to ask that you will make another effort for my release.
>
> Assuring you if pardon is granted I shall return to my home and will conduct myself in such manner that the authorities will have no trouble with me, while I shall ever feel under the greatest obligations to you for your kind exertions in my behalf.[23]

Smith forwarded Brown's letter to the president saying,

> I presume that the Atty General has looked into his case & reported upon it to you. You see from his letter that Brown is a man of good sense & fair education. I am aware that this does not entitle him to special favor. But if you would find it in your heart to pardon the poor old man, I should be glad.[24]

President Grant evidently ignored this request for clemency, rather leaving the process in the hands of the attorney general who was actively dealing with the cases of all men confined to the Albany Penitentiary for Klan activities.

As a concession to his age and health, Brown was allowed to sleep in the prison hospital, but he was not relieved from his workload in the shoe shop. On the morning of 26 February 1873, he was called to be fitted for new prison clothing. Brown, as well as the prison authorities, knew this meant he would not be released during the year. Prior to the fitting, an announcement appeared in the Washington *Chronicle:*

> The Attorney General declines to issue a pardon to Saml. G. Brown who is in the Penitentiary, under 5 years sentence as a Ku Klux, because he moved in good society, was in fact a leader, well posted, and of good education.

When a cousin, Mary Davis Brown, visited his family in April, she found them "in great hopes that cousin Psalm will be pardened & git home soon."[25] Still pressing for release, Brown, urged by his friends, reluctantly wrote to A. S. Wallace in July 1873 asking him to recall their old friendship prior to Reconstruction and to aid him in securing pardon. Members of the family "went to Wallace almost upon their knees" pleading for his release. Congressman Wallace, who had been approached several times on behalf of Brown, always made promises and then found specious reasons for not keeping his word.

Three weeks after Brown's appeal to Wallace (which produced no results), the former received a letter from J. D. Ottz, a Secret Service agent well known in Charlotte. Ottz told Brown that he had seen the president and had his promise of a pardon — if Brown's friends and family would deliver a petition (which might contain a few well-known Republicans' names) by July.

When the petition was complete and included the requested names,[26] Wallace came to Brown's friends feigning friendship. He talked them into letting him have the petition, saying he would add his recommendations and forward it on the next mail. After the deadline of July 1 was past, Wallace admitted he had not sent the petition as he had promised because it "might cause a fuss among his Party."[27] It was learned thereafter that Judge Mackey had urged Wallace to permit the old man to be pardoned (Wallace's recommendation was all that was required) only if Brown revealed the location of his two sons.[28]

Later in July, South Carolina Comptroller Doctor J. Neagle came to the prison to review the institution. Under the guise of concern and compassion, he called for Brown and several others from South Carolina to inquire about their health. Though Brown knew Neagle to be a carpetbagger in the worst meaning of that term, he could not help being elated over Neagle's promise to intercede with President Grant.[29]

At the time Brown's friend Randolph Shotwell of North Carolina was released on 25 August 1873, Shotwell requested Superintendent Amos T. Pilsbury to appoint the aged prisoner to his position as steward, thereby relieving him of the hardship and drudgery of the shoe shop.[30] Pilsbury, Shotwell's keeper and friend, promised Brown that he at least would be appointed assistant steward.[31] When Shotwell, the last of Brown's friends in the Albany Penitentiary, told the old man of his pending release, he nearly broke down and cried. Shotwell believed Brown was so moved partly because all the southern men except himself were being released.[32]

Brown's wife again took up her pen in yet another effort to have her husband freed. She wrote to President Grant on 14 September 1873:

> To His Excellency U. S. Grant
> President of the United States of America
>
> Dear Sir:
>
> Although a stranger, yet a woman and the wife of an unfortunate prisoner, now confined in the Penitentiary at Albany in the State of New York, I take the liberty to address you this short letter, without any apology or preamble. I will briefly state my request and my reasons for it. My husband S. G. Brown was arrested and brought to trial in Dec. A. D. 1871, as a Ku Klux and was sentenced then to a term of imprisonment for five years and was sent to the penitentiary as above named where he has been nearly two years. The object of this communication then is to solicit and ask a pardon of Your Excellency in his case. In giving my reasons for this request, I will state in the outset that what I shall say to your Excellency, shall be strictly true and the whole truth as far as I know, whatever may be the impression, you may have received — derived from the information of others. I will say further in this place, that I have sent two Petitions signed by considerable number of our neighbors, white and black, respectfully asking a pardon in his case, from the Government[,] and both have proved unavailing. I do not mention this fact by way of complaint, but rather to call your attention to a fact, from which I suppose your Excellency must be somewhat acquainted with the particular facts of my Husband's case.
>
> That my Husband attended one meeting of the Ku Klux in our neighborhood, I will not pretend to deny, but that he was in any sense a leader and counseled any of these acts of violence, justly chargeable to the organization I do deny. Our relations as Husband and wife were such, that to me he gave his fullest confidence and repeatedly declared that the raiding must be stopped. Our family consisted at that time of four daughters, one of whom was married and living near us and the others with us and two sons, both of whom were living on farms of their own, and apart from us. I will not attempt to disguise the fact that both of our sons left the

country at the commencement of the trials, and are still absent or that they were members of the Ku Klux organization, but whatever they may have done, I feel certain no act of violence was ever committed or advised by their Father. Our circumstances are limited and as you know we need very much the assistance, comfort and protection of him to whom in the order of nature we must look to for these earthly blessings. My husband has given a written statement as I am informed to the Hon. Gerrit Smith of the State of New York and the Hon. A.S. Wallace of this State that if released he would in no way give any trouble to the government of the United States.

He is now about sixty years old and if your Excellency will listen to and give confidence in the words of his wife, I think I need have no hesitation in assuring your Excellency that should you deem it proper to order his pardon, the balance of his days will be spent in obedience to all the laws, of the Government of the United States.

Respectfully,
M. M. Brown[33]

The following November, North Carolina's ex-governor, William W. Holden, made an appeal to Attorney General George H. Williams on Brown's behalf:

He is an old man. He has been in the Penitentiary some two years. The coming of Winter will be hard upon him. The policy of the government has been one of mercy towards these misguided persons. It may be that this poor old man has been overlooked. I hope, Sir, that you will see the President and have him pardoned.[34]

Senator Robertson and Congressman A. S. Wallace also recommended to the president that a release was in order. Brown finally was granted a pardon on 16 December 1873. He arrived home Tuesday, December 30.[35]

Appendix 10

An Act to Provide for the Protection of Persons, Property and the Public Peace. No. 337

Whereas threatenings, intimidation and violence are used in portions of this State against the peace of the same; and whereas the laws are set at defiance, and the officers of the law hindered, prevented and obstructed in the discharge of their duties; and whereas armed, disguised and lawless persons are threatening, maltreating and assassinating peaceable and defenseless citizens; therefore,

Section 1. Be it enacted by the Senate and House of Representatives of the State of South Carolina, now met and sitting in General Assembly, and by the authority of the same, That if any person shall assault or intimidate any citizen because of political opinions or the exercise of political rights and privileges guaranteed to every citizen of the United States by the Constitution and laws thereof, or by the Constitution and laws of this State, or, for such reason, discharge such citizen from employment or occupation, or eject such citizen from rented house or land or other property, such person shall be deemed guilty of a misdemeanor, and, on conviction thereof, be fined not less than fifty or more than one thousand dollars, or be imprisoned not less than three months or more than one year, or both, at the discretion of the Court.

Section 2. That if any two or more persons shall band or conspire together, or go in disguise upon the public highway or upon the premises of another, with intent to injure, oppress, or violate the person or property of any citizen, because of his political opinion or his expression or exercise of the same, or shall attempt, by any means, measures or acts, to hinder, prevent or obstruct any citizen in the free exercise and enjoyment of any right or privilege secured to him by the Constitution and laws of the United States, or by the Constitution and laws of this State, such persons shall be deemed guilty of a felony, and, on conviction thereof, be fined not less than one hundred or more than two thousand dollars, or be imprisoned not less than six months or more than three years, or both, at the discretion of the Court; and shall thereafter be ineligible to and disabled from holding any office of honor, trust or profit in this State.

Section 3. That if, in violating any of the provisions of this Act, any other crime, misdemeanor or felony shall be committed, the offender or offenders shall, on conviction thereof, be subjected to such punishment for the same as is attached to such crime, misdemeanor and felony by the existing laws of this State.

Section 4. That the Sheriffs, Constables and other officers in the several Circuits or Counties vested with powers of arresting, imprisoning and bailing offenders against the laws of this State, be, and are hereby, specially authorized and required to institute proceedings against all and every person and persons who shall violate any of the provisions of this Act, and cause him and them to be arrested, imprisoned or bailed, as the case may require, for a trial before such Court as shall have jurisdiction of the offense.

Section 5. That the Circuit Courts of this State, within their respective Circuits, in the Counties of which the Circuits are respectively composed, shall have cognizance of all offenses committed against the provisions of this Act, and of all other causes arising under this Act.

Section 6. That it shall be the duty of all Sheriffs, Constables, and other officers who may be specially empowered, to obey and execute all warrants and other processes issued under the provisions of this Act to them directed; and should any Sheriff, Constable, or other officer specially empowered, refuse to receive such warrant or other process, when tendered to him, or neglect or refuse to execute the same, he shall, on conviction thereof, be fined in the sum of five hundred dollars, to the use of the citizens deprived of the rights secured by the provisions of this Act, or be imprisoned in the County jail, in the discretion of the Court. And the better to enable the Sheriffs, Constables, and other officers specially empowered, to execute all such warrants and other processes as may be directed to them, they shall

Act to Provide for the Protection of Persons, Property... 157

have authority to summon and call to their aid the by-standers or *posse comitatus* of the proper County; and all persons refusing to obey the summons or call of the officers thus empowered shall be deemed guilty of a misdemeanor, and, on conviction thereof, be punished. And such warrants and other processes shall run and be executed by said officers anywhere within the Circuit or County in which they are issued.

Section 7. That any person who shall hinder, prevent or obstruct any officer or other person charged with the execution of any warrant or other process issued under the provisions of this Act, in arresting any person for whose apprehension such warrant or other process may have been issued, or shall rescue, or attempt to rescue, such person form the custody of the officer or person or persons lawfully assisting him, as aforesaid, or shall aid, abet or assist any person so arrested, as aforesaid, directly or indirectly, to escape from the custody of the officer or person or persons assisting him, as aforesaid, or shall harbor or conceal any person for whose arrest a warrant or other process shall have been issued, so as to prevent his discovery and arrest, after notice or knowledge of the fact of the issuing of such warrant or other process, shall, on conviction for either of said offenses, be subject to a fine of not less than fifty, nor more than one thousand dollars, or imprisonment of not less than three months, nor more than one year, or both, at the discretion of the Court having jurisdiction.

Section 8. That any citizen who shall be hindered, prevented or obstructed in the exercise of the rights and privileges secured to him by the Constitution and laws of the United States, or by the Constitution and laws of this State, or shall be injured in his person or property because of his exercise of the same, may claim and prosecute the County in which the offense shall be committed for any damages he shall sustain thereby, and the said County shall be responsible for the payment of such damages as the Court may award, which shall be paid by the County Treasurer of such County on a warrant drawn by the County Commissioners thereof; which warrant shall be drawn by the County Commissioners as soon as a certified copy of the judgment roll is delivered them for file in their office.

Section 9. In all cases where any dwelling house, building, or any property, real or personal, shall be destroyed in consequence of any mob or riot, it shall be lawful for the person or persons owning or interested in such property to bring suits against the County in which such property was situated and being, for the recovery of such damages as he or they may have sustained by reason of the destruction thereof; and the amount which shall be recovered in said action shall be paid in the manner provided by Section 8 of this Act.

Section 10. That no person or persons shall be entitled to the recovery of such damages if it shall appear that the destruction of his or their property was caused by his or their illegal conduct, nor unless it shall appear that he or they, upon knowledge had of the intention or attempt to destroy his or their property, or to collect a mob for that purpose, and, sufficient time intervening, gave notice thereof to a Constable, Sheriff, or Trial Justice or Justice of the Peace of the County in which such property was situated and being; and it shall be the duty of such Constable, Sheriff, Trial Justice or Justice of the Peace, upon receipt of such notice, to take all legal means necessary for the protection of such property as attacked, or threatened to be attacked; and, if such Constable, Sheriff, Trial Justice, or Justice of the Peace, upon receipt of such notice, or upon knowledge of such intention or attempt to destroy such property, in any wise received, shall neglect or refuse to perform his duty in the premises, he or they so neglecting or refusing shall be liable for the damages done to such property, to be recovered by action, and shall also be deemed guilty of a misdemeanor in office, and, on conviction thereof, shall forfeit his commission.

Section 11. That nothing in this Act shall be construed to prevent the person or persons whose property is injured or destroyed from having and maintaining his or their action against all and every person and persons engaged or participating in said mob or riot, to recover full damages for any injury sustained: Provided, however, That no damages shall be recovered by the party injured against any of the said rioters for the same injury for which compensation shall be made by the County.

Section 12. That it shall be lawful for the County Commissioners of the County against which damages shall be recovered under the provisions of this Act to bring suit or suits, in the name of the County, against any and all persons engaged, or in any manner participating in said mob or riot, and against any Constable, Sheriff, Trial Justice, or Justice of the Peace, or other officer charged with the maintenance of the public peace, who may be liable, by neglect of duty, to the provisions of this Act, for the recovery of all damages, costs and expenses incurred by said County, and such suits shall not abate or fail by reason of too many or too few parties defendant being named therein.

Approved March 1, 1871

Appendix 11

Union League Oath[1]

"I (each repeating his own name with an uplifted hand) do solemnly swear or affirm (if conscientiously opposed), without mental reservation in me of any kind, that I will support and protect and defend the constitution and government of the United States of America, one and indivisible, the flag thereof, against all enemies, foreign or domestic; that I will vote only for and for none but those who advocate and support the great principles set forth by this league to fill any office of honor, profit or trust, in either the state or general government, and that if ever called to fill any office I will faithfully carry out the principles set forth by this league; and further, that I will protect and defend all worthy members of the Union League of America, and that I never will in any manner or form, divulge or make known to any person or person, not worthy members of this organization, any of the signs, passwords, grips, proceedings, designs, debates or plans or any other council of this organization, unless when engaged in admitting mew members. And with my right hand on the Holy Bible, Declaration of Independence and the Constitution of the United States of America I acknowledge myself firmly bound to the faithful performance of this my solemn obligation, so help me God."

Response by the members—"To this we pledge ourselves."

"Gentlemen, around you is a band of brothers, alike sacredly pledged; this circle is never to be broken by treachery."

Response by the members—"Never."

"Brothers, will you enlarge your circle to admit new members?"

Response by the members—"We will."

"Prepare then for accession to your ranks." (The circle is then opened, and the new members are admitted.)

"With clasped and uplifted hands, repeat after me the freeman's pledge to defend and perpetuate freedom, political equality, and an indivisible Union: I pledge my life, my fortune and my sacred honor, so help me God."

"The candidate will take their places before the altar." Next comes the charge. And next some poor man's whiskey that has never been taken without permission or pay.

Notes

Introduction

1. Christine Leigh Heyrman, *Southern Cross: The Beginning of the Bible Belt* (New York: Alfred A. Knopf, 1997), p. 151.
2. Diary of Dr. James Rufus Bratton (Transcription by J. L. West, York County Public Library, Rock Hill, SC), Part 1, p. 9.
3. "Political Meeting at Belton, SC," *Yorkville Enquirer*, 10 September 1867.
4. Ibid.
5. Ibid.
6. Ibid.
7. Joseph T. Derry, *Story of the Confederate States* (Harrisonburg, VA: Sprinkle Publications, 1996), p. 97
8. York County resident and Congressman Alexander S. Wallace, predicting that a "reign of terror" would prevent a fair election in Anderson County, first used this phrase in the summer of 1868.
9. "Gov. Scott's Letter," *Yorkville Enquirer*, 15 July 1869.
10. "Just A-Rolling Along the Way," *Yorkville Enquirer*, 14 July 1933.
11. Richard Zuczek, "The Federal Government's Attack on the Ku Klux Klan: A Reassessment," *South Carolina Historical Magazine*, 1997 (January): p. 52.
12. Christine Leigh Heyrman, *Southern Cross: The Beginnings of the Bible Belt* (New York: Alfred A. Knopf, 1997), p. 10–11.
13. Howard J. Marchall, *Gentlemen Without a Country: A Social and Intellectual History of South Carolina, 1860–1900* (Chapel Hill: University of North Carolina Press, 1979), p. 304.
14. Robert C. McMath, Jr., *Populist Vanguard: A History of the Southern Farmer's Alliance* (Chapel Hill: The University of North Carolina Press, 1975), p. 63.
15. Ibid., p. 257.

16. *Fairfield Herald*, 20 November 1872.
17. "A Description of the Carpet Bagger," *Yorkville Enquirer*, 28 May 1868.
18. "The Ku Klux Klan — What Is It?" *Yorkville Enquirer*, 23 April 1868.
19. The Holy Bible, Philemon, Chapter V, Verses 10–21.
20. Howard J. Marchall, *Gentlemen Without a County: A Social and Intellectual History of South Carolina, 1860–1900* (Chapel Hill: University of North Carolina Press, 1979), p. 305.
21. Ibid.
22. Mellichamp, 20 April 1876, *George Engelmann Papers*, Missouri Botanical Garden, MO.
23. Richard M. Jolly, *The Story of my Reminiscences* (1924), p. 18. Jolly tells that he was converted, baptized and joined the church at Buffalo Baptist Church in York County (now Cherokee County) during a meeting held by Reverend Thomas Dixon. Dixon's son, Thomas Dixon Jr. wrote *The Klansman* on which the movie *The Birth of a Nation* was based.
24. Elizabeth Fox-Genovese, 19 January 1996, Atlanta, Georgia, at a celebration of Robert E. Lee's birthday.
25. United States Congress, *Testimony Taken by the Joint Select Committee to Inquire into the Conditions of Affairs in the Late Insurrectionary States* (Washington, DC: Government Printing Office, 1872; reprint New York: AMS Press, 1968), pp. 1051–52.
26. "The Ku Klux Klan — What Is It?" *Yorkville Enquirer*, 23 April 1868.

1 — Opening Scenes to Fury

1. "Registration Returns," *Yorkville Enquirer*, 22 August 1867.
2. Manuscript voter registration books, South Carolina Department of Archives and History, Columbia, SC; Philip N. Racine, ed, *Piedmont Farmer: The Journals of David Golightly Harris, 1855–1870* (Knoxville: University of Tennessee Press, 1990) p. 444.
3. "Registration in York District," *Yorkville Enquirer*, 22 August 1867.
4. Richard Zuckek, *State of Rebellion: Reconstruction in South Carolina* (Columbia, SC: University of South Carolina Press, 1996), p. 39.
5. "The Convention Election," *Yorkville Enquirer*, 28 November 1867, Jerry L. West, *Political Actions of York County, South Carolina, Conservative Clubs in 1868* (Sharon, SC: Broad River Basin Historical Society, 1996), p. 10.
6. Dr. J. L. Neagle was born in the Pisgah section of Gaston County, North Carolina, of a respected family. While attending school in Mecklenburg County, North Carolina, he boarded with Rev. Dr. John Hunter who was pastor of an Associate Reformed Presbyterian Church. Suspected as a thief in Hunter's home, he either ran away or was expelled from school. He studied medicine under a Dr. Tracy and practiced under him near Kings Mountain, North Carolina. He married a sister of Mrs. Tracy. About 1867 he moved to Columbia, South Carolina, joined the Republican Party and entered politics, and was elected State Treasurer. "Views and Interviews," *Yorkville Enquirer*, 28 July 1933.
7. Jerry L. West, *Political Actions of York County, South Carolina, Conservative Clubs in 1868* (Sharon, SC: Broad River Basin Historical Society, 1996), p. 10.

The number of registered voters, as well as those voting in favor of or against the proposed constitutional convention varies according to the sources used. See as examples Richard Zuczek, *State of Rebellion* (Columbia: University of South Carolina Press, 1991), p. 41; Carol K. Rothrock Bleser, *The Promised Land* (Columbia: University of South Carolina Press, 1969), p. xii.

8. James E. Sefton, *The United States Army and Reconstruction 1865–1877* (Baton Rouge: Louisiana State University Press, 1967), p. 185. Previously the South Carolina state Constitution required a certain percentage of registered voters to participate in an election for it to be valid.

9. "To the Citizens of York District," *Yorkville Enquirer*, 2 April 1868.

10. For administrative purposes, military authorities divided York District into three regimental precincts. The third precinct was composed of Coate's Tavern, Fort Mill, Pride's Old Mill and Rock Hill. The first precinct was comprised of Bethel, Blairsville, Clay Hill, McConnellsville and Yorkville. The second precinct was comprised of Bethany Church, Boydton, Clark's Store and Wylie's Store.

11. "Registration Returns," *Yorkville Enquirer*, 9 April 1867.

12. "The Conservative Mass Meeting," *Yorkville Enquirer*, 9 April 1868.

13. W. B. Romine, *A Story of the Original Ku Klux Klan* (Pulaski, TN: The Pulaski Citizen, 1934), p. 7.

14. "Sunday Sports in Hamburg," *Yorkville Enquirer*, 28 October 1869.

15. Allen W. Trelease, *White Terror: The Ku Klux Klan Conspiracy and Southern Reconstuction* (Baton Rouge: Louisiana State University Press, 1971), p. 61.

16. Michael W. Fitzgerald, *The Union League Movement in the Deep South* (Baton Rouge: University of Louisiana Press, 1989), p. 2.

17. Julie Saville, *The Work of Reconstruction: From Slave to Wage Labor in South Carolina, 1860–1870* (New York: Cambridge University Press, 1994), pp. 162–63.

18. Ibid., p. 168.

19. Michael W. Fitzgerald, *The Union League Movement in the Deep South* (Baton Rouge: University of Louisiana Press, 1989), p. 6.

20. The Second Military District included both North and South Carolina.

21. Julie Saville, *The Work of Reconstruction: From Slave to Wage Labor in South Carolina, 1860–1870* (New York: Cambridge University Press, 1994), pp. 166–67.

22. Ibid., pp. 184, 186.

23. Ibid., pp. 187–88.

24. "Miscellaneous Reading," *Yorkville Enquirer*, 11 July 1867.

25. "Union League Ritual," *Yorkville Enquirer*, 12 September 1867. Like the Masonic Order and the Ku Klux Klan, as well as other male dominated societies of the 19th century, the league had secret ceremonies, signs, handshakes and signs. One writer claimed members usually opened and closed their meetings by singing "Rally Round the Flag, Boys." Samuel B. Hall, *A Shell in the Radical Camp* (Charleston, SC, 1873), p. 2.

26. "The Union League," *Yorkville Enquirer*, 24 October 1867.

27. Lou Falkner Williams, *The Great South Carolina Ku Klux Klan Trials, 1871–1872* (Athens: University of Georgia Press, 1996), p. 20.

28. Ibid.

29. Samuel B. Hall, *A Shell in the Radical Camp* (Charleston, SC, 1873), p. 35.

30. Ibid., p. 22.

31. Julie Saville, *The Work of Reconstruction: From Slave to Wage Laborer in South Carolina, 1860–1870* (New York: Cambridge University Press, 1994), pp. 188.

32. Ibid., pp. 179–80.

33. A more detailed study of the York County Conservative Clubs may be found in: Jerry L. West, *Political Actions of York County, South Carolina, Conservative Clubs in 1868* (Sharon, SC: Broad River Basin Historical Society, 1996).

34. "Colored Conservatives," *Yorkville Enquirer*, 23 April 1868.

35. Occasionally the word "Union" was injected into the title of the Conservative Clubs.

36. "...whereas the conservative people of the District have united themselves into organizations for the purpose of carrying out the views and principles of the Conservative Union Party of the United States...." *Yorkville Enquirer*, 30 April 1868.

37. "Clark's Fork Conservative Club," *Yorkville Enquirer*, 30 April 1868.

38. "Another Club," *Yorkville Enquirer*, 11 May 1868.

39. "Rock Hill Conservative Meeting," *Yorkville Enquirer*, 11 May 1868.

40. "Conservative Clubs," *Yorkville Enquirer*, 21 May 1868.

41. Ibid.

42. "Conservative Clubs," *Yorkville Enquirer*, 4 June 1868.

43. The election was held in obedience to an order issued by General Canby.

44. "Revision of Registration," *Yorkville Enquirer*, 28 May 1868.

45. "The District Election," *Yorkville Enquirer*, 11 June 1868.

46. Ibid.

47. The 4th Congressional district of South Carolina consisted of Chester, Fairfield, Greenville, Laurens, Oconee, Pickens, Union, Spartanburg and York counties.

48. "Another Democratic Club," *Yorkville Enquirer*, 27 August 1868.

49. "Bethesda Democratic Club," *Yorkville Enquirer*, 27 August 1868.

50. "The Mass Meeting," *Yorkville Enquirer*, 3 September 1868.

51. The Rose Hotel had been renovated in January 1867. Some of its new accommodations included a barbershop billiard room and bar; it probably was more up-scale and larger than the Kings Mountain Hotel. However since William Edward Rose owned the hotel, a Radical Republican who was a key white leader from York County, the crowd would not have assembled there.

52. "The Mass Meeting," *Yorkville Enquirer*, 3 September 1868.

53. "District Mass Meetings," *Yorkville Enquirer*, 3 September 1868.

54. Judson Gwin of the Turkey Creek Club, Captain E. A. Crawford of the McConnellsville Club and E. R. Mills of the Bethesda Club were delegates at the September 18 meeting in Yorkville.

55. "Colored Democrats," *Yorkville Enquirer*, 10 September 1868.

56. "The Compromise of Debts," *Yorkville Enquirer*, 10 September 1868.

57. Ibid.

58. "The Mass Meeting," *Yorkville Enquirer*, 24 September 1868.

59. "Mass Meeting and Picnic," *Yorkville Enquirer*, 1 October 1868.

60. "The Clark's Fork Meeting," *Yorkville Enquirer*, 15 October 1868. The Colored Democratic Club had been formed during the last week of September by a group of freedmen who met at the York County Courthouse. "Colored Democratic Club," *Yorkville Enquirer*, 1 October 1868.

61. Reverend Robert A. Ross was the pastor of the Sharon Associate Reformed Presbyterian Church (Sharon, SC) 1843–93 and often participated in political activities.

62. "The Clark's Fork Meeting," *Yorkville Enquirer*, 15 October 1868.
63. A. M. Grist, "Just A-Rolling Along the Way," *Yorkville Enquirer*, 25 August 1933.
64. "Views and Interviews," *Yorkville Enquirer*, 15 September 1933.
65. "The Republican Meeting," *Yorkville Enquirer*, 15 October 1868.
66. "Meeting at Buffalo," *Yorkville Enquirer*, 15 October 1868.
67. "Soldiers in Yorkville," *Yorkville Enquirer*, 22 October 1868.
68. Some of these counties had whites in the majority while others had a larger number of blacks as registered voters. "Voting," *Yorkville Enquirer*, 29 October 1868.
69. "The Election," *Yorkville Enquirer*, 29 October 1868.
70. "Tuesday Next," *Yorkville Enquirer*, 29 October 1868.
71. "Every Votes Counts," *Yorkville Enquirer*, 29 October 1868.
72. "The Election in York," *Yorkville Enquirer*, 5 November 1868.
73. United States Congress, *Testimony Taken by the Joint Select Committee to Inquire into the Condition of Affairs in the Late Insurrectionary States* (Washington, DC: Government Printing Office, 1872; reprint New York: AMS Press, 1968), pp. 1943, 1955–56, 1959–60.
74. Allen W. Trelease, *White Terror* (New York: Harper & Row, 1971), p. 117; John S. Reynolds, *Reconstruction in South Carolina 1865–1877* (Columbia, SC: The State Co., 1905), p. 104.
75. "Murders and Outrages," *Yorkville Enquirer*, 12 November 1868.

2 — Advent of the Ku Klux Klan

1. The Klan vigilante system originated in the law office of Judge Thomas Jones in Pulaski, Tennessee, on 24 December 1865. W. B. Romine, *A Story of the Original Ku Klux Klan* (Pulaski, TN: The Pulaski Citizen, 1934), p. 4. Romine, who traces its origin to a group of young men in the town, relates that the Klan was more or less a private club for their own entertainment; it later developed into a more serious affair. Judge Jones wrote, "Men who composed the membership of the Klan accidentally discovered the power their order wielded over the minds of the superstitious negroes ... and also over the ignorant and lawless white element, both being rendered unruly by atrocious political influence. In the beginning[,] the position of Law and Order League [apparently an earlier name of the Ku Klux Klan] had never been even remotely anticipated by the members of the order[,] but it was thrust upon them by numerous wanton acts, and the Klan rose as one man to meet the demand." Ibid, pp. 3–4. See also Allen W. Trelease, *White Terror* (New York: Harper & Row, 1971), pp. 3–27. Belton O'Neall Townsend traces the Klan's ideological roots to the antebellum patrol that consisted of nonaristocrats who frequently practiced racial violence. Townsend makes the connection saying, "The Ku Klux Klan, with its night visits and whippings and murders were the legitimate offspring of the patrol ... the chief object of which was to whip severely any Negro found away from home without a pass from his master." Howard J. Marshall, *Gentlemen Without a Country: A Social and Intellectual History of South Carolina: 1860–1900* (Chapel Hill: University of North Carolina Press, 1979), p. 300.

2. The rumor that every freedman would receive "forty acres and a mule" was rife in South Carolina during the early years of Reconstruction. General William

T. Sherman's Special Field Order No. 15 (16 January 1865) specified that land sales on the Sea Islands of South Carolina were limited to blacks only. His order allowed each adult black male to purchase up to 20 acres, plus up to 20 additional acres if he was married. Virginia C. Holmgren, *Hilton Head: A Sea Island Chronicle* (Hilton Head, SC: Hilton Head Publishing Company, 1959), p. 109. See also John Solomon Otto, *Southern Agriculture During the Civil War Era, 1860–1880* (Westport, Connecticut: Greenwood Press, 1994), pp. 49, 56, 58. An informed discussion of black efforts to obtain land appears in Julie Saville, *The Work of Reconstruction: From Slave to Wage Laborer in South Carolina, 1860–1870* (New York: Cambridge University Press, 1994). A state land commission was established early under the reconstruction regime, and an appropriation of $700,000 was made to purchase land and distribute it among poor persons. Fraud defeated the aim of the program; worthless land was purchased and sold at exorbitant prices. York County Republican John L. Neagle was a member of the land commission advisory board and involved in its shady practices. Black hopes for obtaining homesteads rarely were gratified, and the majority of land remained in the hands of the white population. See Carol K. Rothrock Bleser, *The Promised Land: The History of the South Carolina Land Commission 1869–1890* (Columbia: University of South Carolina Press, 1969). The tradition of "forty acres and a mule" also has some local tradition attached. In 1933 ex-Klansman John C. Robinson told that a number of acres located four miles east of Yorkville was seized by the federal government and sold off in small tracts to a number of freedmen on an easy payment plan. Robinson believed this was part of the "Forty Acres and a Mule" plan which was to be a "great drawing card for the ignorant Negroes of that day." "Just A-Rolling Along the Way," The *Yorkville Enquirer*, 12 September 1933.

3. For a limited discussion of black arson, see Allen Trelease, *White Terror* (New York: Harper & Row, 1971), p. xix.

4. Written in pencil by M. S. Carroll in 1924 and found in that year's voter enrollment book of the Beersheba Precinct. Copy in author's possession. In a preface, Carroll states two reasons for writing the recollection: "(1) ...our young people should know and remember these things; and (2) ... to [explain] the necessity for some such organization and [to] justify any acts of violence committed by them...."

5. Recollections of John Daniel McConnell as told to his son, D. E. McConnell. From a private collection.

6. "K.K.K.," *Yorkville Enquirer*, ? April 1868. "G.G.S." is the abbreviation for great grand scribe.

7. "K.K.K.—Mysterious," *Yorkville Enquirer*, 2 April 1868.

8. In York County, the equivalent of the Loyal Leagues was called the Union League.

9. "The Ku Klux—What Is It?," *Yorkville Enquirer*, 9 April 1868.

10. "K.K.K.," *Yorkville Enquirer*, 16 April 1868.

11. Allen W. Trelease, *White Terror* (New York: Harper & Row, 1971), p. 62.

12. "Termite": its use here alludes to secret, clandestine destruction.

13. "The Ku Klux Klan—What Is it?," *Yorkville Enquirer*, 23 April 1868.

14. "From Chester," *Yorkville Enquirer*, 14 May 1868.

15. The particulars of this family tradition evolved about 1901 or 1902 when eight-year-old Jacob H. Clawson II, a son of Doctor Clawson, crawled under the

porch where his father and great-grandmother, Mary Morris McClintoc, were talking. Young Jacob's curiosity had been piqued when he was told to leave the porch where the older family members were conversing. Jacob overheard his father tell Mrs. McClintoc (who had been a messenger for the Klan) how he had gone to Tennessee and brought the organization to York County.

16. Stanley F. Horn, *The Invisible Empire*, 2nd ed. (Montclair, NJ: Patterson Smith, 1969), pp. 216–17.

17. Allen W. Trelease, *White Terror* (New York: Harper & Row, 1971), p. 72.

18. Hope, who testified that he had received the constitution from Major Avery, had organized a Klan (Den) and been elected as a Klan chief (Grand Cyclops). He allegedly became one of the "Pukes" or witness for the prosecution, who turned state's evidence by cooperating with the authorities. As expected, this action generated a great deal of ill will, especially among his in-laws, the Whitesides, who were Klan members. Their antagonism with Hope was expressed in 1875 when he was indicted on suspicion of murder after his wife's 17-year-old niece, then living with them, gave birth to an illegitimate son and died shortly after in convulsions. Several members of the Whiteside family gave testimony that they suspected Hope of murder in order to cover up the child's paternity. They were instrumental in having the girl's body exhumed and her stomach sent to New York for analysis. Although Hope was exonerated after a highly publicized trial, the attached stigma lingered with him for the rest of his life.

19. The history of the Klan's origin written in Pulaski, Tennessee, mentions that "Committees came to Pulaski for initiation and instruction and then returned to their homes to establish the organization there." While no name was given in the account, particularly mentioned is a "messenger who took the organization to South Carolina." W. B. Romine, *A Story of the Original Ku Klux Klan* (Pulaski, TN; The Pulaski Citizen, 1934), p. 9.

20. Stanley F. Horn, *The Invisible Empire*, 2nd ed. (Montclair, NJ: Patterson Smith, 1969), pp. 216–17.

21. "Views and Interviews," *Yorkville Enquirer*, 15 September 1933.

22. John S. Reynolds, *Reconstruction in South Carolina* (Columbia, SC: The State Co., 1905), p. 205.

23. Richard Zuczek, "The Federal Government's Attack on the Ku Klux Klan: A Reassessment," *South Carolina Historical Magazine*, 97 (January, 1996): 48.

24. Interview with Lee Guyton, in B. A. Botkin, *Lay My Burden Down* (Athens: University of Georgia Press, 1989), p. 67.

25. Kirkland Gunn testified that the Burris Klan numbered about 20, and the Byers Klan about 17. Charles W. Foster claimed at the Klan trials that the Mitchell Klan wore ground-length red robes and that their horses' covers were white. After each raid the robes were given to Mitchell for safekeeping until they were needed for the next raid. United States Government, Senate Report No. 41, parts 3–3, Forty Second Congress, Second Session, *Testimony Taken by the Joint Select Committee to Inquire into the Condition of Affairs in the Late Insurrectionary States* (Washington, DC: Government Printing Office, 1872; reprint New York: AMS Press, 1968), 3 (of the SC Volumes): 1704.

26. Ibid., 3 (of the SC volumes): 1256–60; Allen W. Trelease, *White Terror* (New York: Harper & Row, 1971), p. 115.

27. Grist, the editor of the *Yorkville Enquirer*, told the "older whites 'to advise

the young men not to engage in whipping and murdering the colored people.'" Allen W. Trelease, *White Terror* (New York: Harper & Row, 1971), p. 368.

28. "What the Ku Klux Did," *The Herald* (Rock Hill), 7 October 1886.

29. "Allen W. Trelease, *White Terror* (New York: Harper & Row, 1971), p. 363. This figure is comparable to the 1867 voters registration numbers for York County, which showed 2,203 white voters. It cannot be concluded, however, that the entire white voting population belonged to the Klan since some whites were registered Republicans and others undoubtedly took no part in Klan activities or even in the political process.

30. Recollections of John Daniel McConnell as told to his son, D. E. McConnell. From a private collection.

31. Allen W. Trelease, *White Terror* (New York: Harper & Row, 1971), p. 363.

32. Robert Drew Loftis, "Federal Protection of the Freedmen in South Carolina: 1871" (Master's Thesis, the American University 1968), 43.

33. Ibid., pp. 36–37.

34. Using the list of men convicted of Klan activities and the 1860 and 1870 federal censuses for York County will give some sense of the wealth and class of Klan members. The transcripts of the Klan trials reveal that upper or professional classes gave the orders that were carried out by middle and lower classes of whites.

35. Julie Saville, *The Work of Reconstruction from Slave to Wage Laborer in South Carolina, 1860–1870* (New York: Cambridge University Press, 1994), p. 172.

3 — A Threat of Violence

1. Robert Martin and B. W. Duncan to Governor Scott, 25 July 1868, Box 1, Folder 17, Governor Robert K. Scott's Papers, South Carolina Department of Archives and History, Columbia, SC.

2. Allen W. Trelease, *White Terror* (New York: Harper & Row, 1971), p. 631.

3. Richard M. Jolly, *The Story of My Reminiscences* (1924), p. 18.

4. "Governor Scott's Proclamation," *Yorkville Enquirer*, 29 October 1868.

5. Richard Zuczek, *State of Rebellion: Reconstruction in South Carolina* (Columbia, SC: University of South Carolina Press, 1996), p. 60.

6. Ibid., pp. 53–54.

7. John S. Reynolds, *Reconstruction in South Carolina* (Columbia, SC: The State Co., 1905), p. 179.

8. Allen W. Trelease, *White Terror* (New York: Harper & Row, 1971), p. 363.

9. Richard Zuczek, *State of Rebellion: Reconstruction in South Carolina* (Columbia: University of South Carolina Press, 1996), p. 62.

10. Ibid., p. 61.

11. A joint resolution adopted by the General Assembly in 1869 authorizing Governor Scott to employ an armed force for peace, and to use Treasury funds for such purposes, was reported as a fraud upon the people of South Carolina during the administration of Governor Wade Hampton. Vast amounts of money were used to support this organization for purely political purposes. Alrutheus Ambush Taylor, *The Negro in South Carolina During the Reconstruction* (New York: AMS Press, 1971), p. 278.

12. "One Thousand Dollars Reward," *Yorkville Enquirer*, 29 April 1869.

13. "A Mean Act," *Yorkville Enquirer*, 9 September 1869, reprinted from the

Notes—Chapter 3

Chester Reporter. A number of men from western York County would later participate in a violent clash with a black militia near this site.

14. Ibid.

15. Born 1804–05, Sanders, a Baptist minister, served in the Constitutional Convention of 1868 and the House of Representatives from 1868 to 1872. According to the 1870 census, he owned $175 in personal property. Eric Foner, *Freedom's Lawmakers: A Directory of Black Office Holders During Reconstruction* (New York: Oxford University Press, 1993), p. 189. He was appointed census taker for western Chester County for the 1870 Federal Census. "State Items," *Yorkville Enquirer*, 16 June 1870.

16. Ibid. That Sanders took the time to learn to write does not seem a sufficient reason for his loss of favor with his black constituents. Many blacks wanted and expected their ministers to be somewhat learned. The reporter's statement may have been an assumption on his part.

17. "Richard Zuczek, *State of Rebellion: Reconstruction in South Carolina* (Columbia: University of South Carolina Press, 1996), p. 78.

18. "Nelson Hammond (black) wrote to Governor Scott from Yorkville on April 6 that 75 men had been raised for a militia to be known as the "Neagle Guards," and requested it be supplied with arms and its appointed officers commissioned. Hammond's letter lists the following officers: Nelson Hammond, captain; Miles McElwee, first lieutenant; J. A. Newton, second lieutenant; Sloan Johnson, third lieutenant; T. F. Hunt, first orderly sergeant; Robert King, second orderley sergeant. Nelson Hammond to Governor Scott, 6 April 1870, Box 11, Folder 31, Governor Robert K. Scott's Papers, South Carolina Department of Archives and History, Columbia, SC.

19. "From Kings Mountain Township," *Yorkville Enquirer*, 3 February 1870. Although the newspaper reports this incident taking place in Kings Mountain Township, it actually took place in adjoining Cherokee Township, as a later petition to Governor Scott states.

20. "Presentation of the Grand Jury," *Yorkville Enquirer*, 24 March 1870. The attack commonly is assigned an October 1869 date, though it obviously is a January 1870 event. The error results from a statement made during the Klan trials. See *Testimony Taken by the Joint Select Committee to Inquire into the Condition of Affairs in the Late Insurrectionary States* (Washington, DC: Government Printing Office, 1872; reprint New York: AMS Press, 1968).

21. A petition from a number of people in the township stated that Wright had been living in "open adultry [sic] with a white woman" in North Carolina. After being run out of that state, Wright came a few miles across the state line to Hullender's farm where the white farmer erected a cabin for him and his companion. The petition stated the Klan had followed him to the Hullender farm to exercise their punishment. Petition to Governor Scott, 10 February 1870, Box 11, Folder 3, Governor Robert K. Scott's Papers, South Carolina Department of Archives and History, Columbia, SC.

22. Hugh K. Roberts to Governor Scott, 14 January 1870, Box 10, Folder 29, Governor Robert K. Scott's Papers, South Carolina Department of Archives and History, Columbia, SC.

23. William Littlefield to Captain J. B. Hubbard, 24 January 1870, Box 10, Folder 36, Governor Robert K. Scott's Papers, South Carolina Department of Archives and History, Columbia, SC.

24. "From Kings Mountain Township," *Yorkville Enquirer*, 3 February 1870.

25. John R. Faris was a white Republican and a member of the Union League that met in Yorkville. His military company, the first of its kind in the county, consisted of both black and white soldiers. A petition (15 August 1870) was sent from the Antioch Community to Governor Scott requesting that Faris be dismissed, and that he appoint H. K. Roberts captain of the unit. It was reported that Faris had "caused a heap of dissatisfaction among the company" and had "betrayed the trust that we put in him" because he had not advanced soldiers from within the company, instead recruiting others for the positions. Petition to Governor Scott, 15 August 1870, Box 12, Folder 26, Governor Robert K. Scott's Papers, South Carolina Department of Archives and History, Columbia, SC.

26. "Presentation of the Grand Jury," *Yorkville Enquirer*, 24 March 1870.

27. "From Kings Mountain Township," *Yorkville Enquirer*, 3 February 1870.

28. "Our 'Protectors'" *Yorkville Enquirer*, 10 February 1870.

29. "Names Wanted," *Yorkville Enquirer*, 10 February 1870.

30. Cherokee and Kings Mountain townships.

31. Petition of residents of Cherokee Township to Governor R. K. Scott, 10 February 1870, Box 11, Folder 3, Governor Robert K. Scott's Papers, South Carolina Department of Archives and History, Columbia, SC. The petition mentions that a resident of North Carolina, John Moss, was whipped "by a party of Ku Klux" when he stopped for the night at a "house of ill fame." Also whipped by "the same, or a similar, party from North Carolina" was a married man by the name of Nelson Thompson of North Carolina; he was living with another man's wife and "reported to be in the habit of visiting, for licentious purposes, a house of ill fame, and in another instance even to have caused the separation of a husband and his wife...."

32. "Our Protectors," *Yorkville Enquirer*, 10 February 1870.

33. "Gov. Scott vs. The Grand Jury," *Yorkville Enquirer*, 7 April 1870.

34. It was at Forest Hall (now Hightower Hall) that Klansmen were served refreshments after the lynching raid on Jim Williams.

35. Jim Williams was formally known as Jim Rainey; after emancipation he left the county for a while and returned with his new identity. Williams, during the Klan trials, was described as having been extremely bold and aggressive.

36. In South Carolina two plots had made the state nervous over a possible insurrection. The Camden Insurrection of 1816 awakened the upcountry from its imagined security and resulted in the passage of the Repressive Acts of 1818; increased patrols and limited manumission followed. The second incident that firmly established the fear of insurrection in the minds of South Carolina slaveholders was the Denmark Vesey Plot of 1822.

37. Lou Falkner Williams, *The Great South Carolina Ku Klux Klan Trials, 1871–1872* (Athens: University of Georgia Press, 1996), p. 27.

38. Ibid.

39. Ibid.

40. It seems that two shipments of guns had already arrived in Union County prior to 1 September 1870; five boxes were delivered to the Union Depot and six to the Fish Dam Depot in lower Union County. When Governor Scott armed the militia during the summer of 1870 (he then disarmed them the following January), the whites, with good cause, suspected he was trying to secure his own election at the November polls rather than restoring peace. Others believed the militia

presence was to prevent black men "from leaving the Republican ranks and voting with the Reform party" because these companies were observed drilling and parading in areas that contained a large percentage of blacks. If the militias were in the county to keep the peace, the whites surmised they would be marching "through every nook and corner of the county." At best, they considered Scott's militia to be no more than a nuisance. "The Effect of Bayonets," *Yorkville Enquirer*, 6 October 1870. Mobley later became First Vice Grand Councillor of the "United Brotherhood," which replaced the Union League in 1872.

41. While the Union League of York County appears to have been strongest in the eastern townships there is evidence of the league throughout the county. In 1870, a local unit of the league known as "Scott's Council," was organized in Yorkville through the fervent work of Republican Samuel B. Hall. This council may have served as a kind of headquarters for the other county units of the league.

42. One of these men probably was Sherrod Childers, who later confessed he had voted the Radical ticket. Childers was one of three men (another was Mack Sandlin) who fired a pistol and "used boisterous and profane language" at the Bullock's Creek Township home of W. J. Wilson on the night of 9 September 1872; both were arrested for rioting.

43. Briggs had been a member of the Ku Klux Klan prior to his initiation into "Scott's Council," a Union League unit in Yorkville.

44. Hall fell into disfavor with the Republican Party and sometime in 1872 Colonel Lewis Merrill charged him with "Official Misconduct," alleging he had used the office of probate judge to line his own pockets. During the campaign of August 1872 Hall spoke to about 500 from the steps of the courthouse, denying the charges. Louise Pettus, *Samuel B. Hall and Major Lewis Merrill* (Rock Hill, SC: *The Quarterly*, York County Genealogical and Historical Society, 1997), p. 24. He was arrested June 1873 in Charleston on nine warrants, issued by Trial Justice R. L. Cook of Rock Hill, charging him with embezzlement and official misconduct. The affidavits stated that while Hall was the probate judge of York County he received certain sums of money for the sale of estates, for which he failed to account properly. Hall maintained the charges were false. Those charging Hall were: R. L. Lindsey ($240), Robert Coonrod ($269.36), E. J. Montgomery ($142.00), Henderson Martin ($168.96), J. M. Steele ($154.66), W. D. Parks ($73.50), James A. Erwin ($788.76), M. V. Darwin ($171.42), and Thomas McGill ($388.00). "Arrest of Samuel B. Hall," *Yorkville Enquirer*, 3 June 1873. In October of that same year, he pleaded guilty to assault and battery on I. Witherspoon and was sentenced to pay $1.00 plus costs or receive ten days in jail; no particulars of this case were given. The final outcome of the "Official Misconduct" charges was that Hall was fined $1,000 and given one-year imprisonment in the county jail. Louise Pettus *Samuel B. Hall and Major Lewis Merrill* (Rock Hill, SC: *The Quarterly*, York County Genealogical and Historical Society, 1997), p. 24. After Hall defected in the first part of 1873, he wrote an exposé on the workings of the Republicans in York County.

45. Johnson was campaigning for County School Commissioner. Later he was appointed trial justice. On 27 December 1871, a number of people petitioned Governor Scott for Johnson's removal because of incompetence. They claimed he would do "everything to make money by swindling." Governor Robert K. Scott's Papers, Box 18, Folder 39, South Carolina Department of Archives and History, Columbia, SC.

46. "Radical Meetings," *Yorkville Enquirer*, 15 September 1870.

47. John Hannibal White was born in Yorkville, 26 December 1828. He was elected to serve as a representative in the first General Assembly during Reconstruction and earned the respect of both blacks and whites. In 1874, Congressman Cain appointed his son, William H. White, to a cadetship at West Point.

48. Samuel B. Hall, *A Shell in the Radical Camp* (Charleston, SC, 1873), p. 36.

49. O'Connell was appointed a census taker by Governor Scott to "provide for an enumeration of the inhabitants" of York County for 1870. He was a native of Pennsylvania and educated in Rome. Upon his return to the United States he joined the Republican Party and served two terms as a member of the South Carolina legislature from 1868 to 1872 when he failed to receive a nomination from his party. At that time he unsuccessfully ran as an independent candidate. O'Connell died at home 18 January 1875.

50. Samuel B. Hall, *A Shell in the Radical Camp* (Charleston, SC, 1873), pp. 39–40.

51. This listing is taken from a larger list which was made up from an official report of the adjutant and inspector general of South Carolina, reported to the Legislature 22 November 1870; distribution extended to the date of the fall elections but not afterward. United States Congress, *Report of the Joint Select Committee to Inquire into the Condition of Affairs in the Late Insurrectionary States* (Washington, DC: Government Printing Office, 1872; reprint New York: AMS Press, 1968), pp. 543–45.

52. "State Items," *Yorkville Enquirer*, 18 August 1870.

53. "Organize White Companies," *Yorkville Enquirer*, 15 September 1870.

54. "The Militia Question," *Yorkville Enquirer*, 22 September 1870. Doctor Neagle's argument is somewhat weakened by the knowledge that he was a Radical, served as comptroller-general for the state under Governor Robert K. Scott, and won a seat in the South Carolina House in 1868 on the Radical ticket. Like a number of Scalawags, Neagle had questionable character; the *Charleston Mercury* reported 21 February 1868 that Neagle had been expelled from Davidson College for stealing. Benjamin Chad Simpson, *Heroes or Hoodlums: The White Southern Republicans in Reconstruction South Carolina* (College of Charleston, 1997), p. 7.

55. "White Companies," *Yorkville Enquirer*, 22 September 1870.

56. "The Recent Election," *Yorkville Enquirer*, 10 November 1870.

57. Richard Zuczek, *State of Rebellion: Reconstruction in South Carolina* (Columbia: University of South Carolina Press, 1996), p. 89.

58. Allen W. Trelease, *White Terror* (New York: Harper & Row, 1971), p. 356.

59. H. K. Roberts to Governor Scott, 6 December 1870, Box 13, Folder 20, Governor Robert K. Scott's Papers, South Carolina Department of Archives and History, Columbia, SC.

60. Allen W. Trelease, *White Terror* (New York: Harper & Row, 1971), p. 364. On 15 October 1873 the grand jury appointed Hannibal White guardian of the Rountree children: Albert, James, Frank, Alice, Clarenda and Frances. White sent Alice and Clarenda to Shelby, North Carolina, for their education. In hopes to reduce the first payment of $508.16 to White, the grand jury unsuccessfully attempted to prove the illegitimacy of the three boys. "Card from Hon. J. Hannibal White," *Yorkville Enquirer*, 25 May 1876,

61. Watson later became treasurer of York County. In September 1877, after

Wade Hampton became governor, Watson was served a warrant for embezzlement of county funds.

62. "Just A-Rolling Along the Way," *Yorkville Enquirer*, 14 July 1933.

4 — The Klan Wars

1. According to testimony at the trials conducted in Columbia, SC, a mill belonging to Doctor Allison was the first arson target in York County, in October 1870. "The Trial of the Ku Klux," *Yorkville Enquirer*, 13 December 1871.

2. Mary Davis Brown Diaries, 15–16 December 1870, Manuscript Division, South Caroliniana Library, USC, Columbia, SC.

3. Ibid. 24 January 1871.

4. "The Recent Burnings," *Yorkville Enquirer*, 2 February 1871.

5. As late as 1876, a Beaufort state senator advised the Negroes "that the torch at night was their safest and surest weapon." Alfred B. Williams, *Hampton and His Redshirts: South Carolina's Deliverance in 1876* (Charleston, SC: Walker, Evans & Cogswell Company, 1935), p. 54.

6. Allen W. Trelease, *White Terror* (New York: Harper & Row, 1971), p. 364. In October, Rose's home had been attacked by the Klan and riddled with bullets while he was away.

7. "Exaggeration," *Yorkville Enquirer*, 2 February 1871.

8. Allen W. Trelease, *White Terror* (New York: Harper & Row, 1971), p. 364

9. Ibid.

10. John S. Reynolds, *Reconstruction in South Carolina 1865–1877* (Columbia, SC: The State Co., 1905), p. 189.

11. Merrill, an avowed Republican, testified to the bad character of Rose and that he believed Rose had fired the signal volley from the hotel window to begin the fires around Yorkville. United States Congress, *Testimony Taken by the Joint Select Committee to Inquire into the Condition of Affairs in the Late Insurrectionary States* (Washington, DC: Government Printing Office, 1872; reprint New York: AMS Press, 1968), p. 577.

12. Allen W. Trelease, *White Terror* (New York: Harper & Row, 1971), pp. 364–65.

13. "Exaggeration," *Yorkville Enquirer*, 2 February 1871.

14. Mary Davis Brown Diaries, 30 January 1871, Manuscript Division, South Caroliniana Library, USC, Columbia, SC.

15. United States Congress, *Testimony Taken by the Joint Select Committee to Inquire into the Condition of Affairs in the Late Insurrectionary States* (Washington, DC: Government Printing Office, 1872; reprint New York: AMS Press, 1968), 2: 711. James William Avery had served in the 5th SC Infantry along with Dr. Rufus Bratton, the company's surgeon. It was mentioned in the Klan trials that Major Avery helped organize the Klan in 1868 and was the grand chief (probably the grand giant) of the York County Klan. He was arrested and taken to Columbia for trial. Fearing the outcome of the trial, several of Avery's friends planned his escape by leaving a saddled horse nearby. During a recess he escaped from the federal authorities and made his way to Canada. The federal government offered an award of $60,000 for his arrest. His family later joined him, and they lived in peace for ten years. After Reconstruction, he left Canada and settled in Norfolk, Virginia, where he lived until his death in 1892. Samuel Brooks

Mendenhall, *Tales of York County* (Rock Hill, SC: Reynolds & Reynolds, 1989), p. 52.

16. Samuel B. Hall, *A Shell in the Radical Camp* (Charleston, SC, 1873), p. 58.

17. "Interview with Gen. Anderson," *Yorkville Enquirer*, 2 February 1871.

18. William Edward Rose was the father of Edward M. Rose, treasurer for York County. W. E. Rose was born 13 August 1813 in Buckingham, England. He owned an iron foundry at High Shoals, North Carolina, and was proprietor of hotels in Yorkville and Columbia (The Congaree). He served in the Confederate Army, as a member of the Constitutional Convention of 1868, and as South Carolina Senator for York County from 1868 to 1872. Rose was a former member of the Church of England and one of the founders of the Yorkville Episcopal Church of the Good Shepherd in 1855. He died in Columbia 18 May 1893 and is buried in Rose Hill Cemetery in York. Emily Bellinger Reynolds and Joan Reynolds Faunt, *Biographical Directory of The Senate of the State of South Carolina 1776–1964* (Columbia, SC: South Carolina Archives Department, 1964), p. 302.

19. Mary Davis Brown Diaries, 30 January 1871, Manuscripts Division, South Caroliniana Library, USC, Columbia, SC.

20. "Interview with Gen. Anderson," *Yorkville Enquirer*, 2 February 1871.

21. "Exaggeration," *Yorkville Enquirer*, 2 February 1871.

22. "More Ku-Kluxing," *Yorkville Enquirer*, 16 February 1871.

23. "Chief Constable John B. Hubbard reported to Governor Scott on 14 February 1871: "Within last month, two have been shot, eighteen whipped, and various outrages committed. Captain Faris was driven from his home ... and the state arms in his possession [were] seized and carried away." John B. Hubbard to Governor Scott, 14 February 1871, Box 14, Folder 10, Governor Robert K. Scott's Papers, South Carolina Department of Archives and History, Columbia, SC.

24. Letters Received, Box 15, Folder 9, Governor Robert K. Scott's Papers, South Carolina Department of Archives and History, Columbia, SC.

25. Private Clark Robinson Starnes, "My military Reminiscences of the Civil War," dictated 30 January 1921, to his son, William Clark Starnes, for the Ann White Chapter, U.D.C., Rock Hill, South Carolina.

26. Samuel B. Hall, *A Shell in the Radical Camp* (Charleston, SC, 1873), pp. 55–58.

27. Ibid. Samuel B. Hall claims two boxes of cartridges were stolen.

28. "Pat" may refer to Republican Pat O'Connell who only slightly earlier had made a fiery speech in front of Davis' Hotel concerning the military presence. Since the plan was to lay the blame on Sheriff Glenn, the thieves addressed the note as though the sheriff was thumbing his nose at O'Connell. Glenn was indicted in 1872 as a member of the Ku Klux Klan.

29. "Another Outrage," *Yorkville Enquirer*, 23 February 1871.

30. Arms belonging to the black militia in the Rock Hill area, when surrendered, were placed in the custody of a Mr. Russell, an agent of the C. E. & A. Railroad, and stored in the depot.

31. "Rock Hill Correspondence," *Yorkville Enquirer*, 23 February 1871. Shortly after a meeting between W. M. McDonald of Chester County and colonels Yocum and Puffer, McDonald wrote Governor Scott on 16 July 1872 suggesting that Pride "who lives in Rock Hill, a little town in York County and very business [sic] little place" be used to assist Scott "in any matter" in York County. "[He] is a very shrewd and active man in all public matters." Col. Yocum to Governor Scott, 16

Notes—Chapter 4

July 1872, Box 21, Folder 19, Governor Robert K. Scott's Papers, South Carolina Department of Archives and History, Columbia, SC.

32. Samuel B. Hall, *A Shell in the Radical Camp* (Charleston, SC, 1873), pp. 55–58. McCaffrey testified that the ammunition was thrown in Bloodworth's well. United States Congress, *Report of the Joint Select Committee to Inquire into the Conditions of Affairs in the Late Insurrectionary States* (Washington, DC: Government Printing Office, 1872; reprint New York: AMS Press, 1968), 3: 1368.

33. Allen W. Trelease, *White Terror* (New York: Harper & Row, 1971), p. 366.

34. John S. Reynolds, *Reconstruction in South Carolina 1865–1877* (Columbia, SC: The State Co., 1905), pp. 189–90.

35. "More Incendiary Fires," *Yorkville Enquirer*, 23 February 1871.

36. Letter from Hugh K. Roberts to Sheriff Glenn, 6 March 1871, Box 15, Folder 16, Governor Robert K. Scott's Papers, South Carolina Department of Archives and History, Columbia, SC.

37. John S. Reynolds, *Reconstruction in South Carolina 1865–1877* (Columbia, SC: The State Co., 1905), pp. 189–90

38. United States Congress, *Testimony Taken by the Joint Select Committee to Inquire into the Condition of Affairs in the Late Insurrectionary States* (Washington, DC: Government Printing Office, 1872; reprint New York: AMS Press, 1968), 2: 709–10.

39. Allen W. Trelease, *White Terror* (New York: Harper & Row, 1971), p. 367.

40. Christopher, Commander of Company C of the 18th United States Infantry, killed himself 4 May 1874 in his office in the McCaw Building. It was reported he was in "great trouble and his mind in much distress, owing to the recent treatment of his family at the hands of some of his relations at the north...." Reports told that when Christopher's father refused a visit from the captain's family, he began drinking heavily. On the evening of Christopher's death, he and his wife had words concerning his drunkenness. When she did not permit him into her room, he immediately went downstairs and shot himself in the head. W. B. Williams, acting coroner of York County, impaneled a jury consisting of T. J. Bell, I. D. Witherspoon, H. F. Adicks, T. M. Dobson, J. S. Lewis, John J. Smith, Joseph Herndon, J. M. Whitaker, L. M. Grist, J. Ed. Jefferys, Thomas S. Jefferys and T. C. Dunlap; they ruled his death a suicide. Christopher, 41 years old, was a native of Philadelphia. His wife and two children survived him. Lieutenant J. K. Hyer, who was immediately promoted to captain, replaced him. "Suicide of Capt. Christopher," *Yorkville Enquirer*, 7 May 1874.

41. Richard Zuczek, "The Federal Government's attack on the Ku Klux Klan: A Reassessment," *South Carolina Historical Magazine*, 1997 (January): 49.

42. News of the tumult in York reached the Robert J. Brown family at their farm in the Beersheba Presbyterian Church community on February 27: "...a Curerer [courier] has come with the news that the negroes has threatned to rise down below york to night and kill from the cradle to the grave and oure young men is all ordered to go ... ninty yankeyes [have] been sent up to york to day to try to keep peace...." Mary Davis Brown Diaries, 27 February 1871, Manuscript Division, South Caroliniana Library, USC, Columbia, SC. Several days before, on February 24, Governor Scott received a telegram from the headquarters of the Department of the South at Louisville, KY. Brigadier General Alfred Terry notified him, "A company has been ordered from Charleston to Yorkville."

43. Russell, at the time, operated the barroom in Rose's Hotel. Later — sometime in October 1871— Russell was appointed United States marshal for York County, relieving R. L. Hope. "Deputy Marshal Appointed," *Yorkville Enquirer*, 2 November 1871.

44. Samuel B. Hall, *A Shell in the Radical Camp* (Charleston, SC, 1873), p. 59.

45. United States Congress, *Testimony Taken by the Joint Select Committee to Inquire into the Condition of Affairs in the Late Insurrectionary States* (Washington, DC: Government Printing Office, 1872; reprint New York: AMS Press, 1968), 2: 706.

46. Private papers of the W. P. Thomson family, York County, S.C.

47. The Union Reform Party together with other conservatives established the semisecret Council of Safety in November 1870 to "protect the outnumbered white population against the menace of a Negro rising." A printed constitution of the group was distributed in January 1871. Any relationship between the council and the Klan is yet to be discovered. Allen W. Trelease, *White Terror* (New York: Harper & Row, 1971), p. 352. By late February 1871, Republican Edward Rose had in his possession some pamphlets issued by the Council of Safety. United States Congress, *Testimony Taken by the Joint Select Committee to Inquire into the Condition of Affairs in the Late Insurrectionary States* (Washington, DC: Government Printing Office, 1872; reprint New York: AMS Press, 1968), 3: 1288.

5 — Federal Intervention

1. "To Labor Is to Pray," *Yorkville Enquirer*, 11 January 1872.

2. Allen W. Trelease, *White Terror* (New York: Harper & Row, 1971) p. 366; United States Congress, *Testimony Taken by the Joint Select Committee to Inquire into the Condition of Affairs in the Late Insurrectionary States* (Washington, DC: Government Printing Office, 1872; reprint New York: AMS Press, 1968), 3: 1499.

3. United States Congress, *Testimony Taken by the Joint Select Committee to Inquire into the Condition of Affairs in the Late Insurrectionary States* (Washington, DC: Government Printing Office, 1872; reprint New York: AMS Press, 1968), 3:1292.

4. "The Prospects," *Yorkville Enquirer*, 20 April 1871.

5. Dr. William H. Walling to Governor Scott, 23 January 1871, Box 14, Folder 16, Governor Robert K. Scott's Papers, Department of Archives and History, Columbia, SC. Mr. Donald McSwain who owns the land where the Bullock's Creek mine was located relates that the mining operation worked a large number of blacks and thus became a target. The McSwain family tradition relates that the mine was eventually closed due to Klan harassment. Conversation with Donald McSwain 24 December 1999.

6. Florence J. Higgins to Governor Scott, 9 January 1871, Box 14, Folder 1, Governor Scott's Papers, South Carolina Department of Archives and History, Columbia, SC.

7. "Public Meeting at Clay Hill," *Yorkville Enquirer*, 16 February 1871. Republican Samuel B. Hall related that there were no chapters of the Union League in York County by March 1872: "…the K. K.'s said there should be no leagues, and there were none in York County." Samuel B. Hall, *A Shell in the Radical Camp* (Charleston, SC, 1873), p. 74. Although the Union League ceased, another organization rose in its place known as the "Great Brotherhood" or the "United Brotherhood." It was a more secret organization conceived by a Republican power group

Notes—Chapter 5

in Columbia known as the "Ring." The leadership comprised 12 members of the legislature and others who held state offices or positions. "Scott's Ku Klux," *Yorkville Enquirer*, 18 April 1872. According to Hall, the Ring was very weak in influence and "not worth joining." Samuel B. Hall, *A Shell in the Radical Camp* (Charleston, SC, 1873), p. 75. The Ring schemed to buy up as much stock in the Columbia-Greenville Rail Road as they could for $1.75 per share (some were purchased with state bonds); then they bribed Assembly members to put the railroad up for sale for an elevated amount of $700,000.

8. Michael W. Fitzgerald, *The Union League Movement in the Deep South* (Baton Rouge: University of Louisiana Press, 1989), p. 216.

9. Ibid., p. 213.

10. Allen W. Trelease, *White Terror* (New York: Harper & Row, 1971), p. 367.

11. Telegram from General Alfred Terry to Governor Scott, 11 March 1871, Box 23, Folder 8, Governor Robert K. Scott's Papers, South Carolina Department of Archives and History, Columbia, SC.

12. Richard Zuczek, "The Federal Government's Attack on the Ku Klux Klan: A Reassessment," *South Carolina Historical Magazine*, 1997 (January): 50.

13. Richard Zuczek, *State of Rebellion: Reconstruction in South Carolina* (Columbia, SC: University of South Carolina Press, 1996), p. 93.

14. Sheriff Glenn to Governor Scott, 13 March 1871, Box 15, Folder 17, Governor Robert K. Scott's Papers, South Carolina Department of Archives and History, Columbia, SC.

15. Captain Christopher to Governor Scott, 15 March 1871, Box 15, Folder 19, Governor Scott's Papers, South Carolina Department of Archives and History, Columbia, SC.

16. Allen W. Trelease, *White Terror* (New York: Harper & Row, 1971), pp. 353–54.

17. Merrill would remain in South Carolina until June 1873. After suffering from poor health and two extended sick leaves, he retired from military service in 1886. At that time he was recommended to be promoted to lieutenant colonel but Southern Senators who held him in contempt for the money he made ($20,000) for the arrests and conviction of Klansmen, successfully blocked the promotion for four years. Allen W. Trelease, *White Terror* (New York: Harper and Row, 1971), p. 417. Merrill died 27 February 1896 in a Presbyterian hospital in Philadelphia, of a kidney infection. When the *Yorkville Enquirer* gave notice of Merrill's death, the subject of the money earned by the commandant was included in the column. "Lewis Merrill Dead," *Yorkville Enquirer*, 4 March 1896.

18. "Merrill Assumes Post," *Yorkville Enquirer*, 16 March 1871. "Just A-Rolling Along the Way," *Yorkville Enquirer*, 3 June 1932.

19. Telegram from General Alfred Terry to Governor Scott, 27 March 1871, Box 24, Folder 8, Governor Robert K. Scott's Papers, South Carolina Department of Archives and History, Columbia, SC.

20. Ibid.

21. Richard Zuczek, "The Federal Government's Attack on the Ku Klux Klan: A Reassessment," *South Carolina Historical Magazine*, 1997 (January): 50.

22. *New York Daily Tribune*, 13 November 1871, quoted in Allen W. Trelease, *White Terror* (New York: Harper & Row, 1971), p. 405.

23. Richard Zuczek, "The Federal Government's Attack on the Ku Klux Klan: A Reassessment," *South Carolina Historical Magazine*, 1997 (January): 52.

Notes — Chapter 5

24. United States Congress, *Testimony Taken by the Joint Select Committee to Inquire into the Condition of Affairs in the Late Insurrectionary States* (Washington, DC: Government Printing Office, 1872; reprint New York: AMS Press, 1968), 2: 713.

25. "The Negro Ku Klux," *Yorkville Enquirer*, 30 March 1871. One of the robbers, Bill Garrison, was not apprehended until February 1873. "Arrest of Bill Garrison," *Yorkville Enquirer*, 6 March 1873. In October 1872, Elias Evens and Lafayette McCaw were given a pardon for Ku Kluxing and their part in the robbery after serving one half of their three-year sentences. "Pardoned by the Governor," *Yorkville Enquirer*, 31 October 1872. In 1886, another all-black association appeared in the Bullock's Creek Township with the deadly promise to steal from the whites and kill any witnesses. The first and only murder perpetrated by this group was 12-year-old Johnny Lee Good. This association was dissolved after a vigilante group stormed the Yorkville jail and hanged the five murderers.

26. "Meeting at Bullock's Creek," *Yorkville Enquirer*, 23 March 1871.

27. Prior to the Civil War, General Law occupied the professor's chair in the Kings Mountain Military Academy in Yorkville. He resigned so that he might move to Alabama and serve in the Confederate Army from that state. He later returned to Yorkville. In February 1873, he returned again to Alabama and lived in Tuskegee.

28. "Public Meeting of the Blacks," *Yorkville Enquirer*, 6 April 1871.

29. *Yorkville Enquirer*, 11 April 1871.

30. Supposedly Elias Hill was born the same year as Confederate General D. H. Hill and Elias's mother, Dorcus, was nursemaid to her white master's son. Elias grew up with his master's son and was taught by him as he himself learned. Elias received a valuable education and was able to read ancient Greek fluently. After the war was over and until Elias Hill migrated to Liberia in 1872, General Hill would bring the black preacher to his Charlotte home to spend weekends. "Just A-Rolling Along the Way," *Yorkville Enquirer*, 31 October 1933.

31. "To the Citizens of York County," *Yorkville Enquirer*, 25 May 1871.

32. "To the Citizens of York County," *Yorkville Enquirer*, 1 June 1871.

33. "To the Citizens of York County," *Yorkville Enquirer*, 8 June 1871. Reported in this issue was information about an 80-foot flagpole which had been erected at the military post near the Yorkville depot. Another flagpole was erected by the order of Lieutenant Benner in front of Rose's Hotel, then being used as a barracks for the Federal troops. In 1879, the flagstaff at Rose's was deemed unsafe and was removed in March of that year.

34. "To the Citizens of York County," *Yorkville Enquirer*, 15 June 1871.

35. James E. Sefton, *The United States Army and Reconstruction 1865–1877* (Baton Rouge: Louisiana State University Press, 1967), p. 225 quoting from typescript of Winfield S. Harvey's notes found in the Edward S. Godfrey Papers, Library of Congress, Washington, DC. Sefton writes that Godfrey's papers commence in 1868 while the Seventh Cavalry was on the plains. In 1871, Godfrey was a lieutenant in Company K of the Seventh. Later in 1876, he was in command of this company at the Battle of the Little Bighorn. He along with others of Company K managed to survive because they were with Captain Frederick Benteen's battalion which was not with Custer's force. Sefton, p. 225, note 28.

36. Kenneth M. Stampp, *The Era of Reconstruction: 1865–1877* (New York: Vintage Books, 1965), p. 200.

37. The formal name of this committee was the Joint Select Committee to Inquire into the Condition of Affairs in the Late Insurrectionary States. The *Yorkville Enquirer* amusingly entitled it "the sub–Outrage Committee." "The Ku Klux Committee," *Yorkville Enquirer*, 27 July 1871.

38. Richard Zuczek, "The Federal Government's Attack on the Ku Klux Klan: A Reassessment," *South Carolina Historical Magazine*, 1997 (January): 54.

39. Elijah Givens Feemster (1822–96) of Bullock's Creek served in the Broad River Light Infantry during the Civil War. After joining the KKK, he "divulged [its secrets at] the first opportunity offered, and was branded a traitor by Dr. Samuel A. Smith." Jerry L. West; *A Historical Sketch of People, Places and Homes of Bullock's Creek, South Carolina* (Richburg, SC: Chester District Genealogical Society, 1986), p. 25. Kirkland L. Gunn was also branded a traitor. John S. Reynolds, *Reconstruction in South Carolina*, (Columbia, SC: The State Co., 1905), p. 205.

40. Owens was not one of the "Pukes," but he belonged to the Republican Party, was a member of the Union League, and was well known among the local Radicals. It was common knowledge — even with Merrill — that he had taken part in the raid on the probate judge's office. Samuel B. Hall, *A Shell in the Radical Camp* (Charleston, SC, 1873), pp. 55–58.

41. Randolph Abbott Shotwell, *The Shotwell Papers* (Raleigh, NC: The North Carolina Historical Commission, 1936), 3: 403. In a letter to Lyman C. Draper, James Madison Hope of the Blairsville Community suggested that Wallace might give Draper additional information if he would "feed his reconstructed vanity a little...." J. M. Hope to Lyman C. Draper, 31 December 1873, 15 VV: 311, Draper Manuscripts, State Historical Society of Wisconsin, Madison, Wisconsin.

42. Allen W. Trelease, *White Terror* (New York: Harper & Row, 1971), p. 375.

43. Samuel B. Hall, *A Shell in the Radical Camp* (Charleston, SC, 1873), pp. 65–66; "The Barry-Wallace Difficulty," *Yorkville Enquirer*, 3 August 1871.

44. "Street Affray," *Yorkville Enquirer*, 27 July 1871. After an investigation by the Town Council, Snyder was entirely exonerated.

45. Allen W. Trelease, *White Terror* (New York: Harper & Row, 1971), pp. 375–76.

46. United States Congress, *Testimony Taken by the Joint Select Committee to Inquire into the Condition of Affairs in the Late Insurrectionary States* (Washington, DC: Government Printing Office, 1872; reprint New York: AMS Press, 1986), 3:1471–72. The six murders Merrill referred to were of: Tom Roundtree, 3 December 1870; Anderson Brown, 25 February 1871; Matthew Boyce, 1 March 1871; James Williams, about 6 March 1871; Alexander Leech, 7 March 1871; and Lot Campbell (or Miller), date not discovered. United States Congress, *Testimony Taken by the Joint Select Committee to Inquire into the Condition of Affairs in the Late Insurrectionary States* (Washington, DC: Government Printing Office, 1872; reprint New York: AMS Press, 1986), 3:1472. Persons reported as being whipped or otherwise injured were: Tony Wallace (or Hill), 10 January 1871; Sam Simrill, Jordan Tate, Abraham Webb, and Peter Watson, all in the middle of February 1871; John Tate, end of February 1871; Andy Kitcar [Cathcart], 11 March 1871; Martha Woods and Sylvester Barron, both on 27 April 1871; Creecy Adams, 12 May 1871; Martha ?, 27 May 1871; Phebe Smith, 12 May 1871; and Charley Barron's wife, 13 July 1871. United State Congress, *Testimony Taken by the Joint Select Committee to Inquire into the Condition of Affairs in the Late Insurrectionary States* (Washington, DC: Government Printing Office, 1872; reprint New York: AMS Press, 1986), 3:1474.

47. Corbin, a Vermonter, a captain of black troops during the war, became a federal district attorney sometime later. He acted as a legal adviser to the Constitutional Convention of 1868 and was one of the few federal officials who promoted the Republican Party in South Carolina. Joel Williamson, *After Slavery, The Negro in South Carolina During Reconstruction 1861–1877* (Hanover, Wesleyan University Press, University of New England, 1990), p. 364.

48. Richard Zuczek, *State of Rebellion: Reconstruction in South Carolina* (Columbia, SC: University of South Carolina Press, 1996), p. 98.

49. "Personal," *Yorkville Enquirer*, 14 September 1871.

50. "Charged with Ku-Kluxing," *Yorkville Enquirer*, 28 September 1871. Allen W. Trelease, *White Terror* (New York: Harper & Row, 1971), p. 402.

51. "Charged with Ku-Kluxing," *Yorkville Enquirer*, 28 September 1871.

52. "The Circuit Court," *Yorkville Enquirer*, 28 September 1871.

53. Lou Falkner Williams, *The Great South Carolina Ku Klux Klan Trials, 1871–1872* (Athens, GA: University of Georgia Press, 1996), p. 45.

54. "Report of the Grand Jury," *Yorkville Enquirer*, 5 October 1871.

55. Allen W. Trelease, *White Terror* (New York: Harper & Row, 1971), pp. 376–77, 380.

56. When Wade Hampton became governor, the General Assembly authorized a joint committee to ascertain whether any state funds had been illegally used during the Reconstruction. The committee reported that fraud was perpetrated on the people of South Carolina when Governor Scott issued a proclamation on 28 July 1871 offering $200 for each person arrested and convicted under the Enforcement Act. Over $30,000 had been paid out and distributed by the proclamation. Alrutheus Ambush Taylor, *The Negro in South Carolina During the Reconstruction* (New York: AMS Press, 1971), p. 280. Supposedly Merrill was the recipient of the $200 reward offered by Governor Scott for each person convicted of Ku Kluxing. One eyewitness suggested the payment to Merrill was somewhat higher. John A. Leland wrote that Merrill was instrumental in getting an appropriation of $35,000 from the Legislature in 1871–72. Of this sum, he received the lion's share of $21,800 for 109 convictions. John A. Leland, *A Voice from South Carolina* (Charleston, SC, 1879) pp. 209–12. Congress investigated Merrill in 1878 on a matter relating to ill-gotten gains. Ibid. p. 134. Samuel B. Hall called Merrill the "Prairie Bull of Kansas" who was always looking for a spot of green (money) to devour.

57. T. M. Graham to Governor Scott, 12 August 1871, Box 17, Folder 14, Governor Robert K. Scott's Papers, South Carolina Department of Archives and History, Columbia, SC.

58. Doctor L. A. Hill to Governor Scott, 28 October 1871, Box 18, Folder 8, Governor Robert K. Scott's Papers, South Carolina Department of Archives and History, Columbia, SC.

6 — *Colonel Merrill Begins Arrests*

1. Lou Falkner Williams, *The Great South Carolina Ku Klux Klan Trials, 1871–1872* (Athens: University of Georgia Press, 1996), p. 46.

2. Richard Zuczek, *State of Rebellion: Reconstruction in South Carolina* (Columbia: University of South Carolina Press, 1996), p. 98.

3. Mary Davis Brown Diaries, 15–16 October 1871, Manuscript Division, South Caroliniana Library, USC, Columbia, SC.

4. Allen W. Trelease, *White Terror* (New York: Harper & Row, 1971), p. 403. Years later it was reported that Merrill's private secretary Dick Clinton, a Klan sympathizer, had supplied to the Klan leaders a list of names for whom warrants were issued. Upon discovery, he was arrested and served a prison term for his duplicity. *Rock Hill Herald*, 9 April 1904.

5. Mary Davis Brown Diaries, 17 October 1871, Manuscript Division, South Caroliniana Library, USC, Columbia, SC.

6. Ibid., 22 October 1871.

7. According to testimony heard at the November 1871 term of the Federal Court held in Columbia, SC, the Sherer men were sworn in by Chambers Brown while they were on their way to raid the home of Jim Williams. Everyone was dressed in robes except for the Sherers, who evidently had no disguises because they had only recently been inducted. "The Trial of The Ku Klux," *Yorkville Enquirer*, 13 December 1871. When they were released in 1873, their mother was not home to receive them; she had died 13 July 1872.

8. While in Albany penitentiary, William L. Hood and Captain J. W. Mitchell wrote to scalawag Congressman A. S. Wallace assuring him that they always were his friends and would always vote for him if pardoned. R. A. Shotwell classified Hood and Mitchell as having a "weakness of backbone" and surrendering their principles and manhood. Randolph Abbott Shotwell, *The Shotwell Papers* (Raleigh, NC: The North Carolina Historical Commission, 1936), 3: 376–77.

9. "Arrests of Citizens," *Yorkville Enquirer*, 26 October 1871. Allen W. Trelease, *White Terror* (New York: Harper & Row, 1971), p. 402.

10. An obituary printed in the weekly *Union Times*, Union, South Carolina, reported Hugh H. Kell was shot and killed near Fort Worth, Texas, 6 June 1889 .That notice stated, "Many of our readers, no doubt, will remember Hugh in connection with his shrewdness, by which he escaped the clutches of Maj. Merrill and then the U. S. Court during the incarceration and punishment of the Ku Klux, in 1871 and '72." Tommy J. Vaughan & Dorothy Harris Phifer, *Union County South Carolina Death Notices from Early Newspapers 1852–1914* (Spartanburg, SC: Pinckney District Chapter South Carolina Genealogical Society, 1995), p. 36.

11. J. W. Dobson was a dealer in groceries, hardware and plantation supplies and operated a large and successful livery business in Yorkville. He came to Yorkville in 1868, at the age of 20, to work with T. M. Dobson who owned a mercantile establishment. He managed the grocery department of Dobson's store. In 1879, in partnership with R. A. Parish, he opened a grocery store in Yorkville, and after seven years the partnership was dissolved and he continued his business alone. His success went on for at least another decade. *Yorkville Enquirer*, 27 February 1889.

12. "The Situation," *Yorkville Enquirer*, 2 November 1871.

13. In 1856, $1,400 was raised to send seven men (Thomas B. Whitesides, Meek Whitesides, John Whitesides, Ross Bird, C. A. Connor, R. H. McClain and Isaac B. Dunlap) from York County to Kansas to join the ranks of slaveholders and attempt to gain control that territory's legislature. Thomas B. Whitesides was elected to the territorial Legislature in 1857 from Leavenworth County. A few months later, in December, Whitesides and other proslavery legislators were unseated when their election was found to be fraudulent. At that time the Free Staters gained control of the legislature. Whitesides remained in Kansas for several years before returning to York County. *The Quarterly* (Rock Hill, SC,

York County Genealogical and Historical Society, 1998), June and September 1998.

14. Robert Hayes Mitchell was the first man brought to trial; his lawyers, A. H. Stanbery and Reverdy Johnson received $15,000 to defend him. Randolph Abbott Shotwell, *The Shotwell Papers* (Raleigh: The North Carolina Historical Commission, 1936), 3: 200. One of the court recorders for the federal government was Benn Pitman who founded a school of stenography. He was assisted by Louis F. Post, a law clerk in the office of United States Attorney David T. Corbin, who later became Assistant Secretary in the Department of Labor. "Echo of the K.K.K.," *Yorkville Enquirer*, 17 February 1914.

15. Segregated from the white prisoners, black men Samuel Stewart, Minor Moore, Frank Fewell and Cornelius Pride were held in the guardhouse.

16. Mary Davis Brown Diaries, 18 November 1871, Manuscript Division, South Caroliniana Library, USC, Columbia, SC. It is curious that none of the five men she mentions appear on any list of those arrested.

17. Douglas Summers Brown, *A City Without Cobwebs* (Columbia: University of South Carolina Press, 1953), p. 151. Toole was born in Charleston and came to Rock Hill in 1870. He opened the first barbershop in the town and served many of the leading white citizens. His brother, Gray Toole, was personal barber to President Grover Cleveland. *The Herald*, 3 May 1952.

18. "An Act to Provide for the Protection of Persons, Property and the Public Peace," No. 337. V. XIV.

19. United States Congress, *Report of the Joint Select Committee to Inquire into the Condition of Affairs in the Late Insurrectionary States* (Washington, DC: Government Printing Office, 1872; reprint New York: AMS Press, 1968), p. 566.

20. "The Situation," *Yorkville Enquirer*, 2 November 1871.

21. Interview with Lee Guiton in B. A. Botkin, *Lay My Burden Down* (Athens: University of Georgia Press, 1989), p. 68.

22. Visitation may not have been as lenient as the correspondent indicated. On 1 November 1871, a notice was posted to the door of the jail, "On and from this date, none but immediate relatives, (wives, fathers, mothers, brothers and sisters) will be permitted to visit the prisoners in jail. By order of Colonel Merrill." "The Situation," *Yorkville Enquirer*, 2 November 1871.

23. *New York Tribune*, 23 November 1871 (Copy located in Templeton Family Papers, Manuscript Division, South Caroliniana Library, USC, Columbia, SC). This reporter's remarks concerning the jail sharply contrast with the praises sung by the *Yorkville Enquirer*, 12 April 1855, just after construction was finished: "It is a beautiful building, reflecting equal credit on the Commissioners and our townsman Capt. Thomas H. Smith, the architect.... We can now challenge the State to produce a better Court House and Jail than ours. They are both large and commodious, and well adapted to the comfort of the unfortunate inmates...."

24. Contemporary observer John A. Leland emphatically denies the existence of a Klan in Laurens County before or after 1870. He states that the so-called "riot" of 20 October 1870 (the day after the elections) taught the black man in Laurens county that the white man had a limit; once pushed beyond that limit, he would not hesitate to murder. Leland believed the riot prevented any need for the Ku Klux Klan in his home county and that the arrests were contrived for appearance. John A. Leland, *A Voice from South Carolina* (Charleston, SC, 1879),

p. 91. Researchers of the past three decades likely disagree with Leland's assessment.

25. Richard Zuczek, "The Federal Government's Attack on the Ku Klux Klan: A Reassessment," *South Carolina Historical Magazine*, 1997 (January): 55.

26. Allen W. Trelease, *White Terror* (New York: Harper & Row, 1971), p. 404.

27. "Lawson & Eb is gone again...." Mary Davis Brown Diaries, 5 February 1872, Manuscript Division, South Caroliniana Library, USC, Columbia, SC.

28. Mary Davis Brown Diaries, 16 October 1871, Manuscript Division, South Caroliniana Library, USC, Columbia, SC. The town of York must have been in great turmoil with so many men fleeing to escape arrest following the declaration of martial law. Brown mentions her "Cousin Daubson," a merchant in York who was a victim of the pandemonium. She wrote, "...cousin Daubson is badly down, he had laid in a great stock of new goods. His clerks [are] all gone and such excitement that he is not selling. He is boxen up some of his goods and sending them back." Ibid.

29. "Views and Interviews," *Yorkville Enquirer*, 14 June 1932.

7 — The Klan Trials

1. Corbin's assistant was Daniel H. Chamberlain, who subsequently served as attorney general and later governor of South Carolina.

2. Amos Akerman, a native of Georgia, was head of the newly created Justice Department. He was a driving force behind President Grant's southern policy and an advocate of federal protection of civil and political rights. He mysteriously resigned 12 December 1871. Leaving office he commented on the North's fading interest in civil rights and "Ku Kluxery" in the South and suggested that Southern Republicans would find it necessary to cease depending on federal help in promoting their efforts toward civil rights. Radical George Williams, who had little or no experience in law or civil rights enforcement, replaced him. Richard Zuczek, "The Federal Government's Attack on the Ku Klux Klan: A Reassessment," *South Carolina Historical Magazine*, 1997 (January): 58–59.

3. This Act allowed the suspension of the privilege of the writ of habeas corpus in a defined area on the discretion of the president. Richard Zuczek, "The Federal Government's Attack on the Ku Klux Klan: A Reassessment," *South Carolina Historical Magazine*, 1997 (January): 55–56.

4. Ibid.

5. For a full study of the trials see U.S. Congress, *Testimony Taken by the Joint Select Committee to Inquire into the Condition of Affairs of the Late Insurrectionary States* (Washington, DC: Government Printing Office, 1872; reprint New York, AMS Press, 1968) and *Report of the Joint Select Committee to Inquire into the Condition of Affairs of the Late Insurrectionary States* (Washington, DC: Government Printing Office, 1872; reprint New York: AMS Press, 1968).

6. John S. Reynolds, *Reconstruction in South Carolina* (Columbia, SC: The State Co., 1905), p. 202.

7. Lou Falkner Williams, *The Great South Carolina Ku Klux Klan Trials, 1871–1872* (Athens: University of Georgia Press, 1996) pp. 52–53.

8. Others tried for the raid were Sherrod "Bunk" Childers, Banks Kell, Evans Murphy, Hezekiah Porter, Sylvanus Hemphill and William Montgomery. Corbin chose to try Sherrod Childers separately from others.

9. The Ku Klux Klan Act allowed the enforcement of the 15th Amendment and imposed heavy penalties on those who "shall conspire together, or go in disguise ... for the purpose ... of depriving any person or any class of persons of the equal protection of the laws, or of equal privileges or immunities under the laws."

10. Lou Falkner Williams, *The Great South Carolina Ku Klux Klan Trials, 1871–1872* (Athens: University of Georgia Press, 1996), p. 105.

11. Ibid., p. 74.

12. Ibid., p. 113,

13. Ibid., pp. 10–11.

14. Ibid., p. 137–138.

15. John S. Reynolds, *Reconstruction in South Carolina* (Columbia, SC: The State Co., 1905), pp. 203–206.

16. "Although the United States attorneys had secured a conviction in U.S. v. Robert Hayes Mitchell, the trial had largely been a failure regarding constitutional goals...." "The long term goal of changing the social and political structure of South Carolina was a failure." Lou Falkner Williams, *The Great South Carolina Ku Klux Klan Trials, 1871–1872* (Athens: University of Georgia Press, 1996), p. 85.

17. Ibid., p. 41.

18. Richard Zuczek, "The Federal Government's Attack on the Ku Klux Klan: A Reassessment," *South Carolina Historical Magazine*, 1997 (January): 56–57.

19. Leech testified that Doctor Whitesides always had been kind to the freedmen, and that the doctor had given Leech a free bushel of corn when he was in need.

20. According to his testimony, Gunn was born in York County, lived in Yorkville, and joined the Klan in January 1871. He was sworn into the John Mitchell Klan by A. Wesley Smith and John Osborne. Gunn testified that he was present on the first raid known as the "Bill Kell raid" (William "Bill" Kell was a white Republican and president of a chapter of the Union League) and had received his orders from "Night Hawk" John Wallace. The raid was canceled when the men got to the meeting place and found Hugh Kell, the brother of Bill Kell, present. The second raid was on a black woman, Jennie Good, who lived on Dr. John Good's farm. She had made herself "a nuisance to his wife and they thought it a duty of the order to drive her away from there." Mr. Isaac Cole, a descendant of Jennie Good, told this author in the 1980s that she had been brought from Virginia and had eight children fathered by Doctor Good. Seemingly, it was Doctor Good who had made himself a nuisance to both Jennie and his wife. Gunn's testimony at the Klan trials was damning when he said that the purpose of the Klan was "to put down the Radical Klan party and rule negro suffrage." While the United States court was in session and the trials in progress, Kirkland Gunn disappeared during the night and was never heard of after that. In 1906, a skeleton was unearthed in the suburbs of Columbia; it was believed to be that of Gunn. Evidently the skeleton was identified by his near giant frame and teeth and jaw which were described as being able to crack a hickory nut. *The Gaffney Ledger*, 12 October 1906.

21. The secret grip of the Klansmen consisted of the little fingers interlaced and the forefingers placed on the wrists. The bailey word was "say" spelled out s-a-y, to which the reply also came spelled out: n-o-t-h-i-n-g. A shout of "avalanche" was given when a Klansman was in distress; he hoped to hear the response of

Notes—Chapter 7

three whistles. Another means of recognition by fellow members was to tap a man three times on the ear; the tapped man would respond by placing his right hand in his pants pocket and placing his left foot forward. United States Congress, *Testimony Taken by the Joint Select Committee to Inquire into the Condition of Affairs in the Late Insurrectionary States* (Washington, DC: Government Printing Office, 1872; reprint New York: AMS Press, 1968), 3: 1284.

22. United States Congress, *Testimony Taken by the Joint Select Committee to Inquire into the Condition of Affairs in the Late Insurrectionary States* (Washington, DC: Government Printing office 1872; reprint New York: AMS Press 1968), 3: 1848.

23. Lou Falkner Williams, *The Great South Carolina Ku Klux Klan Trials, 1871–1872* (Athens: The University of Georgia Press, 1996), p. 120.

24. Ibid., pp. 95–96.

25. Federal troops came to Doctor Avery's home in Ebenezer on the night of 16 June 1872 to arrest him. When the family discovered the house was surrounded and heard an order given, "Shoot him if he comes out!" Mrs. Avery made haste in hiding her husband between feather mattresses. She placed her children in the bed, went to the door where soldiers were loudly and continuously knocking, and let them into the house. While searching they eventually went to the Averys' bedroom. Mrs. Avery protested, "My little children are asleep. Please do not wake them. They will be frightened half to death if they see you." They acquiesced. After leaving the house the troops searched the grounds and outbuildings, leaving sentinels in the yard until morning. Samuel Brooks Mendenhall, *Tales of York County* (Rock Hill, SC: Reynolds & Reynolds, 1989), p. 53.

26. Reverend Cooper was the pastor of Ebenezer Presbyterian Church, Rock Hill, SC.

27. Lou Falkner Williams, *The Great South Carolina Ku Klux Klan Trials, 1871–1872* (Athens: The University of Georgia Press, 1996), pp. 96–97.

28. Ibid., p. 98.

29. "Pardon of Dr. E. T. Avery," *Yorkville Enquirer*, 1 May 1873.

30. Sentenced to one year's imprisonment.

31. Sentenced to one year's imprisonment.

32. Sentenced to one year's imprisonment and $10 fine.

33. Sentenced to one year's imprisonment.

34. Sentenced to one year's imprisonment and $10 fine.

35. Sentenced to two years' imprisonment and $50 fine.

36. Sentenced to five years' imprisonment and $1000 fine.

37. Sentenced to five years' imprisonment and $1000 fine.

38. Sentenced to six months' imprisonment and $10 fine.

39. Sentenced to three months' imprisonment and $20 fine.

40. Sentenced to two months' imprisonment.

41. Sentenced to one month's imprisonment.

42. Agnes McDill to William D. Knox, 8 January 1872, Knox Family Letters, Manuscript Division, South Caroliniana Library, USC, Columbia, SC.

43. "Transfer of Troops," *Yorkville Enquirer*, 28 March 1872.

44. "Military Arrests in Chester," *Yorkville Enquirer*, 28 March 1872.

45. All the white men were associated with Bullock's Creek Presbyterian Church in York County.

46. "Military Arrests in Chester," *Yorkville Enquirer*, 28 March 1872.

47. "The Military Prisoners," *Yorkville Enquirer*, 18 April 1872.

48. During the Saturday night raid into Union County in which Marion Harris was apprehended, Minor Paris, who was in company with Harris, was shot and killed when he attempted an escape. Captain Christopher's investigation revealed that Lieutenant Brenner, accompanied by Deputy Marshal Duncan, had given the order to shoot when Paris jumped in a nearby bateau and rowed down the river. Paris was struck by several bullets and was found dead when taken from the boat by Lieutenant Brenner. "Citizen Shot by Soldiers," *Yorkville Enquirer*, 18 April 1872.

49. "The Military Prisoners," *Yorkville Enquirer*, 18 April 1872.

50. "The United States Court," *Yorkville Enquirer*, 18 April 1872.

51. Lou Falkner Williams, *The Great South Carolina Ku Klux Klan Trials, 1871–1872* (Athens: University of Georgia Press, 1996), pp. 109–10, 121–22.

52. Richard Zuczek, "The Federal Government's Attack on the Ku Klux Klan: A Reassessment," *South Carolina Historical Magazine*, 1997 (January): 56.

53. In 1869, Mackey became so disillusioned with Republican rule in South Carolina that he resigned as a member of the Charleston city government saying he no longer wanted to be part of that "board of robbers, polygamists, perjurers and forgers, who now rule the city of Charleston." Benjamin Chad Simpson, *Heroes or Hoodlums: The White Southern Republicans in Reconstruction South Carolina* (College of Charleston, 1997), p. 19.

54. "Judge Mackey's Speech," *Yorkville Enquirer*, 16 May 1872.

55. "Arrest of John Benfield," *Yorkville Enquirer*, 14 November 1872.

56. "More Attempts at Robbery," *Yorkville Enquirer*, 7 September 1871.

57. "Circuit Court," *Yorkville Enquirer*, 14 November 1872.

58. Wilson was a white Republican living in the Blairsville community.

59. At a jousting tournament held at Rock Hill on 8 October 1869, "knight" Jones boldly entered the contest under the assumed name of "Ku Klux." "The Tournament at Rock Hill," *Yorkville Enquirer*, 14 October 1869.

60. In 1892 a skull was unearthed on the farm of D. J. Smith of Hickory Grove, about 50 yards from the Broad River. It was surmised to have belonged to a body buried there during "Ku Klux times." "Letter from Hickory Grove," *Yorkville Enquirer*, 7 September 1892.

61. Bascomb Kennedy is not on this list; he, along with Daniel Smith and Martin Hall, were released when a true bill was not returned against them. "The Circuit Court," *Yorkville Enquirer*, 14 November 1872.

62. According to testimony conducted during the trials at Columbia, Chambers Brown held a position known as "Monarch" in a Klan located in western York County. "The Trial of the Ku Klux," *Yorkville Enquirer*, 13 December 1871.

63. Napoleon Miller, known by his friends as "Pole," was identified as holding the position of "Turk" in a western York County Klan unit. "The Trial of the Ku Klux," *Yorkville Enquirer*, 13 December 1871.

64. Randolph Abbott Shotwell, *The Shotwell Papers* (Raleigh: The North Carolina Historical Commission, 1936), 3: 282.

65. "Transfer of Troops," *Yorkville Enquirer*, 27 February 1873.

66. "Returned," *Yorkville Enquirer*, 30 January 1873.

67. "Departure of Troops," *Yorkville Enquirer*, 20 1873. In 1876, the Seventh Cavalry would engage Sitting Bull in battle. From Yorkville they were to travel to Memphis, Tennessee, and then by steamer to Ft. Randall on the

Missouri River. Estimated time of travel was three to four weeks. These troops would be on the Plains a short period before being returned to the South. They served as mounted troops in Northwestern Louisiana during much of 1873 and all of 1874 before being sent to the Dakotas. While in Louisiana, their duties "were similar to those in South Carolina — aiding law officers to enforce court orders." James E. Sefton, *The United States Army and Reconstruction 1865–1877* (Baton Rouge: Louisiana State University Press, 1967), pp. 226–28.

68. "Relieved," *Yorkville Enquirer*, 6 March 1873. Previously, in December 1872, Merrill on a motion of District Attorney Corbin was admitted to practice as attorney, solicitor and counsel of the court. "The U.S. Circuit Court," *Yorkville Enquirer*, 2 January 1873.

69. "Transfer of Troops," *Yorkville Enquirer*, 27 February 1873.

8 — Peace Returns to York County

1. John S. Reynolds, *Reconstruction in South Carolina* (Columbia, SC: The State Co., 1905), pp. 137, 191.

2. United States Congress, *Testimony Taken by the Joint Select Committee to Inquire into the Condition of Affairs in the Late Insurrectionary States* (Washington, DC: Government Printing Office 1872; reprint New York: AMS Press 1968), 3: 1292. "A Gloomy Prospect," *Yorkville Enquirer*, 26 October 1871; "To Labor Is to Pray," *Yorkville Enquirer*, 11 January 1872.

3. James Spratt White IV, "History of the Ku Klux Klan in Upper South Carolina, 1868–1871" (paper prepared in 1963 at Wofford College, Spartanburg, SC, 1963), 43.

4. Major Reno was at the Battle of Little Bighorn in 1876 and commanded several companies of the Seventh Cavalry in the valley and hilltop fight. He was court-martialed in 1877 and died in 1889. Two of the companies of the Seventh Cavalry stationed in York County were massacred in the battle.

5. Richard Zuczek, "The Federal Government's Attack on the Ku Klux Klan: A Reassessment," *South Carolina Historical Magazine*, 1997 (January): 59–60.

6. Though the documentation could not be immediately located, the federal bounty laws were expanded sometime around 1871 to allow bounty hunters to cross state lines to apprehend fugitives; in 1872 the Supreme Court upheld that law. This change may have been made in an effort to capture fleeing Klansmen.

7. Chief Constable Hubbard to Governor Scott, 1872, Box 22, Folder 5, Governor Robert K. Scott's Papers, South Carolina Department of Archives and History, Columbia, SC.

8. Lou Falkner Williams, *The Great South Carolina Ku Klux Klan Trials, 1871–1872* (Athens: University of Georgia Press, 1996), p. 49.

9. Mary Davis Brown Diaries, 12, 13 March 1873, Manuscript Division, South Caroliniana Library, USC, Columbia, SC.

10. Ibid., 23 March 1873. Efforts to arrest Hall probably ceased since he and Mag Brown were married Thursday, May 1. Over 50 people attended the wedding at the Brown home and the following "infare" in spite of a rain that persisted all day. Mary Davis Brown Diaries, 1 May 1873, Manuscript Division, South Caroliniana Library, USC, Columbia, SC.

11. "Sheriff Glenn has sent out after Lawson to day[.] Harkness [R. B. Hartness] wanting to make a witness of him he don't want to be made a witness fore him." Ibid., 27 March 1873.

12. Ibid., 5 April 1873.

13. "the tryal came on to day they could doo nothing.... Lawson is set free." Ibid., 9 April 1873.

14. Lou Falkner Williams, *The Great South Carolina Ku Klux Klan Trials, 1872–1872* (Athens: University of Georgia Press, 1996), p. 123.

15. Ibid., p. 173 n. 29; "The Ku Klux," *Yorkville Enquirer*, 7 August 1873.

16. Lou Falkner Williams, *The Great South Carolina Ku Klux Klan Trials, 1871–1872* (Athens: University of Georgia Press, 1996), p. 123.

17. Williams to the Committee, reprinted in "The Ku Klux," *Yorkville Enquirer*, 7 August 1873.

18. "Imprisonment at Yorkville," *Yorkville Enquirer*, 1 May 1873. Leech served out his term in the Yorkville jail; but Moore and Wallace were sent to the Albany Penitentiary.

19. "The Colored Militia," *Yorkville Enquirer*, 5 June 1873.

20. Lou Falkner Williams, *The Great South Carolina Ku Klux Klan Trials, 1871–1872* (Athens: University of Georgia Press, 1996), p. 110.

21. Ibid.

22. "The Circuit Court," *Yorkville Enquirer*, 17 July 1873. Mackey, a resident of Chester and a member of the Republican Party, had been a district officer in the United Brotherhood that was formed in Columbia when the Union League was forced by the Ku Klux Klan to shut down.

23. "The Colored Militia," *Yorkville Enquirer*, 5 June 1873.

24. Lou Falkner Williams, *The Great South Carolina Ku Klux Klan Trials, 1871–1872* (Athens: University of Georgia Press, 1996), p. 49. Although Williams tells that the arrests continued in 1873, some apparently took place after this date. These later arrests may have been more connected to the events leading up to the 1874 election than earlier Klan activity.

25. "Arrests," *Yorkville Enquirer*, 12 February 1874.

26. "Congressman Wallace," *Yorkville Enquirer*, 20 August 1874.

27. Lou Falkner Williams, *The Great South Carolina Ku Klux Klan Trials, 1871–1872* (Athens: University of Georgia Press, 1996), pp. 125–26.

28. Mary Davis Brown Diaries, 3 November 1874, Manuscript Division, South Caroliniana Library, USC, Columbia, SC.

29. "The Elections," *Yorkville Enquirer*, 5 November 1874.

30. "Reduction of the Army," *Yorkville Enquirer*, 12 November 1874.

31. "Recruits," *Yorkville Enquirer*, 4 March 1875.

32. "Infantry Recruits," *Yorkville Enquirer*, 20 February 1873.

33. The men apparently had a good deal of time on their hands as a number of incidents involving drunkenness were reported. One of the more serious incidents related to Adam Youngblood, an old black man who was attacked and beaten unmercifully by a soldier under Captain Christopher's command. "Deadly Assault," *Yorkville Enquirer*, 30 April 1874.

34. "Circuit Court," *Yorkville Enquirer*, 15 April 1875.

35. "The Latest Ku-Klux Case," *Yorkville Enquirer*, 8 July 1875.

36. Richard Zuczek, "The Federal Government's Attack on the Ku Klux Klan: A Reassessment," *South Carolina Historical Magazine*, 1997 (January): 63. Lou

Falkner Williams, *The Great South Carolina Ku Klux Klan Trials, 1871–1872* (Athens: University of Georgia Press, 1996), p. 111.

37. James Spratt White IV, "History of the Ku Klux Klan in Upper South Carolina, 1868–1871" (paper prepared in 1963 at Wofford College, Spartanburg, SC), 43.

38. Although the nation saw a so-called revival of the Ku Klux Klan in the second decade of the 20th century, that organization, and subsequent groups using the same name, shared only an external resemblance to the Klan of the Reconstruction era. The Ku Klux Klan of the late 1860s and early 1870s was political in purpose, while later organizations were mainly racial.

App. 1— Oath, Constitution and Bylaws of the Ku Klux Klan

1. "The Trial of the Ku Klux," *Yorkville Enquirer*, 21 December 1871.
2. The grand wizard commander-in-chief, head of the "empire," who lived in Memphis Tennessee, governed the Ku Klux Klan. The grand dragon commanded a state, the grand titan one to three congressional districts, the grand giant a county, and the grand cyclops, a den. Thomas Dixon, Jr., *The Clansman* (Norborne, MO: Salon Publishing Co., 1904), Introduction. In York County, local Klan units were known as dens and organized by men of a community or area. At the head of these dens were the grand cyclopses, or chiefs, and subordinate to them were nighthawks.

App. 2— Captain James Williams

1. A partial list of men who were involved in the raid and murder of Captain Williams is gleaned from the Klan trials: Lafayette Hood, Pinckney Caldwell, Josiah Martin, Henry C. Warlick, Robert Riggins, Robert Sherer, Miles Carroll, Elias Ramsey, Hugh H. Sherer, Sylvanus H. Sherer, William B. Sherer, James M. Sherer, Robert Hayes Mitchell, Alonzo Brown, Dr. John S. Bratton, John Caldwell, William Johnson, Chambers Brown, Evan Murphy, W. H. Montgomery, Hezikiah Porter, Eli Ross Stewart and Amzi Ramsey. John W. Mitchell, a Klan chief, actually did not participate in the murder but stayed back with the horses while the rest to the party went to Williams' house. Since he was a magistrate, like Samuel Brown, Mitchell was sentenced to five years and $1,000 fine.
2. "The Trial of the Ku Klux," *Yorkville Enquirer*, 13 December 1871.
3. Some family traditions say that Williams was a carriage driver for John L. Rainey of the Blairsville community.
4. Written by M. S. Carroll of York County. The original document, written in pencil, was found in the 1924 enrollment book of the Beersheba Precinct and remains in the privately held papers of the White family.

App. 3— James Rufus Bratton, M.D.

1. A history of Doctor Bratton, thought to have been written by Mrs. Virginia Mason Bratton, flatly denies his Klan involvement stating, "While a strong sympathizer, yet, Doctor Bratton did not join this organization, but was forced to leave home owing to false charges concerning him...." However, in a memorial to Doctor Bratton presented at the 1899 meeting of the Survivors Association of the

Ex-Confederate Surgeons of South Carolina by Doctor A. A. Moore, president, and attested to by R. Andral Bratton, secretary and son of Doctor Bratton, his membership was not denied. Papers of Dr. J. R. Bratton, York County Public Library, Rock Hill, SC.

2. Diary of Dr. James Rufus Bratton, Transcription by Jerry L. West, York County Public Library, Rock Hill, SC.

3. In a letter written from Miss Ida de Loach, a niece of Doctor Bratton, to Fred Landon, vice president of the University of Western Ontario, regarding Doctor Bratton, she informed him, "...by and large the newly freed slaves behaved well until a federal garrison was set up in York and the former slaves were invited to turn against their former owners.... My uncle was supposed to be a ringleader in ... the Ku Klux Klan ... [and] gave his sanction to their acts especially when a notoriously bad specimen of a Negro proclaimed openly that he would 'kill every Bratton from the cradle to the grave.' This Negro disappeared and officers and men of the federal garrison placed the blame on Doctor Bratton and when affairs became dangerous for him he went to Canada." "Dr. Bratton, Colorful figure of Reconstruction Days, Is Recalled in Letter Exchange," *Camden Chronicle*, date unknown.

4. This intended purchase is highly suspect since some time later Bratton could not raise enough money for bail after he was placed in the Yorkville jail. Mrs. Jean Agee of Richburg says that the family was completely broke, and that Major James Wallace loaned Doctor Bratton's mother, Harriet, enough money to pay the tax on the farm. Mrs. Agee further tells that Harriet Bratton was responsible for keeping the farm going during the Civil War, sending large quantities of farmstuffs to the army in Virginia. She reputedly enticed someone in charge of the state prison to send prisoners to work the farm.

5. "The Abduction of Dr. Bratton," *Yorkville Enquirer*, 1 August 1872.

6. One family account relates that the men went to Florida where they sailed for Canada rather than attempting to pass through Northern states and risk capture. The same account discloses that some members of the Gordon and Avery families were among the refugees.

7. "The Arrest of Dr. J. R. Bratton," *Yorkville Enquirer*, 20 June 1872.

8. "The Case of Dr. J. R. Bratton," *Yorkville Enquirer*, 27 June 1872.

9. The warrant for Avery read: "...he, on the second day of March, A.D. 1871, did, at the county of York, in the State of South Carolina, one of the United States of America, feloniously and of his malice aforethought, kill and murder one Anderson Brown, and hath on account of the said felony fled from the said State of South Carolina, and come into the Dominion of Canada, and is now residing at the city of London." "The Abduction of Dr. Bratton," *Yorkville Enquirer*, 1 August 1872.

10. Bratton testified that he had seen Hester at the scene of the arrest, at the Corpus Christi festival at Mount Hope and also on the G. W. R. station platform. "The Abduction of Dr. Bratton," *Yorkville Enquirer*, 1 August 1872.

11. "The Abduction of Dr. Bratton," *Yorkville Enquirer*, 1 August 1872.

12. "The Arrest of Dr. J. R. Bratton," *Yorkville Enquirer*, 20 June 1872.

13. "The Abduction of Dr. Bratton," *Yorkville Enquirer*, 1 August 1872.

14. In the account of Virginia Mason Bratton, daughter-in-law of Doctor Bratton, she denied that he had any part in the Ku Klux Klan, and that the entire account was so spurious and contradictory to documented facts that little

credence in it was warranted. Papers of Doctor J. R. Bratton, York County Public Library, Rock Hill, SC.
  15. "Arrest of Dr. J. R. Bratton," *Yorkville Enquirer*, 13 June 1872.
  16 "Dr. Bratton Released on Bail," *Yorkville Enquirer*, 20 June 1872. John T. Lowry, W. A. Moore, J. H. Adams, W. B. Steele, P. B. Darwin, S. R. Moore, A. I. Barron, R. F. Clark, T. M. Whitaker, T. M. Dobson, James B. Allison, R. J. Latta and J. M. Lowry secured Bratton's bond. Ibid.
  17. "The Abduction of Dr. Bratton, *Yorkville Enquirer*, 1 August 1872.
  18. "Dr. J. R. Bratton's Case," *Yorkville Enquirer*, 27 June 1872, reprinted from the *New York Herald*.
  19. Sometime during the 1980s, a Canadian historic society (probably the London and Middlesex County Historical Society) contacted the director of Historic Brattonsville for information on Bratton's life in preparation for placing a marker on the building where he practiced. Some protest was made when Bratton's involvement in the Ku Klux Klan became known, and the marker was never erected.
  20. Dixon dedicated his book to his uncle, Colonel Lee Roy McAfee (McAfee was Klan Grand Titan of North Carolina), who lived in the Beersheba Church community of York County. The silent movie *The Birth of a Nation* premiered in 1913, and played three weeks in Atlanta where a revival of the Ku Klux Klan was in progress.

App. 4 — *John Hannibal White*

  1. Part of a "Sketch of John Hannibal White," *Yorkville Enquirer*, 20 November 1873, reprinted from the Columbia, SC, *Union-Herald*.
  2. At the site later known as "Hannibal's Grove" the Radicals gathered to hear and make speeches. Today (2002), "Hannibal's Grove" would have been near the intersection of South Congress Street and Sharon Road.
  3. Emily Bellinger Reynolds and Joan Reynolds Faunt, *Biographical Directory of the Senate of the State of South Carolina 1776–1964* (Columbia: South Carolina Archives Department, 1964), p. 332.

App. 5 — *Elijah Ross Sepaugh*

  1. "Ku Klux Trial," *Yorkville Enquirer*, 5 May 1870.
  2. "King's Mountain Township," *Yorkville Enquirer*, 3 February 1870.
  3. Ibid.
  4. (The newspaper article incorrectly identified him as A. H. Sapock.) "Ku Klux Trial," *Yorkville Enquirer*, 5 May 1870.
  5. Ibid.
  6. Ibid.
  7. Bobby Gilmer Moss, *The Old Iron District* (Clinton, SC: Jacobs Press, 1972; reprint, Blacksburg, SC: Scotia-Hibernia Press, 1989), p. 195; Lou Falkner Williams, *The Great South Carolina Ku Klux Klan Trials, 1871–1872* (Athens: University of Georgia Press, 1996), p.108.
  8. Lou Falkner Williams, *The Great South Carolina Ku Klux Klan Trials, 1871–1872* (Athens: University of Georgia Press, 1996), p. 107.
  9. Ibid., p. 108.
  10. Ibid., p. 109.

11. Ibid.

12. Sheriff Glenn reported to Governor Scott that Mack Byers had been arrested for the murder of Roundtree, and that warrants had been taken out for John Hicks and Samuel Randall. Both were believed to have fled to Cleveland County, NC. Sheriff Glenn to Governor Scott, 14 December 1870, Box 13, Folder 28, Governor Robert K. Scott's Papers, South Carolina Department of Archives and History, Columbia, SC.

13. "The County Jail," *Yorkville Enquirer*, 16 April 1874.

14. "The Case of E. Sapaugh," *Yorkville Enquirer*, 24 December 1874.

15. Lou Falkner Williams, *The Great South Carolina Ku Klux Klan Trials, 1871–1872* (Athens: University of Georgia Press, 1996), p. 111.

16. Bobby Gilmer Moss, *The Old Iron District* (Clinton, SC: Jacobs Press, 1972; reprint, Blacksburg, SC: Scotia-Hibernia Press, 1989), p. 196; "The Case of E. Sapaugh," *Yorkville Enquirer*, 24 December 1874.

17. "Elijah Ross Sapaugh," *Yorkville Enquirer*, 4 February 1875.

18. "Pardon of E. Ross Sepaugh," *Yorkville Enquirer*, 28 October 1875.

App. 6 — York County Men Imprisoned at Albany Penitentiary

1. Randolph Abbott Shotwell, *The Shotwell Papers* (Raleigh: The North Carolina Historical Commission, 1936), 3: Appendix.

2. John C. Robinson was born 18 August 1851, the son of Clark and Margaret Doster Robinson. Although his name does not appear on any list of prisoners sent to Albany, he reported in 1933 that he had been a member of the Avery Klan, pled guilty to conspiracy at the Charleston trials, and served a little over ten months of a two-year sentence. Robinson, who had "J.C.R. A51" tattooed on his right arm, said that while he was in the Charleston jail a number of sailors were imprisoned for mutiny, one of whom was a tattoo artist. Robinson took the sailor's ink and pens and inscribed his arm with his initials and the month and year of his birth. "Just A-Rolling Along the Way," *Yorkville Enquirer*, 12 September 1933.

App. 7 — Prison Life at the Albany Penitentiary

1. Randolph Abbott Shotwell was born in Virginia. He was self-employed as a journalist in Rutherford County, North Carolina, at the time of his arrest. He was "unmarried and so to remain!" While in prison Shotwell was allowed to keep a journal; it was from this account that *The Shotwell Papers*, a three-volume work, was published by the North Carolina Historical Commission in 1936.

2. Randolph Abbott Shotwell, *The Shotwell Papers* (Raleigh: The North Carolina Historical Commission, 1936), 3:113.

3. Ibid., 3:122.
4. Ibid., 3:171.
5. Ibid., 3:122–24.
6. Ibid., 3:124–25.
7. Ibid., 3:138.
8. Ibid., 3:130.
9. "Civil War Veteran Recalls Army Days," The *Evening Herald*, 8 April 1939.

10. Randolph Abbott Shotwell, *The Shotwell Papers*, (Raleigh: The North Carolina Historical Commission, 1936), 3: 136.
11. Ibid., 3:145.
12. Ibid., 3:322.
13. Ibid., 3:284.
14. Ibid., 3:162.
15. Ibid., 4:163.
16. Ibid., 4:149.
17. Ibid., 3:163.
18. "Civil War Veteran Recalls Army Days," *Evening Herald*, 8 April 1939.
19. Randolph Abbott Shotwell, *The Shotwell Papers* (Raleigh: The North Carolina Historical Commission, 1936): 3: 150.
20. Ibid., 3:166–67
21. Ibid., 3:194–95.
22. Ibid., 3:222.
23. Ibid., 3:224.
24. Ibid., 3:322.
25. Ibid., 3:152
26. Ibid., 3:168.
27. "Civil War Veteran Recalls Army Days," *Evening Herald*, 8 April 1939.
28. Randolph Abbott Shotwell, *The Shotwell Papers* (Raleigh: The North Carolina Historical Commission, 1936), 3:433.
29. Ibid., 3:434.

App. 8 — Presidential Pardons

1. Attorney General Williams to Governor Scott, 10 February 1870, Box 22, Folder 24, Governor Robert K. Scott's Paper, South Carolina Department of Archives and History, Columbia, SC.
2. "The Pardoned Ku Klux," *Yorkville Enquirer*, 16 January 1873.
3. Randolph Shotwell said regarding Wright, "The Government takes good care [to release] only those who are too ignorant and insignificant to make their wrongs known to the public ... even mercy is made subservient to base political purposes." Randolph Abbot Shotwell, *The Shotwell Papers* (Raleigh: The North Carolina Historical Commission, 1936), 3: 309.
4. "Ku Klux Pardons," *Yorkville Enquirer*, 30 January 1873.
5. "More Ku Klux Pardoned," *Yorkville Enquirer*, 13 February 1873. Stewart was arrested for bootlegging in 1874. "Revenue Seizures," *Yorkville Enquirer*, 12 February 1874.
6. "The Four Sherer Boys," *Yorkville Enquirer*, 13 February 1873.
7. "The Sherer Boys at Home," *Yorkville Enquirer*, 20 February 1873.
8. "More Ku Klux Pardoned," *Yorkville Enquirer*, 16 March 1873.
9. "Ku Klux Pardoned," *Yorkville Enquirer*, 20 March 1873.
10. "Ku Klux Pardons," *Yorkville Enquirer*, 27 March 1873.
11. "More Pardons," *Yorkville Enquirer*, 3 April 1873.
12. Randolph Abbott Shotwell, *The Shotwell Papers* (Raleigh: The North Carolina Historical Commission, 1936), 3: Appendix.
13. "Pardoned," *Yorkville Enquirer*, 1 January 1874.
14. "Pardoned," *Yorkville Enquirer*, 19 February 1874.

15. "Pardon of Elijah Hardin," *Yorkville Enquirer*, 5 March 1874.
16. "Pardoned," *Yorkville Enquirer*, 17 December 1874.

App. 9 — Samuel Gordon Brown

1. S. G. Brown, 7 February 1814 to 7 June 1888, was the son of John Brown and Elizabeth Gordon Brown. At his home in Sharon, the only copy of the constitution and bylaws of the Ku Klux Klan discovered in the county was confiscated by the Federal government. Brown testified that he had gotten them from his cousin and neighbor, James Albertus Brown, but never took the time to read them. In a letter dated 19 May 1985, Mr. Elmer O. Parker of Columbia wrote that Brown gave the key to his desk to Lieutenant Edward Settle Godfrey of the 11th U.S. Cavalry on the night of 20 October 1871 (the day after his arrest) and a note to his daughter, Jennie, telling her where the material could be found. The files of the National Archives in Washington, DC, contain a memorandum that reads, "The within papers were found by me in the private desk of Samuel G. Brown, of York County, when I sought for them by order of Colonel Merrill...."

2. Just a little less than one month earlier, two of his daughters (Addy and Laura) were baptized on Friday, September 22, during a communion meeting at Beersheba Presbyterian Church. Mary Davis Brown Diaries, 23 September 1871, Manuscript Division, South Caroliniana Library, USC, Columbia, SC.

3. John Alonzo Brown and James Chambers Brown. Chambers Brown was the chief of the Rattlesnake Klan.

4. This meeting supposedly took place 26 February 1871 at the Sharon (A.R.P.) Meeting House. Elmer O. Parker to "My dear Cousin," 19 May 1985 (copy located in author's file). Brown was concerned the order was allowing men into membership who were violent and immoral and taking a course that would spell disaster to all concerned. Historian John A. Leland agrees with Brown: "When all immediate danger of actual conflict was over, from the disarming of the militia and the withdrawal of the constabulary force, the more prudent and respectable withdrew from them, and they fell into the hands and under control of those lawless and reckless spirits, to be found in almost every community — particularly after a protracted and disastrous war." John A. Leland, *A Voice from South Carolina* (Charleston, SC, 1879), p. 87.

5. Colonel Wilson began his practice in Yorkville in partnership with Colonel Isaac D. Witherspoon. This arrangement continued until the death of Witherspoon. At that time he formed a new partnership with I. D. Witherspoon, Jr.

6. Randolph Abbott Shotwell, *The Shotwell Papers* (Raleigh: The North Carolina Historical Commission, 1936), 3:326–27.

7. Ibid., 3:328.

8. Lou Falkner Williams, *The Great South Carolina Ku Klux Klan Trials, 1871–1872* (Athens: The University of Georgia Press, 1996), pp. 116–17.

9. In a letter to abolitionist Gerrit Smith, Brown reported that he was not yet 61, and his wife, in another letter, mentioned that he was 60 years old.

10. Randolph Abbot Shotwell, *The Shotwell Papers* (Raleigh: The North Carolina Historical Commission, 1936), 3:329–30.

11. Ibid., 3:331.

12. Ibid., 3:388.

13. Ibid., 3:349.
14. "Col. Whitley's Ku Klux Report," *Yorkville Enquirer*, 22 August 1872.
15. Randolph Abbott Shotwell, *The Shotwell Papers* (Raleigh: The North Carolina Historical Commission, 1936), 3:245.
16. "Col. Whitley's Ku Klux Report, *Yorkville Enquirer*, 22 August 1872.
17. "The Albany Penitentiary," *Yorkville Enquirer*, 22 August 1872.
18. Family tradition relates that he never belonged to the KKK.
19. Randolph Abbott Shotwell, *The Shotwell Papers* (Raleigh: The North Carolina Historical Commission, 1936), 3: 366.
20. Elmer Oris Parker, "The Case for Squire Samuel G. Brown of York County, South Carolina" (unpublished paper, 1960), 16–18.
21. Ibid., 18–19.
22. "Pardon For Ku Klux," *Yorkville Enquirer*, 8 August 1872.
23. Elmer Oris Parker, "The Case for Squire Samuel G. Brown of York County, South Carolina" (unpublished paper, 1960), 21–22.
24. Ibid., 22.
25. Mary Davis Brown Diaries, 5 April 1873, Manuscript Division, South Caroliniana Library, USC, Columbia, SC.
26. "Twenty-one of the seventy-two signers were Negroes. The first name was that of a Negro who had once been a slave belonging to Mrs. Brown's mother, and by her given to her daughter Mrs. Elizabeth Lyle." Elmer Oris Parker, "The Case for Squire Samuel G. Brown of York County, South Carolina" (unpublished paper, 1960), 18.
27. Randolph Abbott Shotwell, *The Shotwell Papers* (Raleigh: The North Carolina Historical Commission, 1936), 3: 402–03.
28. Ibid., 3:429.
29. Ibid., 3:416–17.
30. Ibid., 3:432.
31. Ibid., 3:438.
32. Ibid., 3:432.
33. Elmer Oris Parker, "The Case for Squire Samuel G. Brown of York County, South Carolina" (unpublished paper, 1960), 23–26.
34. Ibid., 25.
35. "Pardoned," *Yorkville Enquirer*, 1 January 1874.

App. 11— *Union League Oath*

1. "Just A-Rollin Along the Way," *Yorkville Enquirer*, 3 June 1932.

Bibliography

Primary Sources

South Carolina State Records

1867–1868 Voter Registration Books, South Carolina Department of Archives and History, Columbia, SC.
Governor Robert K. Scott's Papers, South Carolina Department of Archives and History, Columbia, SC.

U. S. Government Records

Report of the Joint Select Committee to Inquire into the Condition of Affairs in the Late Insurrectionary States. U. S. Congress, Washington, DC, United States Government Printing Office, 1872.
Testimony Taken by the Joint Select Committee to Inquire into the Condition of Affairs in the Late Insurrectionary States. U. S. Congress, Washington, DC, United States Government Printing Office, 1872.

Books

Jolly, Richard M. *The Story of My Reminiscences.* Gaffney, SC: Richard M. Jolly, 1924.
Shotwell, Randolph Abbott. *The Shotwell Papers.* Raleigh: North Carolina Historical Commission, 1936.

Manuscripts

James Rufus Bratton Diary. York County Public Library. Rock Hill, SC.
Papers of James Rufus Bratton. York County Public Library. Rock Hill, SC
Mary Davis Brown Diary. South Caroliniana Library, University of South Carolina, Columbia, SC.
Draper Manuscript Collection, State Historical Society, Madison, Wisconsin.

George Engelmann Papers, Missouri Botanical Gardens, St. Louis, MO.
Knox Family Letters, South Carolinana Library, University of South Carolina, Columbia, SC.

Secondary Sources

Bleser, Carol K. Rothrock. *The Promised Land.* Columbia: University of South Carolina Press, 1969.
Botkin, B. A. *Lay My Burden Down.* Athens: University of Georgia Press, 1989.
Brown, Douglas Summers. *A City Without Cobweb.* Columbia: University of South Carolina Press, 1953.
Derry, Joseph T. *Story of the Confederate States.* Harrisonburg, VA: Sprinkle Publications, 1996.
Dixon, Thomas, Jr. *The Clansman.* Norborne, MO: Salem Publishing Company, 1904.
Fitzgerald, Michael W. *The Union League Movement in the Deep South.* Baton Rouge: University of Louisiana Press, 1989.
Foner, Eric. *Freedom's Lawmakers: A Directory of Black Office Holders During Reconstruction.* New York: Oxford University Press, 1993.
Hall, Samuel B. *A Shell in the Radical Camp.* Charleston, SC: 1873.
Heyman, Christine Leigh. *Southern Cross: The Beginning of the Bible Belt.* New York: Alfred A. Knopf, 1997.
Holmgren, Virginia C. *Hilton Head: A Sea Island Chronicle.* Hilton Head, SC: Hilton Head Publishing Company, 1959.
Horn, Stanley F. *The Invisible Empire.* Montclair, NJ: Patterson Smith, 1969.
Leland, John A. *A Voice from South Carolina.* Charleston, SC: 1879.
Loftin, Robert Drew. "Federal Protection of the Freedmen in South Carolina 1871," Master Thesis, American University, 1968.
Marchall, Howard J. *Gentlemen Without a Country: A Social and Intellectual History of South Carolina.* Chapel Hill: University of North Carolina Press, 1979.
McMath, Robert C., Jr. *Populist Vanguard: A History of the Southern Farmer's Alliance.* Chapel Hill: University of North Carolina Press, 1975.
Mendenhall, Samuel B. *Tales of York County.* Rock Hill, SC: Reynolds and Reynolds, 1989.
Moss, Bobby Gilmer. *The Old Iron District.* Clinton, SC: Jacobs Press, 1972.
Otto, John Solomon. *Southern Agriculture During the Civil War Era 1860–1880.* Westport, CT: Greenwood Press, 1994.
Parker, Elmer O. "The Case for Squire Samuel G. Brown of York County, South Carolina," unpublished, 1960.
Pettus, Louise. "Samuel B. Hall and Major Lewis Merrill." *The Quarterly.* Rock Hill, SC: York County Genealogical and Historical Society, 1997.
Racine, Philip N. *Piedmont Farmer: The Journals of David Golightly Harris 1855–1870.* Knoxville: University of Tennessee Press, 1990.
Reynolds, Emily Bellenger, and Joan Faunt. *Biographical Directory of the Senate of the State of South Carolina 1776–1964.* Columbia: South Carolina Department of Archives and History, 1964.
Reynolds, John S. *Reconstruction in South Carolina 1865–1877.* Columbia, SC: The State Company, 1905.
Romine, W. B. *A Story of the Original Ku Klux Klan.* Pulaskie, TN: The Pulaskie Citizen, 1934.

Saville, Julie. *The Work of Reconstruction: From Slave to Wage Labor in South Carolina, 1860–1870.* New York: Cambridge University Press, 1994.
Sefton, James E. *The United States Army and Reconstruction 1865–1877.* Baton Rouge: Louisiana University Press, 1967.
Simpson, Benjamin Chad. "Heroes or Hoodlums: The White Southern Republicans in Reconstruction South Carolina," College of Charleston, SC.
Stampp, Kenneth M. *The Era of Reconstruction 1865–1877.* New York: Vintage Books, 1965.
Starnes, Clark Robinson. "My Military Reminiscences of the Civil War." Rock Hill, SC: Ann White Chapter UDC, 1921.
Taylor, Alrutheus Ambush. *The Negro in South Carolina During the Reconstruction.* New York, AMS Press, 1971.
Templeton Family Papers, South Caroliniana Library, University of South Carolina, Columbia, SC.
Trelease, Allen W. *White Terror: The Ku Klux Klan Conspiracy and Southern Reconstruction.* Baton Rouge: University of Louisiana State Press, 1889.
Vaughn, Tommy J., and Dorothy Harris Phifer. *Union County South Carolina Death Notices from Early Newspapers 1852–1914.* Spartanburg: Pinckney District Chapter South Carolina Genealogical Society, 1995.
West, Jerry L. *A Historical Sketch of People, Places and Homes of Bullock's Creek, South Carolina.* Richburg, SC: Chester District Genealogical Society, 1986.
_____. *Political Actions in York County, South Carolina, Conservative Clubs in 1868.* Sharon, SC: Broad River Basin Historical Society, 1996.
White, James Spratt IV. "History of the Ku Klux Klan in Upper South Carolina 1868–1871," Wofford College, 1963.
Williams, Alfred B. *Hampton and His Redshirts: South Carolina Deliverance in 1876.* Charleston, SC: Walker, Evan and Gogswell Company, 1935.
Williams, Lou Faulkner. *The Great South Carolina Ku Klux Klan Trials 1871–1872.* Athens: University of Georgia Press, 1996.
Zuczek, Richard. "The Federal Government's Attack on the Ku Klux Klan: A Reassessment." Charleston: South Carolina Historical Magazine, 1996.
_____. *State of Rebellion: Reconstruction in South Carolina.* Columbia: University of South Carolina Press, 1996.

Index

Abbeville, SC 32
Abbeville County, SC 33, 40, 97
Ackerman, Attorney General Amos 86, 89, 90, 97
Adams, Captain George 59, 67
Adams, J. H. 28, 43
Adams, John (former U.S. president) 1
Adams, John 82
Adickes, Jefferson 55
Agee, Jean 38
Alabama 16, 95
Albany, New York Penitentiary 89, 101, 106, 107, 136, 137, 139–143, 146, 147, 150–154
Alcorn, Misses 70
Alexander, Calhoun 95
Allison, Dr. 64
Allison, Dr. J. B. 90, 91
Allison, Dr. J. W. 27
Allison, Dr. R. T. 28, 29
Allison, Ruff 93
Allison's Store 24, 27
Allison's Store Club 29
American Colonization Society 84
Anderson, Maj. Gen. C. L. 66–68, 70
Anderson, Captain J. W. 59
Anderson, Samuel 28

Anderson, SC 3
Anderson, Thomas A. 103
Anderson County, SC 33, 97
Antioch Baptist Church 24
Antioch Community 49, 50, 61
Antioch Precinct 27
Arkansas 110
Armstrong, Lawson 87
Armstrong, Mingo 55
Ashely River xii
Atkinson, Mrs. 92
Augusta Chronicle 18
Austell, J. H. 91
Avery, Colonel 35
Avery, Dr. Edward T. 32, 55, 90, 99
Avery, Green 55
Avery, Maj. James W. 40, 66, 70, 71, 80, 82, 98, 128, 129
Avery, Kizzy 100
Avery, Mary 100

Baltimore, MD 98
Barber, F. H. 82
Barber, J. G. 61
Barnet, Judge 101
Barnwell, SC 127
Barrett, D. T. 25
Barron, Alex A. 91
Barron, John A. 38
Bascion School House 31
Beamguard, Charles 87

Beamguard, O. C. 87
Beatty, Allen 55
Beatty, William C. 26, 31
Beaufort, SC 32
Beersheba Community, SC 111
Beersheba Presbyterian Church 89
Bell, E. F. 90
Bell, Tom 38
Belton, SC 3, 4
Benfield, John 104
Bennett, James 104
Berry, Major J. H. 85, 86
Berry, James 54
Berry, Levi 74
Berry, Thomas 54
Bethany, SC 16, 70, 82
Bethel Precinct 13, 16, 27, 82
Bethel Township 87, 20
Bethesda Club 25, 27
Bethesda Precinct 27
Biggers, Amos 25
Bigham, Robert Dickson 106
The Birth of a Nation 130
Black, Alexander 82
Black, R. A. 27, 87, 90
Black, Thomas 61, 91
Black, Tim 61
Black, William C. 61, 82
Blacksburg, SC 24
Blackwell, W. Shefflin 102
Blackwood, Columbus 102

Index

Blackwood, Melvin C. 102
Blair, Frank P. 25, 29
Blair, James 27
Blair & Seymour Flag 27, 29
Blairsville, SC 27, 64, 89, 98, 141
Blairsville Club 24
Bloodworth, _____ 70
Bluffton, SC 9
Bond, Judge Hugh L. 98, 100, 103, 135, 145
Boyce, Peter 75
Boydton, SC 16, 59
Bragg, General 127
Bratton, John S. 28, 55, 58, 71, 82, 124, 127
Bratton, Dr. James Rufus 2, 3, 27, 28, 35, 40, 71, 81, 82, 85, 94, 98, 106, 110, 123, 124, 126–130
Bratton, Napoleon 71
Bratton, William 126
Brattonsville 71, 123, 126
Breckinbridge, General 2
Brian, James 28
Briar Patch Muster Ground 124
Bridges, Alexander 102
Briggs, B. F. 25, 59
British Navy 126
Broad River 63, 123
Brown, Alonzo 106
Brown, Anderson 71, 79
Brown, Chambers 106, 123
Brown, Davis 111
Brown, Joe 95
Brown, John 93
Brown, John A. 106
Brown, Lawson 64, 89, 93, 96, 112
Brown, Margaret 111, 112
Brown, Mary Davis 64, 66, 67, 73, 74, 89, 91, 93, 100, 111, 112, 123, 152
Brown, Mary Margaret Byers 149, 154
Brown, Peter 106
Brown, Robert Jackson 96
Brown, Samuel G. 27, 38, 40, 82, 90, 102, 106, 112, 137, 145, 146, 148, 149, 151–154
Brunson, R. J. 38
Bryan, Judge George S. 98, 103, 129
Buffalo Club 24

Buffalo Precinct 27, 82
Buffalo Creek 31
Bullock's Creek, SC 59, 78, 82, 84, 88
Bullock's Creek Club 24
Bullock's Creek Precinct 27
Bullock's Creek Presbyterian Church 24, 73
Burnett, John F. 102
Burnett, William P. 102
Burris, Robert 40
Byers, Charley 40
Byers, Edward 149
Byers, Mack 61, 91
Byers, William Bolivar 55
Bynum, James 25
Byrd, Sam 55

Cahill, Frank 74
Caldwell, Bob 95
Caldwell, James M. 106
Caldwell, John 106, 150
Caldwell, Pinckney 63, 87, 103, 106, 136, 137
Caldwell, Robert J. 106
Caldwell, Robert L. "Bob" 124
Caldwell, William 90
Camders, R. L. M. 78
Camp, W. E. 91
Camp Sherman 74, 76
Campbell, Dr. A. P. 27, 43, 82
Campbell, Rev. W. H. 8
Canada 73, 100
Cantrell, Dillard N. 102
Cantrell, John 102
Cantrell, Tibion 102
Carmel Hill Church 73
Carmel Hill Militia Company 73, 74
Carroll, Addison 106
Carroll, D. H. 90
Carroll, Milus "Miles" Smith 34, 35, 101, 106, 123, 124, 137, 143
Carroll, Pinckney 106
Carter, Anderson 74
Carter, Henry 74
Carter, William 95
Canby, General E. R. S. 16
Cash, W. J. 8
Castles, F. T 103
Cathcart, Andrew 104
Caveny, W. M. 91
Caziarc, Louis V. 44
Cedartown, GA 95

Cellers, George 50
Central Democratic Club 27
Chalk, Wade 74
Chambers, J. C. 28, 90
Chambers, John 95
Chambers, Louisa 100
Charleston, SC 4, 7, 16, 86, 98, 101, 102, 103, 104, 112, 136
Charleston, USS 101
Charleston County, SC 113
Charleston Courier 59, 109
Charleston Republican 18, 60, 83, 134
Charlotte, NC 2
Charlotte Railroad 75
Cherokee County, SC 9, 10, 24, 33, 49, 63, 102
Cherokee Township, SC 46, 51–55, 58, 75
Chester, SC 2, 25, 26, 29, 30, 32, 37, 72, 73, 75, 76, 102, 107
Chester Brass Band 26
Chester Conservative Clan 38
Chester County, SC 10, 41, 44, 48, 49, 75, 79, 80, 89, 93, 95, 97, 109, 111, 123, 143
Chester Democratic Club 29
Chesterfield County, SC 89
Childers, Bank 106
Childers, Sherrod 42, 88, 91, 101, 106, 137, 143
Christopher, Captain John 71, 72, 74, 76, 79, 80, 107
Civil War 3, 5, 9, 12, 18, 34, 41, 61, 123, 126
The Clansman 130
Clark's Fork 54
Clark's Fork Club 24
Clawson, Dr. Charles 38
Clay Hill League 78
Clay Hill, SC 27, 82–84
Cleveland County, NC 50, 54, 66, 70, 75, 103
Coate's Tavern, SC 82
Colcox, Will[i]e 93
College of South Carolina 126
Columbia, SC 2, 25, 50, 51, 55, 57, 61, 68, 70, 72, 80, 84, 87, 97, 100, 112, 114, 145

Index 203

Conservative Democratic Clubs 17, 22, 23, 24
Constitutional Convention (1865) 16
Constitutional Convention (1868) 35, 49
Cook, Calvin 102
Cook, Captain James H. 59
Cook, Lenn 95
Cooper, Robert E. 100
Corbin, District Attorney David T. 86, 90, 97, 98, 100, 110–112, 116, 135
Cornwell, Isaac Bell 128–129
Coward, Col. Asbury 25, 26, 66, 67
Crenshaw, E. A. 2
Crawford, Edward A. 71
Crawford, John O. 28
Crosby, Allen B. 98, 106, 115
Crosby, Dennis 64
Cudd, Andrew 102
Cukulcan (Mexican god of light) 17, 18
Culp, Green 106

Darby, James 103
Darlington, SC 32
Darlington County, SC 33
Davidson College 102
Davis, President Jefferson 2, 128, 129
Davis, Thomas 27
Dawson, Walker 138, 144
Democratic State Central Club 47
Democratic State Committee 47
Department of the South 31, 79
Devinney, Greyson 95
Devinney, John 95
Dixon, Thomas, Jr. 130
Dobson, Butler 106, 115
Dobson, J. W. 90, 96
Dobson, Rufus 106, 115, 116
Donald, James A. 138, 144
Douglas, Thomas A. 81, 90
Dover, Daniel 103
Dover, Felix 138, 144
Dover, Miss 53
Dowdle, W. G. 55
Downing, E. J. 91
Drennan, H. H. 55

Eastern New York Shoe Co. 141
Ebenezerville, SC 55
Edgefield, SC 32
Edgefield County, SC 33, 89, 97
Edwards, King 102
Edwards, Moses 82
Elliott, Congressman 62
Ellis, Primus 29
Enloe, J. G. 27
Epping, J. P. M. 4
Etta Jane, SC 94
Ezell, Aaron 102

Fair, John 116
Fairfield County, SC 49, 58, 97
Fairfield Herald 7
Faris, Captain John R. 21, 25, 51, 53–55, 68, 106, 116
Faris, M. P. 95
Farrow, Colonel T. Stobo 26
Faulkner, J. H. 27, 82
Faulkner, Robert 87
Fayssoux, J. H. 61
Feemster, Andrew 74
Ferguson, Samuel 106
Fewell, Frank 91
Fewell, S. A. 90
Ficken, John F, 135
Finely, James 116
"Forest Hall" 58
Forrest, General N. B. 34, 36
Fort Mill, SC 48, 82
Fort Mill Precinct 27
Foster, Charles W. 59
Fowler, Wade 114
Frankfort Springs, PA. 149
Freedmen's Hospital 133
Fulton, J. B. 103
Fulton, W. M. 138

Gaffney, John W. 103
Gaffney, SC 4
Gaffney, W. G. 90, 91
Gaffney, W. W. 82, 90
Gage, J. P. 90
Gage, Martin 74
Gaines, Rev. T. R. 29
Gardner, John 106
Gardner, Levi 106
Gardner, Marion 102
Gardner, R. H. 90
Garrison, Peter 25, 43

Garvin, Rufus 106
Gaston, E. L. 95
Gaston, Lee 102
Gaston County, NC 66, 74
Georgetown, SC 32
Georgia 111
Gilbraith, R. D. 90
Gist, Col. James F. 73
Glenn, Sheriff R. H. 25, 67, 69, 70–72, 74, 79, 96, 112
Godfrey, Edward Settle 102
Goins, Reuben alias Shedd 116
Good, Charley 63
Good, Edward 95
Good, Holbrook 106
Good, M. 102
Gore, Green 74
Governors Island, New York 115
Gowdysville, SC 114
Graham, John A. 90
Graham, T. M. 88
Grant, President 33, 62, 68, 80, 84–86, 88, 89, 93, 107, 108, 116, 128, 129, 147, 149–153
Greene County, Tennessee 94
Greenville County, SC 97
Gregory, Rafe 74
Griffin, Isaac 116
Grist, Lewis M. 2, 31, 32, 36, 37, 51, 52, 56, 57, 60, 66, 68, 103
Gunn, Alex 55
Gunn, Kirkland 99
Gunning, Harvey "Harve" 93, 106
Guthrie, R. E. 27
Guyton, Henry 39
Guyton, Lee 30, 63
Gwinn, O. J. 106

Hale, Captain Hale 107
Hall, Martin 93, 111
Hall, Samuel B. 59, 69, 70
Hambright, Galbreath 138, 143
Hambright, J. M., Jr. 91
Hambright, J. M., Sr. 91
Hambright, Mrs. 53
Hamburg, SC 18
Hammett, Martin 102
Hampton, James 90
Hampton, General Wade 35, 47, 98, 117

Index

Hannibal White's Grove 30
Hardin, Elijah 138, 144
Hardin, Ira 27
Hardin, L. M. 91
Harper, J. R. 90
Harris, Frank C. 25, 38
Harris, Marion 103
The Harris Plantation 55
Hartness, R. B. 124
Harvey, S. J. 90
Harvey, Winfield S. 110
Hayes, Allison 143
Hayes, E. A. 138, 143
Hayes, Henry 124
Hemphill, S. G. 55
Henderson, Louis 102
Hendrick, John 74
Herndon, J. Pink 90
Hester, Joseph G. 128, 129
Hicklin, William Cloud 41
Hickory Grove, SC 39, 82, 84, 95
Hickory Grove Club 24
Hicks, John 61
Higgins, Florence 78
Hill, Elias 83
Hill, Dr. L. A. 88
Hoffman, John T. 146
Holden, William W. 154
Holder, Frederick C. vii
Holland, Rev. R. A. 40
Hood, George Davis 90
Hood, J. P. 82
Hood, J. Simpson 95
Hood, John Halsey 90
Hood, "Squire" 95
Hood, William Lafayette 90, 106, 138
Hood's Store 82
Hoodtown, SC 90
Hope, Albertus 38
Hope, Russell L. 55
Hopper, Romulus 104
Horn, Stanley F. 38
Horton, W. M. 55
The Howard Amendment 26
Howe, Julius 106, 137, 144
Howell, Darvin G. "Dock" 63
Howell, Lucy Zipporah Smith 5, 63
Howell, S. 102
Howell's Ferry 63
Howell, 's Ferry Road 124
Hubbard, J. B. 49, 54, 59, 111, 114

Huck, Captain 126
Hullender, Henry J. 10, 49, 50, 51, 134
Hully, Abner 74
Hunter, Dr. John B. 90, 93
Hutchison, A. E. 28
Hyer, Captain 115

Jackson, Dr. 38
Jefferys, J. E. 25
Jenkins, Colonel 126
Johnson, Eb 93
Johnson, Captain Henry 59
Johnson, Miles 59, 72, 134
Jo[h]nson, Rev. 101
Johnson, Reverdy 136
Johnson, Tom 86
Johnson, William "Will" 106, 123
Johnson, Will[i]e 93
Johnston, J. D. 55
Jolly, C. M. 46
Jolly, Richard M. 9, 46
Jolly, William 102
Jones, Colonel Cadwalder 28
Jones, Captain 91
Jones, Dudley, Jr. 106
Jones, Iredell 38, 47, 90
Jones, J. D. 115
Jones, John 102

Kansas 80
Kee, Captain W. L. 59
Kell, Banks 106
Kell, Hugh H. 90, 106
Kell, W. E. 25
Kerr, Colonel Robert M. 27
Kerr, William 61
Kings Creek 31, 82
Kings Mountain battleground 54
Kings Mountain Hotel 27
Kings Mountain Railroad 2, 75, 107
Kings Mountain Township 51
Kirby, Andrew 98
Kirkpatrick, Andrew 91, 106, 150
Kirkpatrick, J. Craig 95
Kirkpatrick, J. M. 103
Kirkpatrick, John B. 103
Knox, John 95
Knox, William D. 102

LaMaster, Bill 95

Lancaster County, SC 29, 90, 97, 126
The Lantern 42
Latham, F. G. 91
Latham, Henry 88
Lathan, Rev. Robert 25, 26
Lathan, S. B. 30, 38
Latta, Bert 124
Latta, Mary 124
Laurens County, SC 32, 33, 61, 89, 93, 97, 110
Laurensville, SC 61
Law, General E. M. 25, 26, 83
Leander, J. 27
Leckie, Joseph 137
Leckie, William 103
Lee, Captain John 59, 73
Leech, Charles 99
Leech, Edward 106
Leech, George C. 106, 112
Leech, J. E. 115
Leech, Joseph W. 106, 115
Lessley, Thomas H. 87
Lessley, William D. 87
Lexington County, SC 33
Liberia 83, 84
Lindsey, Dr. John F. 66, 81
Littlefield, William 50, 51, 52, 58
Loftis, Robert Drew 41
London, Ontario 98, 128
Long, James 58
Louisville, KY 79, 80
Love, Gim 93
Love, J. T. 102
Loyal League 36, 37
Lowery, Mr. 75
Lowery, William 143

Mabrey, Jess 95
Mackey, Judge T. J. 103, 104, 113, 114, 152
Malleny, Mary vii
Manigault, G. 128
Martin, Andrew J. 104, 143
Martin, Henderson 27
Martin, Josiah 102, 106, 137
Mason, Robert 55
Massey, L. H. 28
Massey, Rebecca 126
May, R. T. 90
May, W. S. 90
Mayrant, R. P 32
May's Drugstore in Yorkville 35
McAfee, Colonel L. M. 29

Index 205

McAfee, Marion 106
McCaffrey, Ed 70
McCall, Reuben 91
McCallum, Peter 28
McCallum, William 103
McCants, John 55
McCarter, Samuel 70
McClain, Quintinelle 90
McClain, Rufus B. 70, 106
McClure, D. C. 102
McClure, Major E. C. 25, 29
McConnell, A. F. 90
McConnell, J. D. 35, 41, 124
McConnell, Sally 125
McConnellsville 15, 58, 66, 75, 82, 124
McConnellsville Club 25, 27
McCorkle, Colonel W. H. 26, 27, 28
McCullock, Miles 138, 143
McDill, Agnes 102
McDill, J. H. 90
McDill, Nixon 102
McElwee, J. Newman 28
McElwee, Rev. William Meek 149, 150
McGill, John 54
McGill, Thomas 27
McGill, Tony 53
McGill, William 28, 82
McGill's Store 55, 68
McKenzie, Major A. A. 27
McKinney, D. D. 82
McKnight, Jeff 95
McKnight, Ross 95
McLain, Rufus 40
McMaster, F. W. 100
Mead, John W. 16, 21, 43
Meade, General George G. 31
Mellichamp, ___ 9
Memphis Appeal 18
Memphis Ledger 38
Merrell, Lewis 2, 41, 80–82, 84–88, 89, 91, 107, 110, 113, 145, 146, 151
Metts, Walter B. 82
Mexican War 18
Milledgeville, GA 127
Miller, John S. 90, 99, 102
Miller, Napoleon 106
Miller, S. N. 64
Mills, Josh 74
Minor, James 29, 33

Missouri 25
Mitchell, John Whitley 40, 82, 90, 102, 137
Mitchell, Joseph 106
Mitchell, Robert Hayes 91, 99, 106, 138, 143
Mobley, June 59
Montgomery, John 137, 144
Montgomery, Tom 95
Montgomery, William H. 101, 106, 143
Moore, ___ 112
Moore, D. D. 27
Moore, H. M. 138
Moore, J. P. 82
Moore, Captain Jacob 59
Moore, Jacob B. 91
Moore, John L. 102
Moore, Jonathan 82
Moore, Minor 91
Moore, R. Springs 28
Moore, Robert 136, 137
Moore, Theodore A. 29
Moore, Captain Thomas 59
Moore, W. A. 28
Moore, Walker 137
Moore, William 126
Morrow, John 106
Moseley, H. C. 86
Moss, Berry 91
Moss, J. M. 91
Moss, Jerome P. 103
Moss, Riley 91
Moss, Sillis 91
Moss, William 91
Mt. Zion Academy 126
Murphy, E. J. 138
Murphy, Evans 101, 106

Nal. K. Xulkuk 18
Neagle, John L. 16, 43, 50, 60, 65, 152, 153
Neel, James 106
Neely, D. R. 91
Neely, L. H. 91
New Center, SC 102
New Hope Church 73
New House Post Office 54
New York 25
New York Tribune 18, 80, 92
New York World 148
Newberry, SC 32, 110
Newberry County, SC 33, 49, 61, 89, 93, 97
Northern Pacific Railroad 107
Noyes, S. F. 54

Oates, William 28
O'Bannon, Sophia 127
Oconee County, SC 97
O'Connell, M. 25, 48
O'Connell, P. J. 30, 43, 59
Ogden, Captain 92, 93
Ohio 85, 129
Oklahoma City, OK 11
Oregon 63
Orr, Governor 4
Osment, Emsley 94
Ottz, J. D. 152
Owens, Alfred 62
Owens, Captain 80
Owens, Scott 90
Owens, William K. 70, 85, 88

Pagan, James 47
Paris, Texas 63
Parker, J. 91
Parrish, Cal 93
Parrish, Frederick 102
Parrish, Theodore 27
Patterson, Edward 50
Patton, John R. 28, 82
Pennsylvania 85
Philadelphia, PA 78
Phillips, Captain J. C. 27, 82
Phillips, James 46
The Phoenix 41, 72
Pickens County, SC 97
Pilgrim Church 48, 49
Pilsbury, Amos T. 141, 142, 146, 147, 153
Pilsbury, Louis D. 142
Pine Grove Club 24
Plexico, J. E., Jr. 90
Plexico, J. E., Sr. 90
Plexico, J. L. 90
Plexico, John 95
Poag, J. S. 91
Poinier, Samuel T. 86
Porter, Hezekiah Z. 91, 101, 106, 137
Porter, James B. 87
Porter, W. D. 112
Postel, Isaac 99, 100
Postel, Mrs. 99
Pressly, J. B. 91
Price, Thomas J. 102
Pride, Col. C. J. 69
Pride, Cornelius 91
Pride's Old Mill 82
Princeton University 142
Pursley, John D. 54

Index

Rainey, Amzi 98
Rainey, Samuel 123
Ramseur, D. S. 143
Ramsey, E. S. 90
Ramsey, Elias 42, 106
Ramsey, John 91, 106, 150
Ramsey, Lewis 90, 91
Ramsey, S. R. 90
Ramsey, William 42
Ramsey, William F. 102
Randall, P. W. 103
Rattaree, James 90, 91
Rattaree, John 82, 90
Rattlesnake Klan 123
Rawlinson, Mr. 85, 86
Rawlinson's Hotel 85
Reconstruction Acts 16, 26
The Red Shirts 35
Reno, Marcus A. 110
Republican Convention (1869) 30
Revere House 128
Reynolds, ___ 95
Reynolds, John S. 47
Richburg, SC 38
Richmond, VA 126
Richmond Dispatch 36
Riggins, Robert T. 90, 103, 104, 106, 137, 144
Robbins, Thomas J. 95
Roberts, Hugh K. 51, 62, 70, 71, 75
Robertson, Senator 154
Robinson, James C. 143
Robinson, John C. 138
Robinson, Joseph C. 137
Robinson, S. W. 116
Robinson, William 90
Rock Hill, SC 2, 16, 27, 32, 38, 42, 47, 58, 61, 69, 73, 78, 82
Roddy, J. H. 55
Roddy, W. L. 27, 28
Romine, W. B. 17
Rose, Edward K. 65, 70
Rose, William Edward 2, 26, 43, 67, 71–73
Rose Hill Cemetery (York, SC) 30, 114
Rose's Hotel 2, 65, 66, 71, 87, 123
Ross, Rev. R. A. 28, 29, 82
Roundtree, Harriet 61
Roundtree, Thomas 61, 62, 87, 103, 135
Russell, David S. 72

Sadler, K. P. 82
Sadler, S. C. 91
Salem Church Cemetery 63
Sanatobia, Mississippi 95
Sanders, Anthony 74
Sanders, Green 74
Sanders, John 48
Sanders, Lee 49, 74
Sanders, Sancho 49
Sanders, T. M. 103
Sandlin, Mack 88
Savannah River 111
Scaife, Amos 102
Scoggins, Ann 111
Scott, Sen. John 85
Scott, Governor Robert K. 5, 12, 33, 45–50, 52, 54–56, 58, 60, 62, 65–68, 70, 74, 78, 79, 80, 86, 88, 111, 128, 134, 143
"Scott's Council" 82
Scruggs, Chesterfield 102
Scruggs, Monroe 102
Seaborn, R. K. 90
Second Military District 19, 31
Self, John C. 102
Selma, Alabama 127
Sepaugh, Elijah Ross 103, 104, 134–136
Sepaugh, Henry 135
Seymour, Horatio 25, 29, 33
Sharon, SC 27, 82, 150
Sharon A. R. P. Church 150
Shaw, R. W. 64
Shelby, NC 29
Sherer, Hugh H. 88, 90, 101, 106, 137, 141, 142
Sherer, James B. 101
Sherer, James M. 87, 90, 106, 137
Sherer, Jane 90
Sherer, John Hicklin 90
Sherer, Richard 90
Sherer, Robert 106
Sherer, Sylvanus H. 90, 91, 101, 106, 138
Sherer, William B. 90, 91, 101, 106, 137
Sherman, Gen. William Tecumseh 71, 127
Shotwell, Randolph 139, 142, 147, 151, 153
Sigmon, John 96
Simpson, J. C. 25

Simpson, W. D. 32, 33
Simpson, Wesley 74
Sims, Billy 73
Sims, Joe 73
Sims, Joseph 103
Skeal, Aleck 74
Smarr, J. D. 102
Smarr, Madison 40
Smith, A. L. 70
Smith, Adolphus 91
Smith, Alex 40
Smith, Daniel 106
Smith, Ed 95
Smith, Frank 106
Smith, Garland 95
Smith, Gerrit 150, 151, 154
Smith, Jefferson 106
Smith, Jim 95
Smith, Joe 63
Smith, John 43
Smith, Phoebe 87
Smith, Dr. Samuel A. 73
Smith, Walker 95
Smith, Wesley 103
Smith, William 137
Smyrna, SC 84
Snyder, William H. 40, 86, 91
South Carolina 5th Infantry 126
Spartanburg, SC 26
Spartanburg County, SC 9, 44, 49, 61, 62, 66, 78, 79, 80, 86, 89, 93, 97, 103, 109, 110
Spencer, Leander 91, 103, 137
Spencer, W. T. 91
Spencer, William L. 103
Splawn, Stephen D. 102
Springs, A. Baxter 28, 47, 82
Stanbery 101
Starnes, Clark R. 69
Starnes, Wylie 91
Steele, G. E. M. 90
Steele, Minor 90
Steele, Robert M. 114
Stevenson, Rep. Job 85, 86
Stewart, ___ 137, 143
Stewart, Captain Andrew 59
Stewart, D. M. 91
Stewart, Eli Ross 101, 106, 143
Stewart, Samuel 91
Stewart, W. B. 54

Index

Stowers, William 28
Strain, James L. 94
Sturgis, Samuel 99
Sumner, Charles 111
Surratt, Gilbert 46
Surratt, Henry 102

Tate, Charles 102
Tate, Christenbury 102
Tate, M. L. 55
Taylor, John 96
Tennessee 18, 38, 95
Terry, Gen. Alfred 71, 79, 80
Third Military District 31
Thomas, J. Newman 87
Thomas, Colonel John P. 25, 26, 28
Thomas, William C. 87
Thomas, William M. 87
Thomason, Butler 90, 93
Thomason, Harriet 90
Thomason, Hiram C. 64, 90, 93
Thomason, Dr. Horace D. 66
Thomason, Jane 65
Thomason, Wille 93
Thompson, Jerry 63
Thompson, Presley 63
Thomson, Dr. Addison 73
Thomson, Richard 73
Thorn's Ferry 81
Tindall, Junius B. 102
Tomlinson, John 38
Toole, Henry 90, 91
Trelease, Allen 38, 41, 42, 46
Turkey Creek 95, 102
Turkey Creek Club 27
Turner, Ed A. 103

Union, SC 32, 73, 84
Union County, SC 33, 41, 44, 45, 49, 59, 61, 62, 74, 79, 80, 89, 93, 95, 97, 102, 103, 104, 109, 110, 114
The Union Herald 131
Union Leagues 4, 17–22, 36, 42, 63, 78, 82
The Union Times 68
University of Pennsylvania 127
U.S. Seventh Cavalry 80, 84, 107, 110
U.S. Eighth Infantry 31
U.S. 18th Infantry 107

Vance, Z. B. 29
Vassey, Jonas 102
Vassey, Taylor 102
Virginia 20th Regiment 127

Wade, Martin 103
Walker, A. T. 103
Walker, Captain Andy 59
Wall, James 102
Wall, John C. 102
Wallace, _____ 112
Wallace, Alexander S. 30, 31, 33, 68, 83, 85, 87, 98, 114, 143, 147, 151, 152, 154
Wallace, George D. 115
Wallace, J. F. 25
Wallace, J. Henry 90
Wallace, John 136
Walling, Dr. William H. 78
Warlick, Henry C. 101, 106, 138, 143
Warlick, J. P. 90
Warm Springs, NC 40
Warren, Hugh 64
Washington, DC 85, 133
Washington Chronicle 152
Waters, J. J. 91
Watson, Miles 104
Watson, John C. 87
Watson, John L. 48, 61, 73, 85
Watson, Mrs. 104
Wear Muster Ground, SC 49
Webber, Joseph G. 82
Westmoreland, Maria Jourdan 146, 147
Whig Party 22
Whisonant, C. 25
Whisonant, Jerome 137, 144
Whisonant, John 137, 144
Whitaker Club 24
White, George 103
White, J. Hannibal 16, 30, 43, 59, 67, 131–133
White, James 90
White, John 90
White, Colonel John M. 28
White, William H. 91, 103
Whitesides, C. W. 137
Whitesides, Ruff 89
Whitesides, Dr. Thomas B. 99, 102, 137
Whitesides, W. B. 91
Whitesides, W. C. 90
Whitesides' Mill 29
Whitley, Colonel 147, 148

Wilkerson, J. T. 90
Wilkerson, Thomas 106
Wilkerson, W. S. 90
Wilkes, Berry 74
Wilkes, Captain James 73, 74
Wilkes, Sylvanus 74
Wilkes, Vincent 74
Wilkesburg, SC 73
Williams, David 82
Williams, Fred 75
Williams, Attorney Gen. George H. 100, 107, 111, 112, 136, 143, 147, 154
Williams, George W. 38
Williams, Captain James "Jim" 34, 58, 59, 70, 71, 75, 79, 87, 98, 99, 106, 123–125
Williams, Lou Falkner 146
Williams, P. S. 104
Williams, Rose 124
Williams, Miss Willie 5
Williamson, J. B. 43
Wilson, J. Blackburn 114
Wilson, J. P. 90
Wilson, Colonel W. B. 26, 29, 31
Wilson, William Blackburn 145
Wilson, William J. 88, 106, 116
Wilson, Wilson 116
Winbush, Lucius 30
Winder Hospital 126
Windsor, James 73
Winnsboro, SC 73, 126
Witherspoon, Captain Isaac D. 26, 29, 81
Wood, John L. 87, 90
Wood, Samuel 90
Wood, William 65
Woods, Richard 103
Worth, Major W. S. 31
Worthy, Warren 74
Wounded Knee, SD 115
Wright, Billy 49, 50, 53
Wright, George S. 137, 143
Wright, Henry 96
Wright, Sam 96
Wright, T. J. 95
Wright, William 134
Wylie, Colonel J. D. 29
Wylie, R. W. 91
Wylie's Store 24, 27, 29

Yokum, Captain 50

York County Conservative
    Clubs 25–27
Yorkville, SC 2, 17, 20, 22,
    23, 31, 32, 53, 58, 60, 64–
    66, 68, 70–72, 74, 75, 80–
    82, 84–87, 89, 90–92, 96,
    99, 101–104, 107, 108, 110,
    112, 115, 123, 124, 126–
    129, 131, 132, 136, 145
Yorkville Colored Club 29
Yorkville Conservative Club
    23, 24–27
Yorkville Enquirer 2, 11, 20,
    23–25, 28, 32, 35–37, 39,
    43, 45, 48, 51, 55–60, 63,
    66, 77, 82, 83, 85, 90–
    92, 96, 106, 109, 113, 115,
    134
Youngblood, S. C. 82

Zuczek, Richard 110

www.ingramcontent.com/pod-product-compliance
Lightning Source LLC
Chambersburg PA
CBHW032054300426
44116CB00007B/738